The New Financial Advisor

BY

NICK MURRAY

Also by Nick Murray

For advisors:
The Craft of Advice: Essays 1995-1998

For clients:
Simple Wealth, Inevitable Wealth: How you and your financial advisor can grow your fortune in stock mutual funds

For financial wholesalers:
On Becoming A Great Wholesaler

Printed in the United States of America
Library of Congress Control Number: 2001118475
ISBN: 0-9669763-2-0

This book is for

Rebecca Giovanna Dickerson

Firstborn of my firstborn,

light of my life

"There is a simplicity

that lies beyond sophistication."

– JOHN W. GARDNER

"The practice is the teacher.

Your practice is *your* teacher."

– MAURINE STUART

"I learn by going where I have to go."

– THEODORE ROETHKE

TABLE OF CONTENTS

———————•———————

AUTHOR'S PREFACE

———————●———————

In the summer of 1996, I sat down to revise my book *Serious Money*, which had been written five years earlier — and found that it couldn't be done.

Serious Money, whose subtitle was *The Art of Marketing Mutual Funds*, had itself been occasioned by a revolution in financial services: the sudden, unprecedented migration of the investing public from individual stocks and bonds to mutual funds. Our industry, at that juncture, found itself in a most curious conundrum: we had a product which the whole world wanted to buy, but which we really didn't know how to "sell." That is, we lacked a consistent way of persuading people to own the right mutual funds for the right reasons. And we were plagued at every turn by the phony issue of "load vs. no-load" — which its proponents chose not to state correctly as the question of help vs. no help. *Serious Money* was my attempt to build a track for this mutual fund revolution to run on.

Five years later, though, the world, the industry, the markets and the issues had left *Serious Money* behind. The packaging of money management (as well as of passive investing) had proliferated wildly beyond the basic mutual fund, and a dazzling array of new pricing mechanisms had come to the fore. But, even more importantly, by 1996 it was clear to me that not one but two entirely *new* revolutions were afoot. And that, each in its own way, these two forces would completely and irreversibly change the way financial advice would be delivered in the future.

First, though few people knew it and still fewer accepted it, the financial services industry was on the threshold of converting from a commission basis to a fee basis. I thought, then as now, that this was the healthiest thing that had ever happened to the craft of advice, but that it would necessitate a sea change in the way advisors related to their clients, and in the way we built and managed their portfolios in the context of their long-term goals.

The other, no less important revolution I believed I saw on the horizon was the final collapse of the old, exhausted, counterproductive Glass-Steagall synthesis — the fragmentation of a family's financial life into three uncoordinated pieces: banking, insurance and investments. As financial services converged, we could transcend a system of competing products, and enter a new era of seamless financial planning.

These two glorious revolutions — and the ways in which they would reinforce and feed off each other — became the basis for a new book, *The Excellent Investment Advisor*, published in the autumn of 1996.

Then, after five more years, it happened again.

With an eye toward editing *EIA* for its fourth printing — 90,000 copies into the mission — I concluded that it was, by then, missing as many important developments as it contained. And that, just as *Serious Money* needed to be replaced with *EIA*, the latter now cried out to be superseded by the book you hold in your hands.

To name just a few of the critical events and ideas which occurred post-*EIA*, I would cite:

- the emerging market breakdown of 1997, and the global financial crisis of 1998
- widespread acceptance of (and, briefly, a virtual mania for) indexing as a core investment policy
- the phenomenon of 24/7 "news" coverage of markets and finance, with its disastrous effects on investors' attention spans
- the advent of the Internet, both as a means to suicidal do-it-yourself overtrading *and* as the "industry" which gave rise to the greatest financial bubble and crash in history
- the formal repeal, in effect, of Glass-Steagall, paving the way for huge convergent mergers across the whole spectrum of financial services (Citigroup being the first, the largest, and in some ways the paradigm)

- globalization and its discontents
- the bundling by large investment firms of virtually all their retail products and services into a coordinated, fee-based platform, and the aggressive push by those firms into formal financial planning
- the rise of CPAs in financial services as partners and/or competitors of traditional advisors
- the first generalized bear market *of normal duration* in almost 20 years: an 18-month, 36.8% decline in the S&P 500 (at this writing)
- the Alzheimer's pandemic in the developed world, and its dire consequences for a family's financial planning

These are many, but by no means all, of the occasions for my reluctant decision to put *EIA* out to pasture. To industry veterans struggling to make their peace with these events, as well as to a new generation of twenty-first century advisors just arriving in our great profession, I felt I owed a fresh perspective. **The New Financial Advisor seeks to reconcile the timely challenges of institutional change with the timeless constraints of dealing with immutable human nature.**

This is not a comprehensive financial planning manual. (Even if I were competent to write such a book — which I am most certainly not — it would be out of date before the ink was dry on the paper.) Nor is it a treatise on the comparative analysis of investments. (At the level of the individual investor and his or her family, portfolio management is a refinement, quite subordinate to far more critical behavioral issues which we will examine in great detail.)

Rather, the book you're reading intends to be a systematic career blueprint — regardless of where in your career you find yourself at the moment. The career in question is that of an advisor who helps a finite number of successful households/families to build, protect, preserve, harvest and bequeath multigenerational wealth. Such wealth is possible only pursuant to one particular investment philosophy, carried out *in the context of a formal, written, comprehensive financial, investment and estate plan.*

The New Financial Advisor will be the steward of that plan — not its author, necessarily, and certainly not "the expert" on all of the plan's myriad technical aspects, but **the relationship manager** between the family and the experts. This is not a job description which many of us have much experience of, for the simple and compelling reason that it isn't a job that's ever really existed before. *The New Financial Advisor* will offer you not merely competence in, but mastery of, this marvelous new role you are to play in the lives of the clients who embrace your stewardship.

I hope and believe that on virtually every page of *The New Financial Advisor* you will find evidence of my firm conviction that we are living — and you are practicing the noble craft of financial advice — in a golden age. With very few exceptions, the changes I'll try to synthesize for you are extremely salutary: good for the client and good for the advisor, *for the same reasons.*

And so I invite you, hereby, to excellence in our calling. Like its two predecessors, this book offers a system of beliefs and behaviors which can and will carry you to the top of the financial services profession, and allow you to remain there for as long as you wish — for as long, in other words, as you are willing to pay the high price which excellence demands.

My advice is to pay it. Excellence is, by definition, very rare, but it feels wonderful. (To know that you have helped a family achieve economic freedom, and to enrich your own family thereby, is simply one of the great human experiences. And no one but you can limit your capacity to have that experience.) Mediocrity, also by definition, is quite common, and it feels awful. (Ours is a business which punishes mediocrity with the most exquisite tortures — chief among them the knowledge that excellence was always within reach.)

Seek excellence. Deserve excellence. Enjoy excellence. And may this book be a comfort and a guide to you on that journey.

The manuscript of this book was completed on Monday, September 10, 2001; the process of editing and publishing it took place over the weeks following the terrible events of September 11. Where necessary, all the numbers in the book were adjusted to reflect events through the end of September. I'm happy and proud to tell you that not one word of the equity philosophy espoused by this book was changed — because not one word needed modification. This time, it's *not* different. Optimism is *still* the only realism. God bless America.

FOREWORD:
THE GIFT AND THE CHALLENGE

———————●———————

Through the end of 1999, there had never been a month in which net inflows into equity mutual funds reached $30 billion. The record was $28.9 billion, set in the annual January cash cascade of 1996, and almost exactly equaled in January of '97.

Then, in four epic months in 2000, as the markets roared toward (and through) one of the greatest speculative blowoff tops of all time, equity fund inflows went like this:

January	$44.5 billion
February	$55.6 billion
March	$39.9 billion
April	$35.3 billion

Knowing absolutely nothing else about equity mutual fund inflows/outflows, you might well be prompted to form a speculative hypothesis. To wit, that there may be some horrific, perverse relationship between the enthusiasm of the American public for equities and the near-term direction of equity price movements.

Wait. As Al Jolson always said, "You ain't seen *nothin'* yet!"

Because if you think equity fund investors' euphoria at the top may be bone-chilling, you're still not necessarily prepared for the awful reality of their proclivity to panic liquidation at market bottoms.

Start by looking at the end of the world: October 19, 1987, the single worst day in the history of the American stock market. It took about 18 months for the market to recover to its pre-crash level. *Need I tell you that equity mutual funds were in net liquidation for 16 of those 18 months?*

Ancient history, you say? OK, suppose we fast-forward to the *next* end of the world, the confrontation in the Gulf/oil spike/banking crisis/ monster layoffs/last real recession apocalypse of 1990. The market topped out in mid-July. *Equity mutual funds were in massive net liquidation in August and September.* The market bottomed on October 11.

How about the Russia default/emerging market meltdown/hedge fund blowup of 1998? This one is a classic of the genre. Equity mutual funds hadn't seen even one month of net liquidation since August/September 1990. *Ninety-four consecutive months of net equity fund inflows had ensued.* You already know what's coming, right?

Market topped out on July 17. *August saw by far the biggest one-month net outflow in history: $11.5 billion.* Market bottomed August 31, and made a new high within two months. And we never saw another month of net liquidation...**until 2001.**

For in February and most particularly in March 2001, as the markets went into a thermonuclear selling climax, equity fund liquidations set new records. After outflows of $2.8 billion in February, *net liquidations hit $20.3 billion in March.* The market bottomed on April 4, and rallied 19% in the next six weeks.

Consider the 94 months of equity inflows from the 1990 bottom until that one. Then take all the people who panicked out of their equity mutual funds just in this historic month of March. Estimate how many man-hours — excuse me: person-hours — those people expended in those 94 months: comparing performance statistics, analyzing expense ratios, reading *Morningstar* and *Money*, watching CNBC, switching funds, and all of the other wheel-spinning, left-brain analytical activities of the "new," "educated" mutual fund "investor." (Who was really the worst species of speculator, and hadn't even the minimal self-awareness to perceive this.)

I'd bet that the sum of those utterly wasted hours is greater than the number of person-hours that went into sending the Apollo 11 spacecraft to its landing on the moon and bringing it safely back.

Why were all this time and energy so heartbreakingly misspent? For one simple reason, which — without excellent professional advice — Americans will never grasp. **Financial success is not driven by the performance of investments, but by the behavior of investors.** And the enemy of successful investing isn't "underperformance," whatever that means; it's The Big Mistake.

Career life insurance advisors, for their part, will regale you with similar tales of behavioral self-destruction from their own bitter experience: the person who doesn't buy life insurance because he "has enough money;" the person who doesn't want her children to inherit anything because "it would just spoil them;" the person who tearfully thanks the advisor for helping him protect his family, and then never makes the second premium payment.

However anecdotally, you can begin to infer from these horror stories a great — if inexplicable — psychological truth. Namely, that **our fellow citizens, regardless of how affluent or well-educated they may be, are hard-wired to fail financially.** Sooner or later, they make The Big Mistake. Some make it several times, in several ways. And some just keep making the same mistake over and over again.

Why is this true? Why, in the world's first — and by far most successful — capitalist democracy, are its citizens critically deficient in financial/emotional literacy?

In part, I think, it's because we have no tradition of financial education. Peter Lynch once observed that no one can get an academic high school diploma without (however briefly) knowing what a cosine is, but that no high school graduate need have ever been taught the difference between a stock and a bond.

Heavily unionized teachers receive limited salaries, but enjoy comprehensive benefits and retirement plans. Thus the biases of the educational system remain deeply rooted in the collectivist traditions of the 1930s–1960s, in which one's lifetime financial support was ultimately not one's personal responsibility: the government, the union and/or the employer would provide. Why (and how) would you teach something of which you have little experience, and which the students needn't really know because it's someone else's responsibility?

This isn't just a repudiation of the deep human need for (and the great American tradition of) self-reliance. It's a complete denial of modern reality. Government social schemes will be in full retreat for at least the next generation, as the number of aging, ailing beneficiaries of these systems swamps the taxpaying capacities of the contributors. In a vibrant, mobile, knowledge-based global workforce, unions become not merely less powerful but less relevant. And, also responding to the rigors of globalizing competition, big employers are unable and unwilling to burden their cost structures with elaborate company-funded retirement programs.

Thus, all of the prevailing economic, governmental and social trends of our time have the concerted effect of challenging the family to rely more and more on its own resources — while the educational system still makes no provision for teaching our citizens what those resources are, or how to use them.

So people end up trying to get a handle on their financial lives (a) after — and perhaps long after — the game is already afoot, and (b) in their very limited spare time. Inevitably, they seek to obtain a lot of information quickly and in its most simplified, digestible form. And that impulse, in turn, delivers them to the tender mercies of journalism.

The bull market of the 1990s, and the resulting public hunger for all the latest market information all the time, spawned a new form of saturation media coverage. CNBC, CNNfn, and a blizzard of web-based "news" services became a part of the culture — sponsored in large part by Internet trading croupiers, no-load/direct access investment and insurance providers, futures/options speculative programs, hair-trigger trading "systems," and other "information"-based, high-turnover purveyors *whose unifying theme was anti-advice.*

"Seize the power." "Rule the Street." "Every second counts." "Points can be made in a heartbeat." "If your broker is so smart, why is he still working?" These actual advertising slogans, and dozens like them, became woven into, and ultimately indistinguishable from, "news" coverage of markets — which finally degenerated into a battle to see who could flash the largest number of totally meaningless data on the screen in a 60-second period. The harried part-time manager of his own personal finances thus found no useful long-term perspective, but instead was subjected to the lowest forms of the worst do-it-yourself, trade-what's-hot, beat-the-market noise ever heard on the planet. *Perversely, the more information he got, and the faster he acted on it, the worse an investor he became, and the more behavioral mistakes he made.*

Financial journalism has much to answer for with respect to its contributions to the great stock market bubble of the late '90s. But, in a very real sense, the viewer was complicit, in that he was asking the media to do something neither they nor anything else can ever do: make one a good investor, not to mention a financial success, quickly and easily. Journalism reports the "news," but for the greater truths of planning and investing, one has to look somewhere else.

Finally, having pointed a finger at the education system and another at journalism, it would be unfair of me not to acknowledge the somewhat unhelpful way in which the financial services industry has tended to interact with the family in years past.

Because we worked in relatively narrow, fragmented segments of the Glass-Steagall synthesis — I a commissioned investment salesperson, you perhaps an insurance agent or a banker — we could not concern ourselves overmuch with the whole scope of financial planning. Indeed, we often didn't know if a family's financial needs outside of our product line were even being addressed. I shudder to think how many six- and seven-figure investment accounts I once had, in complete ignorance of how much debt the investor was carrying, how much insurance he owned, or even whether he had a will or not. I couldn't sell solutions to those problems even if I discovered them, and therefore they weren't — couldn't be — my concern.

To the man with a hammer, every problem looks like a nail. To me, in my Glass-Steagall straitjacket, every problem once looked like an investment issue. To a banker in his, every problem looked like an opportunity to make a loan or issue a CD. To an insurance agent in hers, everything looked like a life and/or disability insurance need. We competed with — rather than complementing, nor even cooperating with — each other. (When I was training at E. F. Hutton & Company, a third of a century ago, "I'm buying life insurance" was an *objection*. And I was taught to "overcome" it: "Buy term and invest the difference," or "Borrow out the cash value and invest it for bigger returns.")

That was the hand we were dealt. But it tended to leave the family battered from pillar to post by a whole lot of bitterly conflicting advice. Little wonder, then, that America has so much trouble doing the right thing financially: its advisors were supposed to be part of the solution, but too often we ended up being part of the problem.

But as culpable as these three cultural factors may be, they can't completely explain the deeply ingrained proclivity of Americans to blow themselves up. We will have occasion, as this book progresses, to look at other cultural contributors to the malaise, most particularly the way widely accepted usages of language ("safety," "risk" and "income," to name three of the usual suspects) distort reality. In the end, though — and this is absolutely crucial — **it is human nature itself which renders people incapable of succeeding on their own.**

Procrastination; wishful thinking; the inability to budget; overconfidence giving way to panic and vice versa; the search for "proof" that doesn't exist; a neurotic overreliance on past "performance" as a guide to future outcomes; the speculator inside nearly every investor, struggling to get out; the simple inability to trust an advisor — these and a dozen other very basic, very human instincts doom the individual. It isn't so much that he doesn't "want" to succeed (whatever that means); it's that he can't. He has an unconscious emotional need, and perhaps a whole complex of needs, that take precedence over the desire for financial success, and make it impossible. (We ourselves are far from immune to such self-defeating psychological needs, as we'll see in vivid detail when we talk about prospecting.)

In summary, then: to the vagaries of human nature, add a singularly (if oddly) unhelpful cultural context — and consider one other issue, which almost (but not quite) goes without saying: *the dense and constantly shifting complexities of the financial planning process itself.* These factors, taken together, form the first of the two great premises upon which this book is to be built: **people simply cannot do it themselves.**

Pause here a moment, if you will, to let yourself be encouraged and empowered by this critical perception. Ours is not a service which a family could perfectly well perform for itself, but chooses to pay someone else to do, like mowing their lawn, cleaning their house or driving them to the airport. What we do is much more akin to the paradigm of medicine: it is quite literally a matter of financial life and death, and the family is incapable of saving its own life.

And thus you see what the second and final premise of this book must be. They cannot do it themselves...**but you (and your firm) can do it for and with them.**

Yet both these points need immediately to be qualified by the fact that they state the *reality* of the situation. The problem is that you and I interact primarily with human nature, and therefore don't often have the luxury of engaging with reality. We deal, instead, with *perception*. And the *perception* by the prospective client family that our two great premises are true *for them* becomes the key to our relationship (just as the absence of that perception becomes an insurmountable obstacle to *any* real relationship).

Thus: **they cannot do it themselves**...but they have to acknowledge and accept this fact before we can help them. **You and your firm can do it for and with them**...but only if they want to be helped, and by you. It's nowhere near enough for you to know that your prospect family is, financially speaking, mortally ill. *They're all mortally ill.* The problem is that almost everyone you're ever going to prospect will turn you aside, with some or another form of denial:

- I'm not sick.
- I'm sick, but the thing you don't understand is that I don't really want to get better.
- I already see a doctor (and I'm not taking the medicine she prescribes, any more than I'd take it from you).
- I'm sick, but you don't know how to cure me.
- I'm sick, but I can self-medicate my way back to health; I don't need you.
- I'm sick, but I can find a cheaper doctor than you.
- I'm sick, but I'm too busy to think about it right now; I'll get treatment some other day.

At the point where we encountered one of these forms of resistance, those of us who were classically trained in the old transaction-oriented, commission-based, product-pushing synthesis started "selling."

We'd get a referral. On the appointed day, a 300-pound guy, wheezing heavily with every labored step, would shamble into our office, and a colloquy not unlike the following would take place.

Doc: How are you feeling?

Patient: Not so hot. No energy, breathing hard,
           coughing a lot, headaches, pains in my joints,
           trouble sleeping...

Doc: Tell me about your lifestyle.

Patient:	Normal activities. Watch TV, stuff like that.
Doc:	Eating habits?
Patient:	Eggs in the morning, cheeseburger for lunch, steak for dinner...normal American food.
Doc:	Smoke or drink?
Patient:	Moderately. Two packs of Camels and a fifth of Jack Daniel's.
Doc:	Every day?
Patient:	Not every *single* day...
Doc:	(Weighs patient, checks blood pressure, listens to heart and lungs) OK, we're just going to put you on a somewhat lower fat/cholesterol eating program. Here's some chewing gum that'll help suppress the urge to smoke, and a prescription to start taking your blood pressure down. Oh, and I'd like you to begin walking on a treadmill; I'll give you a program for 30 days, and then let's see how you're doing, OK?
Patient:	I don't need you turning me into a bleeping vegetarian. Just give me some medicine that'll help me stop breathing so hard. And a sleeping pill.
Doc:	(Leaping around the office, hanging up charts, graphs and scattergrams) Wait! Don't you care about your family? I can *prove* that this blood pressure medicine works! And look at this clinical study of the benefits of walking! And here's a major report on smoking and lung disease; you gotta read this! Do what I prescribe, and I *guarantee* you're gonna get better. Just one signature, and a small check to get you started...you can afford this! Waddya say?!?

If the "doctor's" supplication seems distasteful and even grotesque, (a) you're right, but (b) this is essentially what we were trained to do: reason/argue/prove/persuade/cajole people into doing the right thing, no matter how deeply committed they were to doing the wrong thing and/or to resisting us and our advice. It is a key tenet of this book that the New Financial Advisor can only help people who genuinely want to be helped. And so, in a very real sense, *we're going to have to learn to transcend "selling."*

It is what it is. You can't cause water to run upstream, nor make people love their families more than they do — enough so that they'll accept an appropriate financial plan. You can't make past performance indicate future results. You can't prove the sun's coming up tomorrow, much less which mutual fund or "wrap" account manager is going to "outperform." You can't predict whether interest rates, the stock market or the dollar will be up, down or dead in the water a year from today. You can't know when people are going to pass away, nor what the estate tax rate will be when they do. And you can't guarantee *anything.*

All you can say is all you can say:

> "No airplane can take off without a flight plan; no ship can sail without a plotted course — and no household/family can contemplate a successful financial journey, especially across more than one generation, without some sort of comprehensive financial, investment and estate plan. No one actually plans to fail financially; it's just that most people fail to plan. My job — indeed, my mission in life — is to help households/families like yours make just such a comprehensive plan...and then guide them through the completion of that plan, year after year.
>
> "At the human level — at the level of you as the family talking to me as the financial planner — planning is almost always less complicated and easier to do than people expect.

"We start by assessing **where you are**: what you own, what you owe, what you earn, and what your expenses are. This is simply collecting baseline data: it doesn't deal with where you're going or how you're going to get there. But it does give us a clear — and shared — understanding of the very first thing you have to know in any journey: *exactly where you're starting from.*

"From there, we create a sort of wish list of your hopes and dreams — what you would like to accomplish financially, for yourself and for the people you care about.

"This also turns out to be pretty straightforward, because it usually focuses on a very few threshold issues. When and how do you want to retire? (Maybe you *never* want to retire; you want to work forever, but in a business that you own and love.) What are you going to need or want to do for your parents as they grow older? Who do you have to, or just want to, educate? Children? Grandchildren? What's your philosophy about legacies: heirs, charities? **What would you do if you could?**

"Then we get out a calculator, and see if we can turn those hopes and dreams into concrete financial goals. (1) What will the things you want to do cost, and when? (2) What's the gap between where you are and where you want to get to, and how much time have we got to close that gap? (3) Can you put away enough money, and can that money earn a sufficient return, to close the gap in the time allotted? **Can we get there?**

"If we find that we can, then you've already got the foundation and the framework of a financial plan. If we find that we *can't* fund all your dreams in the time we've got, then we have to consider some trade-offs. Maybe we wanted to get you an income of $6,000 a month over Social Security and your 401(k) payout, *and* we wanted to pay for the college education of your granddaughter. When we put a pencil to it, perhaps we find that we can do most, but not all, of both: $5,000 a month and the little girl's college, or $6,000 a month and half her tuition...trade-offs like that. So you have some decisions to make. But again, when that process settles out, you've substantially framed up a plan.

"Along the way, as the plan takes form, we'll want to insure its outcome against the risk that you wouldn't be around — or wouldn't be physically able — to complete it. A plan that's unsinkable *unless it hits an iceberg* isn't really unsinkable. And it isn't really a plan. It's more in the nature of a bet, and prudent people don't bet on the financial fate of their families.

"At that point, I'll work up an investment portfolio that has some history of producing the kinds of long-term returns we've calculated that we'll need. We'll let the accountants and attorneys — yours, my firm's or both, as you see fit — work out the technical end: wills, trusts and the like. **And there will be your and your family's comprehensive plan.**

"For whatever it's worth, I promise you I won't deliver a plan that's less than complete, or doesn't do what we agreed on, or simply isn't the very best we can do. We'll just keep sending the experts back to the drawing board, to work on it until it's right.

"Then it just becomes a question of giving the plan enough time, enough money, and enough faith. We'll update the plan at least annually — more often if your circumstances really change, or when tax laws do — but we have to try to resist the temptation to tinker with it, or micromanage it, or change it just for the sake of changing it.

"That's how it works. What I can't describe — what you may not fully understand until you experience it — is the tremendous weight of concern that's lifted from you when you know you have a first-rate plan in place. No one can relieve you of the *responsibility* for your family's financial success, but a plan — and, if I may say so, a planner — can take away so much of the anxiety and the worry involved.

"Well, that's my story. That's what I do, and I hope you can see how much I love doing it, and why. Now, before we proceed any further, I'd be happy to answer any questions you have at this stage."

So says the New Financial Advisor — able, in this brave new post-Glass-Steagall world, to pull all the threads of a financial life together, and to offer the family what it's always needed: **one plan, from one planner.**

Was the advisor — in this low-key, comfort-building, roughly five-minute statement — "selling" anything? Well, yes and no. He certainly wasn't "pitching" a portfolio, an insurance program, or even a specific plan. But he surely *was* selling the one thing the client family absolutely has to buy. He was selling himself. Because people never actually buy the plan; *they buy the planner.*

Financial planning — to people outside the industry, and even to some misguided souls within it — appears to be a left-brain intellectual "sale" based on the subtly nuanced technical complexities of the plan itself. In fact, it's the ultimate right-brain emotional "sale," in which the family decides to accept the planner's invitation *to stop being afraid* of what's going to happen to them financially. How can the planner "prove" that the clients should make such a decision? She can't, of course. That's the great thing about this whole approach: in effect, *it forces the family to make an act of faith in you* as the steward of their financial fate. And one mission of this book is to convince you that that's the only kind of client relationship worth having.

As this golden age of financial planning dawns, the New Financial Advisor is offered a gift and a challenge. But these two things come in a package; you must accept both or neither.

The gift is the power to create and maintain, for some number of families, that which all Americans say they are seeking and cannot find on their own: a measure of true and lasting financial peace. And in doing great good for other families you will do wonderfully well for your own. Because we advisors are permitted, without any externally imposed limit, to build our own fortunes *in the act of* helping our clients achieve, hold and grow theirs.

And the challenge, of course, is finding those clients who deserve the priceless gift you bring, out of all the numberless people you'll encounter who won't accept it. For many are called, but few are chosen.

It goes without saying that you have to deserve success — that you must put in the time and the energy necessary to master the new craft of financial advice, as well as the dogged determination it takes to show your and your firm's mastery of that craft to enough prospects.

Yes, you have to deserve great clients. But — and this is the central message of the book you've just started reading — *they have to deserve you, too.* Upon that elegant equation is all true excellence built.

This is how it's done...

BECOMING DOCTOR NOAH

chapter one

ONE

———————•———————

What does comprehensive financial/investment/estate planning do for a family? When you and your affluent clients get up from the table and shake hands over the completed plan, what's true about the family's financial situation that probably wasn't true before? I can think of seven key things:

- If a breadwinner (much less *the* breadwinner) dies prematurely, the family's lifestyle will not be fatally compromised: they will stay in their home; education plans will remain financially on track; the family's business, if it owns one, won't have to be sold precipitously at a disadvantageous price.

- Similar outcomes will prevail in the event of disability.

- The children and/or grandchildren of the family will be able to afford the very best education for which they can qualify, without still being saddled with student loans when they themselves have children.

- The current generation of the family will be able to retire at its own time and on its own terms, with a high degree of confidence that it will never outlive its income — that its dignity and independence will not be undermined by up to three decades of rising living costs.

- The current generation will, if necessary, be able to contribute meaningfully to the support of its parents. Moreover, this generation will never become a financial burden to *its* children, even if extended nursing home stays are required.

- Even as retirement income rises to offset inflating living costs, this generation's capital will continue to grow over time, endowing meaningful legacies to the succeeding generations.

- Estate taxation won't force the sale of a family's important assets (homes, business, etc.). This liability will be funded out of the residual capital, and/or it will be insured.

At the human level — where the New Financial Advisor speaks with her deserving client family — these great goals are starkly beautiful in their simplicity. *These are the real things that real people really yearn to accomplish, and don't know how.*

The *new* New Financial Advisor — the person just entering our profession and intent on doing it the right way — may be daunted and dismayed by the volumes of technical and product knowledge necessary to these Seven Glorious Outcomes *which he does not have.* Where to begin? What to learn? How much studying must he do before he can even *talk* to people about these things without making a fool of himself?

And the neophyte has it relatively easy. Consider the (however narrowly) experienced advisor, rising from the wreckage of her particular Glass-Steagall fragment — especially if it's investments or insurance. She may well feel even more bereft, because she is skilled in pursuing some of these great goals, *and therefore keenly aware of how ignorant she is of the others.* The neophyte may be completely lost, but he is, for that reason, completely open: he has no biases or preconceptions. *The fragment survivor has a comfort zone,* and is being pulled out of it, which generates a lot of anxiety, particularly to the extent that she was already successful in her fragment. Moreover, she's watching her firm vectoring all its time, energy and resources (product development, advanced training, advertising) into the new planning paradigm. They trained her to be narrowly specialized; now they're abandoning that approach — and her, or at least that may be how it feels. That's gotta hurt.

And indeed, the perception that *on some level* financial planning is an enterprise of significant complexity is true. The corollary perception that *someone is going to have to master all those complexities*, if you're going to deliver a plan that achieves these great goals, is equally true.

The liberating, life-enhancing, energy-releasing news this book offers the New Financial Advisor is:

(1) you don't ever have to operate on the technical level, and

(2) you don't ever have to master those dense, shifting technical complexities...*unless and until you decide you want to.*

There is an above-the-line and a below-the-line in financial planning. Above the line is where real people live, work, love, hope for the future, and speak human language to each other, and to you. Below the line is where the experts live, toiling among the intricate gearworks of variable second-to-die insurance, modern portfolio theory, Section 529 plans, family limited partnerships, the efficient frontier, and insurance trusts. The experts speak expert language to each other, and to you.

You are the relationship manager between the two cultures. And, in a very real sense, you are the translator between the family — the passengers of a plan — and the experts — the engineers of the plan — who can't effectively communicate with each other. This is a great, and a rare, and an ultimately invaluable skill — or skill set, really. **The world is full of experts, but great communicators are always in short supply.**

Revel in this. Draw strength from it. And know that, for the duration — or until you're darn good and ready — *you needn't be the expert*...nor even one of the experts.

These days, regardless of what kind of financial services firm you're with, or what its size is, chances are you have very significant technical support at the local, regional and home office levels. (Some of you have armies of these people.) Moreover, there are legions of underutilized wholesalers roaming the countryside — representing insurance and annuity companies, mutual funds, and "wrap" money managers — just dying to bring their own and their employers' resources to bear on your behalf in the hope of earning your business. (That's one of the great things about being on the right side of a classic distribution bottleneck, in which a jillion product originators are desperately trying to get attention from a few, rapidly consolidating outlets — like you and your firm.)

Granted, you have to learn to ask the right questions — but there aren't very many, and there's a ton of data-gathering software that'll walk you through them, even as you sit with your prospects. Granted, as well, that you have to learn to ask the right questions *in the right way* — a way that communicates your genuine concern, and thus closes the emotional distance between you and the prospects. (We'll talk a lot in this book about how to do that.) But that's almost as far as you have to go. Let the prospects' accountant/attorney talk directly to your support people. Better yet, let them *meet* with you and your support people. You just go on talking to the family; keep their (and your) eyes on the prize — the completed plan — and let the experts hammer out the details. That's not your job. Say it loud, and say it proud:

I FLY 'EM.
I DON'T BUILD 'EM.

Now, maybe one day you'll turn out to be like Chuck Yeager, who went into World War II right out of high school and ended up testing generation after generation of high-performance aircraft alongside other pilots who had advanced engineering degrees. (Funny, though: it wasn't an engineer who broke the sound barrier.)

Yeager was the *original* "I fly 'em, I don't build 'em" guy. But as he evolved into the pre-eminent test pilot of his time, Yeager and his team developed a new approach. When they were given an experimental plane to test, before Yeager flew it they'd go into the hangar, take the plane apart down to the last nut and bolt, and then put it back together again. When they were finished, Chuck usually knew more about that plane than did the engineers who designed and built it.

Maybe that'll be you someday. Maybe time, experience and your love of what you do (and whom you do it for) will produce in you a relationship manager who understands the whole plan better than the "experts" in the different disciplines who put it together. (And maybe you recoil in horror at the mere thought of this, so violently that you just decided you want "I fly 'em, I don't build 'em" on your tombstone.) In either event, I say: fine. Let's just wait and see.

But you can't start out trying to be both a relationship manager *and* an expert. There aren't enough hours in the day, and there isn't enough energy in your bones.

And above all, you can't use the quest for technical expertise as the pre-condition of your business-building effort. You don't learn so that you can *then* do; that's an anxiety reaction and an avoidance behavior. **You learn by doing, or I solemnly assure you that you'll never learn at all.** (Or, worse, you'll abandon our calling altogether, and become just another salaried "expert.")

I believe, for example, that the New Financial Advisor should earn the CFP designation. CFP is a very good program, and getting better all the time. It gives you a broad range of core competency across the spectrum of financial planning issues, and that can be an important confidence builder. Moreover, CFP is remarkably widely recognized and respected by the public. They may not know exactly what it means, or how you got it, but they surely sense that it didn't come in no Cheerios box. It says to prospects that you have a serious commitment to planning.

But I can't tell you how much of my e-mail traffic boils down to, "I'm paralyzed; I'm suffering from rejection shock; I don't have enough accounts or enough money under management; please tell me the right way to prospect. And oh, by the way, I'm taking the CFP course." In other words, "I'm filling up the time I psychologically can't use to prospect by studying to learn a whole bunch of new things I'll *still* be too paralyzed to talk to people about." Here you see the quest for more knowledge as the toxic, time-wasting vicious cycle it can turn into, if you don't keep it under tight control at all times.

At the level where the New Financial Advisor interacts with an affluent household/family, financial planning isn't about *knowing* anything. It's about *doing* something: inviting people to find lasting and even multigenerational financial security by trusting you and your firm to create a comprehensive plan. The work of the New Financial Advisor — the glorious work which he believes he was sent into the world to do — isn't done when he's looking into the screen of a computer. It's done when — and only when — he's looking into the eyes of another human being: specifically, the eyes of someone whose household/family is going to be lost, sooner or later, without a plan and a planner. Which means *everybody* — again, whether they know it (or acknowledge it) or not.

Now: how do you "sell" that?

How do you "sell" the idea, "You don't know me from Eve, but your household is mortally ill financially, and unless you take this serum I'm offering you, you're gonna die destitute, and your children are going to inherit the wind"? How does the doctor "sell" that 300-pound smoker/drinker/red meat eater the self-awareness and the will — not to mention the sheer *readiness* — to abort the suicide run that he's so clearly on?

And while you're mulling *that* over, go back to the beginning of this chapter and re-read The Seven Glorious Outcomes — some, most or all of which will become true when a family embraces you and your plan. Freedom from the fear of dying too soon, or becoming disabled? *And* freedom from fear of running out of money in retirement? *And* the ability to intervene meaningfully in the education — not to mention the very lives — of your children...and theirs? I ask again, in wonder and amazement, *how do you "sell" that?*

My answer — this book's answer — is threefold: (1) you don't, (2) because you can't, and (3) it's beneath your dignity. Once more, with feeling: you can only help people who want — and are ready — to be helped...*by you.* In other words, you don't "sell" a plan for multigenerational financial freedom; you allow a finite number of deserving families to buy one from you.

Finding such people may not be particularly easy. What else is new? Excellence is never easy. On the other hand, *once you decide that mediocrity is unthinkable*, your only choices are excellence and quitting. So whatever the price of excellence — and it'll be spelled out in detail for you very shortly — start preparing to pay it.

And take courage from two critically important realizations. First, you're not looking for that many people: 250 reasonably affluent households/families should more than suffice to carry you to the top of the profession. Second, somewhere around halfway through the process of finding the right people, *they themselves will begin to help you recruit the rest.* ("How do you get referrals?" advisors have wailed from time immemorial. The answer is simple. Once again, not easy, but simple: *do great work for people who actively appreciate it.*)

The point is that — **provided only that you have enough qualified prospects from whom to choose** — you can, should, and will select those households/families who (a) meet your minimum account size, (b) acknowledge that they need a plan and ask you to prepare one for them, and (c), most important, are people you like — or at least respect — and want to work with.

In this new golden age of financial planning, why would an advisor subject herself to people who didn't, to some greater or lesser extent, meet these criteria? The answer — the *only* answer — is that she hasn't got enough prospects. She can't choose the clients she wants, so she's forced to accept the customers she can get, however she ends up getting them.

She takes accounts that are too small, and accounts who argue. She takes accounts who carp about her fees. She takes querulous, frightened accounts who call up at every downtick, and "performance" maniacs for whom no return is enough. She takes accounts who have other advisors and who constantly compare her unfavorably to them. She takes accounts who solicit her recommendations, and then find reasons not to act on them. She takes accounts who always want to know what she thinks of the market. She takes accounts who can't read their statements, and who ask the same questions over and over again. She takes accounts she doesn't respect. She takes accounts she doesn't like, and who don't particularly like her. She's so exhausted, frustrated and anxious that she has little energy left with which to prospect, no consistent prospecting plan, and no real hope that her sporadic prospecting activity will get her anywhere. (She's right; it won't.) It may sound to you like this advisor has a whole panoply of issues, but fundamentally there's just the one: *she hasn't got enough prospects.*

At the beginning of 2001, I started a newsletter/spot coaching service called *Nick Murray Interactive* (www.nickmurrayinteractive.com). The idea is that I try to generate some helpful current commentary each month, and I'm there as the subscriber's virtual sales manager/sounding board. As this service grew, and I began getting a steady flow of e-mail questions, I found that more than half of all the inquiries fell into two general categories. One was paralyzing prospecting anxiety, in all its hydra-headed forms — some of which the questioner was conscious of, and some not. (An example of the latter: "I've been in the business a year and a half; I haven't opened many accounts or raised much money; do you think I should take the CFP course?") And the other large sample of related questions had to do with "problem" clients. It took almost six months, but suddenly I had an epiphany. To wit, these are not two different issues; *they're one and the same: not enough prospects.*

I had focused too closely on the individual idiosyncrasies of each "problem" client — the second-guesser, the fee carper, the nervous nellie, the techie know-it-all — to notice that all these situations came down to the same two questions, which in turn had the same one answer. (1) Why did you let this bat into your belfry in the first place? "I needed the business." (2) Why, since he won't listen — won't stop his toxic perseverating about...whatever — don't you fire him? "I need the business."

Why do advisors "need" bad accounts? Because they haven't got enough good accounts. And why don't they have enough good accounts? Because they haven't done the high (but selective) volume of prospecting necessary to find and recruit those accounts. But doesn't it hurt to grind yourself up making a mediocre income (at best) serving troglodytes about as badly as they seem to want to be served? Yes, says the struggling advisor (although he may not consciously hear himself saying this) but the "rejection" I encounter in prospecting hurts even more.

Let me assure you of two cosmic certainties. (1) There are enough — and more than enough — good client relationships out there, awaiting your (and your firm's) claim, to take you to the top of this profession. (2) In the long run, *not* doing what's necessary to find them hurts infinitely worse than doing it. The psychologist Aaron Hemsley (about whom much more in the next chapter) always says, "All chronic production issues are behavior issues." To that I would add that the behavior in question is prospecting. All the real problems advisors encounter in this profession are traceable to not having enough good prospects. The converse is even more wonderfully true: *having an abundant flow of quality prospects solves all your problems.*

Reading this wonderfully focused, tremendously refreshing truth may prompt you to say, "OK, I totally buy into that. Now, how do I prospect?" That's the wrong question. Or, more accurately, it's premature. It's a question that has to be answered, surely, and in the next couple of chapters it will be. *But behavior has to be rooted in belief.* What you propose to say and do must be driven by who you are. Otherwise, you're just a set of techniques. And believe me, boys and girls: ain't no technique in the world gonna stand up to the psychological battering you experience when you prospect three hundred 300-lb. Camels/Jack/ribeye guys *in a row*.

Persistence and determination are indeed omnipotent, like the fellow said, but you need to have a very clear idea of what it is you're persevering *at*, or you're not going to make it. So the threshold question isn't "How do you prospect?" In fact, it isn't even one question: it's three of 'em.

WHO ARE YOU?

WHAT DO YOU WANT?

WHAT IS YOUR PLAN FOR EARNING WHAT YOU WANT?

Let's consider these issues one by one, and then see if we can derive a coherent persona/plan for you, as you begin (or resume) the quest for excellence as the affluent family's primary financial advisor.

(1) *WHO ARE YOU?* Ours is a profession that attracts a startling proportion of other-directed people: folks who, having no real idea who they are, drift into a business of seeking acceptance and approval from other people, unconsciously *hoping someone else will tell them*.

The trouble with this is that if you're getting your identity from other people — vesting in them the power to tell you you're OK by buying your product, portfolio or even plan — you're setting yourself up to fail. Because the huge preponderance of people you encounter aren't going to buy what you're selling — a signal to the other-directed advisor that he's *not*, in fact, OK. Hence, the "pain of rejection" that struggling advisors talk about (or, even more sadly, don't talk about).

When this kind of personality hears enough "no" (i.e. gets "rejected" often enough), the world's overwhelming verdict that he isn't OK paralyzes him. Ultimately it drives him out of the profession, sends him scurrying to immerse himself in the CFP course, or traps him on a gerbil wheel of permanent, self-enforced mediocrity — a state of toxic equilibrium in which the pain of being nobody and the pain of more prospecting just about balance each other out.

You have to have a fairly strong personal and professional sense of self to become outstandingly successful. This is probably true in any walk of life, but it's drop-dead critical in a profession that requires you to command the respect, trust, loyalty and even affection of some of America's more affluent households/families. And developing that powerful internal guidance system is a process — of age, of experience, of knowledge, and of wisdom...all of which take time. Identity doesn't come in cans, like Popeye's spinach.

But even as you're developing that completely new thing in nature that is your unique identity, you can pretty much instantly — and therefore quite easily — become *authentic*. On your first day out of the training program — or even after years of struggle picking stocks, or selling insurance, or trying vainly to handicap mutual funds based on their "track record" — you can make a definitive statement of who you are and what you intend to be. And the beauty of this statement is that it becomes perfectly true *in the instant that you believe it to be true* — and the moment you irrevocably commit to devoting all of your professional time and talent to making it stick. The statement, as I have some reason to hope you've already guessed, is:

I'M A DOCTOR.

I find myself in a society that's pandemically ill financially — a society even whose better-educated, more affluent families are following a life-threatening fiscal lifestyle, and who will surely perish, probably in this generation but certainly in the next, without the intervention of a humane healer *like me*.

I'm not going to hold myself out to the world as a universal specialist — a ranking expert in all diseases and injuries. First of all, it wouldn't be true, and I would never tell a patient something that wasn't true. (He would pay me and then die anyway, and I refuse to live like that.) Second, there is no concept of a universal specialist in the paradigm of medicine: instead there are general practitioners supported by teams of extremely (though narrowly) capable specialists at the hospitals with which the GPs are affiliated. (That reminds me a lot of myself in relation to the great financial institution I'm employed by, as well as to the top-flight insurance/investment/mortgage product providers my firm works with.)

As a general practitioner, the primary skill set I'll be required to employ is *diagnostic*. That works for me, too, because in the financial area there are only a very few, easily identifiable risks that I have to be on the alert for: dying too soon or living too long, loss of income due to disability or unemployment, not putting away enough money or putting it away in the wrong places.

And, like the GP who serves her patients as the first line of defense against the more common health mistakes (smoking, drinking, bad diet, insufficient exercise), I can easily do an enormous amount of good simply by helping people avoid the more common, most destructive investment errors: panic, overconfidence, underdiversification, overdiversification, speculation/trading, investing for yield instead of for total return, and leverage.

When the specific treatment my patient family needs is beyond my competence — which, in the early going, I serenely expect will be virtually all the time — I'll call in the specialists. But I'll be there through the whole course of treatment — explaining, encouraging, and sometimes just holding their hands. That's really important, because I notice that my patients have trouble understanding what the specialists are saying. And I find in the specialists an insufficient capacity for empathy; they tend to see my patients as cases rather than as the sick, frightened human beings that they are.

Over time — as my knowledge, experience and wisdom grow — I'll be able successfully to treat more (and more complex) diseases, and to heal more grave injuries. But I'll never let my ego — or my professional relationship with my patients — get tangled up in the issue of *who* effects the cure. My job is to make sure my patients get better in the most humane way — which is ultimately all that matters — *not to cure them myself*.

Finally, I can never cure — and will never dissipate my time and energy trying to cure — people who do not want to be cured, now, by me and my colleagues. A doctor empathizes; a doctor — up to a point — explains; *a doctor does not "sell."* Modeling my authentic professional self on the doctor:

- I'll tell people the absolute truth all the time. I'll never sugarcoat it; I'll never tell them what they want to hear. As empathetically as humanly possible, I'll give it to 'em straight.

- I will relate to my patients by understanding what they need to do, and then recommending strongly that they do it. I will not, among other things — once I think I've correctly diagnosed the illness — ask them what *they* want to do.

- I won't be responsible for any other treatment but the one I recommend. If they choose to try alternative medicine, or a drug I don't know (or if they elect to buy a mutual fund I've never heard of), I can't stop them. But they can't have recourse to me about that choice when it doesn't work.

- I will not argue, try to "prove" anything, guarantee an outcome, or even predict the course of their illness. I will tell them what works best most of the time in their case, and I'll tell them what the next step is if that doesn't work. (If they have to invest $3,000 a month at the index 11% return to retire comfortably, that's what I'll tell 'em. I certainly won't predict that they'll get 11%. And I'll not fail to make it clear that if they get 8% for the first five years, for instance, they'll have to invest more money, or re-tire on less.)

- I will never try to gain a patient by competing pri-marily on the issue of price.

- Though I will tell people what I believe they should do, and will strongly encourage them to do it, I will expend no extraordinary effort trying to "make" them do it. "Do not try to teach a mule to dance," said Mark Twain; "it wastes your time, and upsets the mule." I will help who wants help; I will at-tempt to teach no mules to dance.

Your professional skills in financial planning are only going to grow. Your personal identity as a planner is only going to mature. And, al-though you may find it difficult to believe at the moment, these two de-veloping aspects of your deepest self are ultimately going to merge: in a very real sense, you become what you do. But while you're waiting for that marvelous process to work itself through, you can still have a very effective interim answer to the question "Who am I?" by lining yourself up with the beliefs and behaviors of the medical GP.

(2) *WHAT DO YOU WANT?* The great Zen master Lawrence Peter Berra said, "If you don't know where you're going, you might not get there." Excellence in our profession usually has a very specific set of goals toward which it's driving; the more definite your purpose, the sim-pler it is to work consistently — and without a lot of flailing — in pursuit of it. Moreover, specific long-term goals in which you (and your family)

deeply believe make adversity easier to overcome; setbacks and reversals become stones in the road that you run over rather than brick walls you crash into. Finally, your quantified goals will usually dictate a clear plan of action, but it won't work the other way around. That is, you'll have trouble crafting a specific plan in support of vague or poorly thought out aims ("making a lot of money," "getting to the top").

The logical place to start — because a long chain of subsidiary decisions falls into line behind it — is what you want to earn. What income should the doctor — the affluent family's primary financial advisor, the person who saves their financial life not once but many times over the years — require in exchange for the incalculable amount of good she does? Well, why not $500,000? (Note to reader: that last question was *anything but rhetorical.*)

Next, simply gross up your required earnings. If you practice in one of the large investment houses, chances are you net about half your gross revenues. For that matter, if you're a sole practitioner in a nice office with modern resources and a competent, reasonably compensated staff, you too may be netting around half your gross. So why don't we use 50% as a reasonably conservative "plug" number? Thus, for you to earn half a million dollars, the practice would have to gross a million. Now, how would it go about doing that? In other words, what's your answer to the last of our three threshold questions?

(3) *WHAT IS YOUR PLAN FOR EARNING WHAT YOU WANT?* Please note that the verb "earning" is not used in this question — nor anywhere else in this book — merely as a synonym for "making money." It is used interchangeably with the word "*deserving.*"

If my ethical standards are shabby enough — if I have no compunction about letting people do things they want to do that I know are bad for them — I can make a fair amount of money in this business. (Of course, I'll have to keep finding new accounts as the old ones finish blowing themselves up.) But do I, in the sense of deserving it, *earn* that money?

Surely not. So this third question is really asking what you plan to do — what real value will you give, what constant effort will you expend — in order to *deserve* $500,000, or whatever dollar answer you got to the second question.

This is no small distinction, and we will have occasion to revisit it many times in this book. Mediocrity tends to see a lot of grey in ethical issues. Bedeviled, I think, by the steadfast refusal of so many people with whom he talks to accept his genuinely good advice, the journeyman ends up walking the path of least resistance, not noticing — or simply choosing to ignore — that it is the road to professional hell. To him, ethical concerns become a nuisance; they just get in the way, and keep him from obtaining what he wants. This is part of the mediocrity's tragedy (excellence was always so near that he might have reached out and touched it), because adherence to high standards is actually an immense wellspring of strength and power.

Whenever you turn aside (or are turned aside by) business that is beneath your standards, you make an equivalent deposit of good business in a great cosmic bank. And there it sits, awaiting your claim. Indeed, Ralph Waldo Emerson, in his essay "Compensation," takes the position that your deposit does a lot more than just sit there: "Compound interest on compound interest," says the sage of Concord, "is the rate and usage of this exchequer."

A 60-year-old couple is referred to me, and on the appointed day they arrive, bearing a $700,000 inheritance check. They know that, even at today's tepid interest rates, this capital might yield them a "safe" $50,000 a year. And combined with Social Security and their other retirement plans, this is — they're quite sure of this — "all the money we'll ever need." Sadly, it is nothing of the kind. The problem is that I know this, that they do not, and that the system ("compliance") would only smile upon these "conservative" investors as they dug their financial graves with a fixed-income shovel — and upon me as I helped them.

But instead of enabling them to do what they want to do, I try to help them do what they really need to do: put the lion's share of the windfall in equities, so that their income and capital have some reasonable chance of growing to offset the depredations of three decades of rising living costs.

I give them all the empathy of which I'm capable ("I understand just how you feel; you wouldn't be human if you didn't feel this way"). I give them a beautiful 1975 10-cent postage stamp — my non-argumentative proxy for the idea of the cancer of inflation in everyday life. I give them a copy of my book *Simple Wealth, Inevitable Wealth* and ask them to read it together.

And when I follow up, they tell me they went to their bank, which was only too happy to sell them CDs, a fixed annuity, and some bond funds.

The journeyman will try this once and learn his lesson. "I lost the sale," he says, "because I foolishly tried to be a better advisor than these people deserved. And besides, come to think of it, who am I to predict that they won't lose money in equities, or how much inflation there'll be? Maybe I could've put them in bonds, and then talked about equities when they got to know me better and trust me more. *I'll never make that mistake again.*"

The doctor says, "It's a shame those poor folks wouldn't take the medicine; now they're going to die. Since the medicine in these cases never changes, perhaps there might be some marginal improvements I could make in the way I prescribe it; let me look at that. But of course, now there's $700,000 around here somewhere with my name on it, *simply awaiting my persistence and courage in finding it.*

"I deserved that $700,000 account — I earned it in the very best sense — I just didn't get it *from these particular people.* But only a depressive would conclude that that meant he wasn't going to get it, *period.* Having deserved/earned an account of this size, I will now surely obtain it *from people who also deserve me.* All I have to do is to keep actively look-ing for them.

"This is no strain, for two reasons. (1) I know this account is around here somewhere, and that the only way I can possibly fail to find it is *if I stop looking.* (2) I just got a tremendous surge of real, lasting strength from the pride I feel in not compromising my principles — in not taking blood money. A lesser advisor would have accepted that account, and become not a doctor but a drug dealer — peddling the narcotic illusion of 'safety' in bonds to that doomed couple, and using the excuse that they were going to buy that drug from *someone.* Yes, they were, but it wasn't me, and I feel great about that. So let me now go back, stronger than ever, and work **my plan for earning $500,000.**"

What's that, dear reader? We haven't even begun to derive that plan yet, you say? O, ye of little faith. Because, while it may be true that we've yet to *quantify* the plan, its much more important *qualitative* ele-ment is now in place. Lasting excellence isn't a number, it's a quality. And your steadfast refusal to compromise your standards — in perfect faith that that refusal *must* be rewarded — is that very quality. Your career — the vessel you will build to carry a finite number of deserving families, along with yours, to the promised land of financial peace — is The Ark. And I assure you that, in agreeing to live by the mighty law of compensa-tion, *you have just laid the keel of The Ark.*

The rest of the plan — the numbers part — you can virtually scratch out on the back of an envelope.

Briefly: we've agreed that you need a million dollars of gross in-come to the practice. The composition of that amount is a moving target — or targets, really — since you can't know at the outset what part of your revenue will come from insurance commissions, what part from invest-ment management fees, what part from fee-for-service plans *without* the asset management, and so on. Moreover, the structures of insurance com-missions and of investment management fees are themselves in constant flux.

So the simplest and potentially most conservative approach might be to assume that your revenues will just be one percent of the assets under management — treating other forms of fees and commissions as a windfall, outside the scope of the plan. That assumption yields the equally simple conclusion that you need to be managing a hundred million dollars.

It's only at this point that the process gets even the least bit tricky, because now you start having to make decisions which are both quantitative *and* qualitative. The big one, of course, is: how many people can you save? How many households/families can you safely take into The Ark without swamping it — and you?

Granting that you can stay in radio contact with a lot of support onshore (the "experts"), and even granting that you can staff The Ark with a crew, on board to assist you directly, the fundamental responsibility (and the huge preponderance of the rewards) are yours. People are buying you — because if they're not, either they're going to go over the side in the middle of a storm, or mutiny and run your Ark up on the rocks. (This, in turn, implies that if you're selling the seaworthiness of The Ark, as opposed to your own seamanship, you're setting everybody up to fail at the critical moment — especially you.)

So: how many people can you navigate to safety, still having enough time and energy to care for each cabin individually, and still having a life? All my years and all my experience tell me it isn't more than about 250 households/families (especially since you may, and I very much hope you will, be dealing with more than one generation of a family). So we seem to be talking about a hundred-million-dollar Ark, with 250 staterooms, the average stateroom costing $400,000 of (possibly transgenerational) assets.

The last question in this sequence, then, becomes: what does the smallest stateroom cost? You have to have a minimum account size — I would hope that'd almost go without saying — so what's it going to be? Remember that, in the act of letting someone on The Ark with less than the minimum, you accept the responsibility to find another household/ family with that much more. Take a $300,000 passenger and you immediately need a $500,000 one. Much more ominously, when your good-natured heart goes out to a $100,000 account, realize that you're now under the gun to find a $700,000 one, or you'll already be behind plan. And so forth.

In the end, I think this particular configuration of The Ark — $100 million/250 staterooms/one percent revenue/$400,000 average — pretty much forces you to accept no household/family that doesn't bring (or can't bring within the next year or so) $250,000 aboard.

Of course, now that you see what a $500,000 income (at 50% of gross revenues) entails, you may elect to reconfigure your Ark. I wouldn't like to see you choose some of these options, but you should at least be aware of the potential tradeoffs, so that you can make an informed — and authentic — decision. It is, after all, your Ark, and you have to skipper it.

You could try to standardize your planning services (like Henry Ford's Model T, the buyer can have any color he wants as long as it's black), hire some more deckhands, put a partition in each stateroom, and board 500 $200,000 households. You'll surely find an Ark with twice as many passengers to be about 10 times harder to navigate, but maybe you just have to go prove that to yourself.

Or you might decide to settle for less income. You could deliver the entirety of your lifetime accumulation of empathy and expertise to 150 $400,000 families — because, I guess, that's all you thought you could earn/deserve. Your practice will gross $600,000 and net you $300,000. (You probably know what I think of that one already, and it's unprintable anyway, so why don't we just pass over it.)

On the other hand, you could — in the sense that no one but you can stop you — decide that the very best way to defend your necessary

$400,000 average standard *is simply to make it the minimum as well.* Well, won't that cause you to overshoot your $100 million goal at some point? Yes — and more quickly than you may be able to imagine. Wouldn't that be wonderful? (That question is rhetorical.)

And you *could* take a very deep breath, see where all this may be leading, and wonder out loud why, in the long run, you wouldn't just aim for 100 one million dollar families. (That question isn't the *least* bit rhetorical. Moreover, you will — even if only unconsciously — answer it someday.)

But enough permutations: let's assume you want to continue to explore the implications of The Ark as originally configured. The first and most obvious implication to the New Financial Advisor is how overwhelmingly the odds are in her favor. She only has to find 250 households/families out of — what? five million? seven? — U.S. entities who fit the profile. A second, and almost equally important, implication is how rapidly her world is filling up with candidates — the number of American millionaires is compounding at an almost absurdly greater rate than is the population itself. (The millionaire next door, in Tom Stanley's and Bill Danko's formulation, is more and more likely to be living *literally* next door.)

And the third implication — perhaps most important of all — is that, weighted for both assets *and* income, the whole world is turning 55 years of age. That is, the population with the perfect planning profile — a lot of assets; a lot of income which needs to, and can, be invested; *and a very pressing sense of harvest time beginning to run out* — is multiplying like rabbits.

(What's so special about 55? Does a 40-year-old have any less objective need to do financial planning than a 55-year-old? Of course not. But remember, we deal with perception, not reality. The New Financial Advisor doesn't have the luxury of testing her prospects primarily for need. She has to find people who will readily board The Ark —

and, believe me, *the 55-year-old can feel in his bones that the rains are coming.*)

And so, finally, the analogy of the practice of medicine and that of The Ark come together, in the authentic persona of you.

In the paradigm of medicine, we found that the critical variable was no function of the patient's pathology, nor of the gravity of his wound. It was: did he want to be cured, by you, now? In the analogy of The Ark, we noted that mere financial wherewithal — and even the need for planning — might be variables on which to configure the vessel, but that they were no reliable indication of anyone's readiness to board. Once again: the household/family has to believe it's going to rain financially for 40 days and 40 nights, has to believe that The Ark will preserve them, and has to realize that you were sent to them on a mission of mercy: to save them and a small number of their kind, out of the millions who will (not may: *will*) ultimately be engulfed by the deluge.

The patients in your clinic — the sinners on the shore — they're not choosing you. *You're choosing them.* Because, of course:

YOU'RE DOCTOR NOAH.

IN SUMMARY

[Each chapter in this book is followed by a bullet-point summary of its key points. The intent is twofold: to let you pause for review before going on, *and to give you, in effect, a mechanism for re-reading the book in its entirety any time you want to.* You'll find that you can read all the chapter summaries straight through in about 20 minutes.]

- Real people really yearn for The Seven Glorious Outcomes of financial planning. And unlike investing or buying insurance, they intuitively know they can't do it themselves. There can be no plan without a planner; *there can be no lasting financial peace without you.*

- Your clients don't need you to be the expert. There is no business sense — and indeed no common sense — in your trying to be the expert. You are the relationship manager between your client families and the legions of experts within (and even outside) your firm. You are the translator between people — whose needs are simple, and who speak human — and the experts — whose solutions are complex, and who speak expert. **You fly 'em; you don't build 'em.**

- Expertise — all you want, and far more than you need — will come in time, through practice. You learn by doing; *it never works the other way around.*

- How do you "sell" The Seven Glorious Outcomes? How do you "sell" true and lasting financial peace? You don't, because you can't, and it's beneath your dignity. You allow a finite number of deserving families to buy peace from you.

- It won't be particularly easy. Excellence is never easy. But mediocrity is unthinkable, as well as unbearable. And the only other alternative is quitting. Choose excellence; prepare to pay its price.

- All your professional problems stem from not having enough quality prospects. The converse is, if possible, even more true, and wonderfully so: an abundance of quality prospects solves all your problems.

There are enough quality prospects out there to carry you to the top of the profession. Not seeking them out hurts *infinitely* worse, in the long run, than the (self-induced) "pain of rejection."

- The question isn't "Who do you prospect?" It isn't even "How do you prospect?" The questions are: who are you; what do you want; what is your plan for earning/deserving what you want?

- You're a doctor. The whole population is sick. You have the power to cure it. That's not the issue. The issue is: saving your time and energy for patients *who want to be cured, now, by you.*

- As a doctor, for as long as you like, you can be a general practitioner. The specialists can be called in as needed; you are the humane healer your patients must trust and believe.

- A doctor empathizes. A doctor — up to a point — explains. *A doctor doesn't "sell."*

- Your practice is The Ark. Build it from a specific blueprint: your income goal, grossed up to a top-line revenue figure, divided by a ballpark fee as a percentage of assets. This calculation will tell you the amount of assets you must raise. Divide that figure by your span of control: the number of households/families you can take on The Ark without swamping it (and your personal life). This gives you your average stateroom size. Set a minimum as close to your average as you can stand.

- When you turn down undeserving, tainted business, the mighty law of compensation puts at least an equivalent amount of clean business in a great cosmic bank, with your name on it. You just have to go and find it. The only way you can possibly fail to find it is to stop looking.

- At the pro forma configuration in this chapter, at least five million households need a stateroom on The Ark, and there are only 250 staterooms to go around. (Moreover, the population in need is growing geometrically.) They're not selecting you; *you're selecting them.* **You're Doctor Noah.**

DECIDING WHO DESERVES TO GO ON THE ARK

chapter two

TWO

The e-mail I received in the spring of 2001 said, "I've been in the business 29 years, all of them with (*name of one of the greatest investment banking, brokerage and asset management firms ever*). I've been back in production for a while after almost a decade in management. I know you always say it's a numbers game, but my questions are: how do you prospect? Does cold-calling still work? What do you say? How about mailings?" And other questions you might expect to hear from someone in the first month of a training program.

At first, I confess, my reaction was, "How can this guy have been in the business for nearly 30 years — with a firm that's gone nowhere but up, to astonishing heights — and not have learned *anything* about prospecting? How did he function as a manager? When people came to *him* and asked how to prospect, what on earth did he tell them?" Then I thought: no, there's got to be something else going on here.

While I was pondering this gentleman's predicament, a second e-mail arrived — this one from a registered sales assistant to a successful planner (also at a very fine firm) who was about to go on her own. "I'm having trouble developing a prospecting plan," this young woman reported. "In your book *The Excellent Investment Advisor*, you say that a person just starting out may be very daunted by the enormity of what she doesn't know yet, and I'm feeling that very keenly. How do you recommend I prospect?"

Yes, I thought, you've quoted almost exactly the first sentence of the first chapter of *EIA*: it does indeed aver that the neophyte may be dismayed by a perceived absence of technical knowledge. *And the very next sentence is, "Don't be."* Whereupon the entire rest of the book advances the thesis that it isn't what you know that counts, but what you do, and that all the knowledge you need will come in time and/or be available from an "expert."

And yet this young woman had seized desperately on that first sentence: she had chosen to live in an essentially illusory problem, as a justification for not being ready to start prospecting. But she *must* have read more than the one sentence, so why was she still stuck inside it?

And then, just as the conundrum of this young advisor's selective helplessness began to seem not all that different from the 29-year veteran's plight, came the final entry in this toxic trifecta of prospecting anxiety. (Although you do have to look at this one extra closely, because it never states the real issue.) "I've been in the business a year and a half, and have gotten my (here the writer reeled off four or five different licenses: securities, options, life insurance, etc.). To get to the next level as your book suggests, don't you think it would be valuable to get my CFP designation?"

Note that he'd told me absolutely nothing that really mattered (what he had actually done to build a practice in that year and a half, and how it was going). Instead, he gave me a brace of facts that couldn't possibly matter less (what tests he'd passed). And then he tried to use my own book to get me to confirm to him that learning more things/passing more tests would somehow get him to "the next level." Only trouble is, of course, that *that's the diametric opposite of what the book said.*

What do we learn from these three stories (which appear to be so disparate, but are really the exact same story, told three different ways)? And, even more pointedly, what do they have to do with you, as you begin/re-start your career in the persona of Doctor Noah, off to recruit 250

deserving passenger families for The Ark ahead of the rains? My answer is implicit in this parable:

> Guy hasn't been feeling so good, so he goes to a doctor for a complete physical examination. Doctor does every test known to medical science: EKG, bloodwork, stress test, X-rays, MRI, you name it; tells the patient to come back in a week for the results. A week later, guy returns; doctor comes around his desk, sits down next to the patient, holds his hand, and with deep empathy says, "I wish I had better news, but I don't. I wish there were an easier way to tell you, but there isn't. I'm sorry: it's terminal." Guy blinks, looks at the doc for a moment, and says, "What do you mean it's germinal?"

You see, I can't expect you to have noticed this, but the eerie subtext of the three e-mails I've just cited is that the writers all indicated familiarity with my work — *and then asked me to tell them it wasn't true.* They knew perfectly well what I had said ("It's terminal"). But they simply couldn't emotionally bear the truth, so they asked me to confirm that I had actually said something else entirely ("What do you mean it's germinal?"). All three e-mails essentially ask me to do exactly the same thing: say it isn't so. **Save me from "no."** And the really sad thing about this is that they don't hear themselves saying it. They're so conflicted about prospecting that they can no longer touch their pain, or identify their problem for what it actually is.

An ancient Chinese proverb says that the beginning of wisdom is calling things by their right names. So, using the cry "Save me from 'no' " as our Rosetta stone, let's go back to the three e-mails and see if we can decipher them. Some of the conclusions we'll reach are pretty obvious (once you know the code); some may be a bit more speculative, or circumstantial. But what I hear is this:

- The 29-year veteran is saying, "I don't have time for a numbers game. Moreover, I'm humiliated to even need to prospect after all these years; I shouldn't have to sit here getting my brains beat out like some rookie fresh from the training program. Give me a secret formula — a list of prospects, a method of prospecting, a magical incantation of words — that will short-circuit the iron law of large numbers. Even though my three decades in the business and your book all tell me it's a numbers game, *please tell me it's really not.*"

- The young woman seizing one sentence out of a 400-page book — the entirety of which vitiates that one sentence — is saying two things: "You can't expect me to prospect until I get more knowledge, nor until I have a 'prospecting plan.'" What the heck *is* a "prospecting plan," anyway? In this person's fantasy, it's a means of generating a lot of "yes" without hearing a lot of "no." Deep down, she knows this doesn't exist, and that realization has her scared to death.

- The guy with 18 months in production and nothing to show for it but a bunch of licenses wants me to give him permission to hide out in the CFP course. He really knows how wrong this would be — that is, on some level he realizes it's a symptom of a pathological call reluctance — or he'd just go ahead and do it. So he's trying to get me to agree that my book says you get to the next level by learning something, when he knows it says — that is, I say — *exactly the opposite.*

Can I prove to you that these are the unconscious thought processes of my three electronic correspondents? Of course not. Does that mean I could be misinterpreting their messages — reading something into them that isn't there? *Of course not.* After a third of a century, first of being crushed by prospecting anxiety, then slowly and painfully (and with a lot of help) overcoming it, and then observing it in other people, I can spot it even (and especially) when its victims can't. *What do you mean it's germinal?*

Look: **prospecting is the most important thing you'll ever do.** And unless you inherit, or buy, or in some other way instantly acquire a book of clients, the cruel necessity of prospecting is the only path to success in our profession. But **prospecting is also the most anxiety-producing thing you'll ever do.** It gets right down into your unconscious and — unless and until you find a healthy way of dealing with it — rattles the cage of every fear, insecurity, self-doubt and self-esteem issue you've got chained up in there. *If you don't know who you are, prospecting is simply the worst method ever devised for trying to find out.*

Believe me. I know.

The details of my nightmare are always different — the locations change, and the characters are never the same. Early in 2001, Bear Stearns's Ace Greenberg appeared in the dream; I can't imagine how he got there.

But the basic situation — the anxiety dynamic of the nightmare — is always exactly the same. At my current age, I'm suddenly back in "wirehouse" production, sitting in a boardroom wearing a suit...*no* idea how I got there.

And I have no business — no accounts, no prospects, no one to call. As the fear seizes me, I try to act busy. After all, the brokers around me know I'm supposed to be a top producer...but I'm a complete imposter...and the others are starting to realize it. (This last time, it was Greenberg who noticed that I wasn't doing any business.)

Why do I tell you this? Because I want you to know that, when I write about the depression, pain and hopelessness that can engulf us when we're prospecting unsuccessfully, *I know whereof I speak.*

I became a stockbroker in 1967, not quite 24 years old. I knew virtually nothing about money, people or life, but I had a little sales experience of a sort. And the market had been going up for 20 years — stocks were hot, and if you could knot your necktie and had no felony convictions, you were hired. So there I was: a newly minted cold caller, touting the stock idea of the day.

And things actually went OK, in a nickel-and-dime sort of way, for a year or so. Then in 1969 and 1970, the market did something it hadn't done for quite a while: it went down a whole lot — slowly. Suddenly, nobody wanted to talk to me anymore, and I was racked with the pain of losing money for people.

Somehow I survived, and in 1971 and 1972 the market rallied very strongly — almost back to that magic Dow 1000 it'd touched four years earlier. I re-built my book — indeed, built it bigger, better and stronger, though that's still not saying much. Then came 1973-74, the greatest market/economic disaster of the post-WWII period, and the second worst of the century.

By the end of 1974, after seven solid years in production, I was living on borrowed money, my business in ruins, few significant prospects, and zero confidence. Prospecting? I was in agony every time I picked up the phone.

But somehow, against all reason, I held on. Maybe it was because I had no idea what else to do, or where else to go. Surely, it was because I had a wife who refused to give up on me when I had all but given up on myself. I was fighting paralysis, and at times almost beyond despair. *But I was still there.*

And then, seemingly out of sheer exhaustion, the market simply stopped going down. The Dow Jones Industrials made their umpty-umpth new low in December — but the broader-based New York Stock Exchange index didn't. We waited, but the other shoe didn't drop, even as tax-selling season came and went. It was over.

I started to be able to call people again — I'd actually inherited a lot of interesting accounts from the legions of brokers who'd quit the business — and just kept telling anyone who'd listen that the war was over. And when the market took off with a roar in 1975, I never looked back.

But even today, a quarter century later, my recurring nightmare of those desperate years is still not gone. Don't cry for me, E. F. Hutton. The truth is, I never left you.

I share this true fable with you not just as a form of therapy, but as a way of telling you that I know the monster I'm sending you out to fight. Why do you think I spent all that time and energy in the last chapter, trying to get you to see how indispensable you are to a family's financial/ investment survival — trying to inculcate in you the essential perception that prospects aren't choosing you, *you're choosing them?* Yes, because those things are ultimately true, but not *just* because they're true. I did it — as you will have to do it for yourself, over and over, sometimes every hour, *sometimes every minute* — to steel you against the psychological rigors of prospecting. Because prospecting, as the film star Bette Davis said about old age, ain't for sissies.

Let's make sure we agree on the essential things that can be known, for absolute certain, about prospecting to build a financial planning practice.

- At the outset, and perhaps for a number of years,
  much or most of your time and energy will be spent
  in the deeply unnatural act of approaching people
  you don't know, and encouraging them to consign
  their family's financial fate to you.

- Almost everyone at whom you metaphorically jump out of the bushes like that will recoil in horror — or maybe just denial, or procrastination; it matters not — and say "no." But not *quite* everyone.

- All your achievements, all your professional (and much of your personal) happiness, will turn out to flow from the very first word in the last bullet point: *almost* everyone will say "no" in the early years. But the few good people who say "yes" — and the other good people to whom those few refer you — will board The Ark. And when, in the fullness of time, the 250 staterooms in The Ark are all occupied, you and they will sail off to the promised land of The Seven Glorious Outcomes.

- Prospecting is, therefore, nothing more or less than heaven's own original numbers game.

- You just have to keep prospecting until The Ark is full. If you do keep prospecting, your success is assured. (Anything that isn't impossible is inevitable: that's the first law of science, and the first law of prospecting to find the 250 families.)

- Unfortunately, the converse is also true: if you *don't* keep prospecting, The Ark will never be filled — or it will be full of undesirables who will swamp it and you at a critical moment...like the next bear market. And the next...

- Your intellect knows that success is the inevitable result of a refusal to stop prospecting. The sad fact is, however, that your intellect isn't running your prospecting effort. Your emotions are. That is, your unconscious is. So success or failure isn't the result of what you know, but of *how you feel*.

- If and when prospecting makes you feel bad enough — when the umpty-umpth tomahawk of "no" feels like it's crashing down on your skull as you run the gauntlet, trying to save people who don't want to be saved — you will stop prospecting. The hope of future happiness will not be able to offset the actuality of this moment's pain — and you will act to stop that pain.

- This has nothing to do with "motivation." In order to be free of any limit to your income, you voluntarily accepted a job — nay, a noble calling — in which there's no salary. That took a level of guts, determination, self-confidence and desire for personal achievement which are not to be found in one-tenth of one percent of the population at large. *You are motivated enough for six lifetimes*.

- But even the rat in the psychology experiment — the hundredth time he pushes the button for a food pellet and gets an electric shock instead — will stop pushing the button. No matter that in the long run he'll die if he can't get some nourishment: right here, right now, *it just hurts too much to push that button*.

- Now for the second best bit of news I've reported to you so far in this discussion. (The very best news, as I hope you won't have failed to notice, is that whatever isn't impossible is inevitable. And 250 $400,000 families may not be easy, but it sure ain't impossible, either.) To wit: *the button isn't wired*. Your unconscious just *thinks* it is. That is, "rejection" — the name given by journeymen to the phenomenon of a whole bunch of "no" — doesn't actually, objectively hurt.

Doc says, "Walk the treadmill; chew the gum; ease off on the bourbon." Patient says, "I'll think about it," leaves, and never comes back. Is the healer — who said and did *exactly* what he was supposed to — hurt by this "rejection"? I don't think so. "Human nature," he shrugs; "you can lead a horse to water, but he may go right back to Jack 'n' Coke." And remember, your patient is merely going to live in penury if he says no to you; *the doctor's patient is gonna die.* So why does "rejection" hurt you and not the doctor?

- *Because you allow it to.* That's as close to "why" as you need — or are likely — to get. Forgive me, but "why" is a ticket to five years worth of psychoanalytic navel-gazing, at the end of which (a) you'll either know "why"...or you won't, and (b) the knowledge of "why," *if* you attain it, will vaporize your call reluctance/hypersensitivity to "rejection"...*or it won't.*

  "Why" misses the point, anyway. The point is that the electric shock isn't generated by pushing the button, but by your own *internal, unconscious reaction* to the experience of pushing the button and having nothing happen. *You're* generating the pain...*and you can stop.* Not all at once, maybe; not by waving an attitudinal magic wand, but by consistently and progressively altering the way you process the experience of "no." *To disbelieve this is to despair,* and thereby to render your situation literally hopeless.

- You can, I repeat, completely change the way you experience "no" — and you'll have to, because *you can't change the incidence of "no" itself.* The frustration of the 29-year veteran, the fear of the fledgling planner faced with leaving the nest, and the utter denial of the guy trying to study his way to the next level, are all rooted in the unconscious need to avoid facing this simple truth.

  "How do you prospect?" is, as we've seen, code for: give me a formula that will meaningfully reduce the statistical incidence of "no." So is the illusion of a more effective "prospecting plan" based on more "knowledge." So is the quest for three more letters after your name instead of (not in addition to) doing the real work of prospecting.

  The real work of prospecting is actively and even joyfully listening to a whole lot of people say "no" until that glorious day when the 250th household/family says "yes." Enough "no" will inevitably yield enough "yes." And the only way in this world to hear a "yes" is wholeheartedly, enthusiastically and above all consciously to choose to run the risk of hearing "no."

- It doesn't matter who you prospect, how you prospect, or what you say: almost everyone you approach "cold" will say "no." This is human nature, and it's immutable; nothing you say or do can change it. So if you can't change human nature, and you can't change any one human being (from wanting to say "no" to wanting to say "yes"), what *can* you change?

Why, yourself, of course.

The bad news — and it isn't really bad news, it's just a natural fact, like gravity or tides — is that you have no power whatsoever to change another person. The good news — and I believe choirs of angels burst into song when one New Financial Advisor truly accepts this — is that *you have limitless power to change yourself.* You can't alter the incidence of "no," *but you can completely change the experience.*

- There are two ways progressively to change the experience of "no" without in any way changing its incidence. The first is attitudinal, and the second is behavioral. That is, you can (and must) begin by changing what you *believe* about what you're doing; then you can gradually change what you're actually doing. There is ample evidence that these two modifications, *both of which are entirely under your control*, inexorably if gradually lead to a lessening of one's internally generated sensitivity to "no," and therefore to a steady increase in one's prospecting activity. They lead, in other words, down the only proven path to excellence in our profession.

ATTITUDE ADJUSTMENTS

(1) DOCTOR/NOAH. This deliberately mixed metaphor helps the New Financial Advisor stay focused on the great saving and healing power that he possesses. Having already discussed this power at some length, we need only make three summary observations here — although before reading on, you'd be well advised to look back at the litany of affirmations which begin on page 35, vectoring the advisor's psychology

toward the paradigm of medicine.

(A) Financial planning, unlike investments or insurance, is something which even semi-rational people know they can't do themselves — and which, with each passing day, they need more and more. There is great *perceived* value-added in a planner that does not necessarily attach to an investment advisor nor to an insurance professional. Realize and reaffirm to yourself daily, before you start prospecting, the vital importance of what you do. Any number of people may refuse to accept this great power you have, *but no one can take it away from you.*

(B) You are a physician — a humane healer, functioning for as long as you like as a general practitioner. Acting primarily as a diagnostician, you needn't know the answers; you just have to know where (and from whom) to get them. *And you do.*

One difference between you and the doctor is that her patients come to her, and already know they're sick. You have to go find patients, and they have to be both educable and ready. On the other hand, the huge preponderance of the doctor's potential audience is, on any given day, not sick, and therefore not in need of her services. *The entire monied population around you is fatally ill* — with too little life insurance, its retirement fund invested in bonds instead of equities, and no long-term care insurance (just to name three common symptoms). Your task — virtually your only task, at this point — is finding 250 families who admit they have the disease, and who want to recover. The ones who don't...don't. But what's that got to do with *you*, doctor?

(C) Noah's job would have been a lot easier if God had told everybody — or at least not just him — that it was going to rain for 40 days and 40 nights. (On the other hand, this would have defeated God's purpose, which was, you'll remember, to wipe everybody out and start over again. But I digress.) In the event, only Noah knew that all mankind was doomed, but he couldn't get anyone outside his own family to believe him. OK, so nearly everyone you prospect — even (and especially) the ones who *think* they have "enough" money — is going to turn you aside. Suck it up. You only have to convince 250 households/families out of five to seven million who meet our financial criteria. And the danger of running out of money in retirement is a *whole* lot easier to sell than that 40-days-40-nights precipitation probability forecast.

(2) DO GOOD/DO WELL. You and I are among the only people who've ever lived on the earth who get to do well for ourselves and our families by doing good for others. Most people, if they get a choice at all, are forced to choose between one and the other.

There's no measurable way of knowing how much good a schoolteacher does, for instance, nor where (or even *if*) that good will end. A biology lab teacher spends a few extra minutes each week with a little girl who seems to love that science. The little girl grows up to be a doctor. And *her* little girl grows up to be the scientist who unlocks the riddle of Alzheimer's...years after that caring teacher is under the earth. *The teacher worked 35 years for a civil servant's wages*...because, when she reached that first fork in the road, she was forced to choose between doing well and doing good. Police officers and firefighters are even more horrific examples of this phenomenon, as we were reminded so terribly at the World Trade Center. For less than a skilled plumbing contractor makes, they get up each day and go out to save lives, never knowing if their children will see them again this side of Jordan.

You and I never had to make that choice; by some miracle, we were shown another way. I know that financial security, by itself, can't bring anyone genuine peace, but I know that the converse is also true: peace is nearly impossible to find and maintain when a home is haunted by financial worry. You and I were given a way — no, The Way — to do marvelously fulfilling work and to build wealth for our own families by slaying the dragon of financial fear — thus, perhaps, at least clearing a client family's path to peace.

Are you not thunderstruck by this, if only once a day (never mind all day every day)? Is the combination of the importance of what you do, the desperation with which good people need it done, and the utter limit-lessness of the income you can earn doing it *not enough to leave you breath-less for just one breath between every sunup and sunset?* Because if it's not, I think I know what your trouble is. (Hint: it's not that your manager gave you a "bad list" to call.)

Get back in touch with gratitude. *Gratitude is the ultimate attitude adjustment*, and no sadness, anxiety or depression — in other words, no amount of "no" — can stand up to constant, deeply felt professions of this noble emotion.

(3) ENLIST IN A HOLY CRUSADE. Remember the Blues Broth-ers? Every time Jake told someone, "We're getting the band back together," Elwood laconically added, "We're on a mission from God."

If you just have a job, or even a career — if you're just selling a product, a portfolio or even an essentially technical plan — you're likely to become very discouraged when almost everyone you approach doesn't want it (and/or you). But if you have a calling — if you, too, are on a sort of "mission from God," albeit without the whole Chicago police force chasing you — you won't care how many are called, nor how few are chosen. You won't stop testifying to the truth, as you've been given light to see the truth.

Personally, I had to wander in the desert for a lot of years, waiting for a sign. But then it was revealed to me that I'd been sent into the world to bear witness to the healing power of equities vs. the slow, metastasizing cancer of bonds. The scales fell from my eyes, and I saw that, in retire-ments of 30-plus years, only the rising dividends and values of equities could keep the current generation ahead of inflation while continuing to grow their heirs' patrimony. (And, conversely, I saw that taking a fixed-income investment strategy into 30 years of a rising-cost retirement is suicide.) When I do battle for equities, I'm not just selling much higher long-term returns. I'm crusading for good (stocks) and against evil (bonds).

This is my calling: I'm saving people's financial lives. (I'll demonstrate this truth in exquisite detail later on in this book.)

Multigenerational financial peace through comprehensive planning: now *there's* something to devote one's life to. Make it *your* calling, embark on *your* crusade...and you'll never stop, because you'll be unstoppable.

(4) GO THE EXTRA MILE/HOLD NOTHING BACK. Every single time you get the chance, do more and better work for a prospect than you have to — even if it's more than he deserves. *Never hold back.* Flush the prospect, if that's what your heart tells you to do; but while you go on talking to him, give him everything you've got. The joy of doing everything you do in the best possible way you can do it will make you strong and enthusiastic, and those qualities will radiate from your voice and your bearing. They'll also make you impervious to the slights of undeserving prospects, in that you'll never give in to the impulse to lower yourself to their level. Most important, these qualities will make you very, *very* attractive to good prospects, whose genuine need and desire to be helped may be ignited by your wholehearted willingness to be that help.

Serve everyone to whom you speak completely or not at all. Remember: no good that you do — or even attempt to do — is wasted. It may be lost on any one undeserving prospect, but it is stored up in that great cosmic bank of compensation we discovered earlier. And it's compounding away, even as we speak...

(5) TAKE EXTRA CARE TO REMAIN ETHICALLY UNCOMPROMISED. When you're desperate to open an account and do some business — any business — it's usually a sign that you've lost touch with the conviction that 250 good households/families are out there waiting for you. Which would be bad enough by itself, but in that desperation the temptation to cut ethical corners is at its worst. Be afraid — be very afraid — of ethical compromise. It's a downward spiral. **Every act of weakness weakens you still further.** You may write a piece of business by cutting an ethical corner, but the price you pay is a withdrawal from the cosmic

bank of compensation. And if you keep doing that, you write a lot of wrong tickets for a lot of wrong people — and your compensation account goes slowly but inexorably to zero. Don't do it. As former U.S. Senator Alan Simpson said at Harvard a few years ago, when he was introducing former President Gerald Ford, "If you have integrity, nothing else matters. And if you don't have integrity, nothing else matters."

(6) DISCONNECT THE ACTIVITY OF PROSPECTING FROM ITS OUTCOME; DO THE WORK FOR THE JOY AND PRECISION OF DOING THE WORK — A LITTLE BETTER EVERY DAY. I'll have much more to say in just a little while about disconnecting the act and the outcome, when we cover the *behavioral* aspects of desensitizing yourself to "rejection." But since attitude has to come first (inasmuch as belief ultimately dictates behavior), it's not too soon to start thinking about this issue.

Living in (and for) the *outcome* of prospecting is just setting oneself up to fail. If the only "good" prospecting call is one in which the prospect says "yes" — an outcome over which I have no control — then an approach that results in "no" is a "bad" prospecting call. And that means almost every prospecting approach I made in a third of a century was "bad." (Once again: my fortune and my happiness are implicit in that one glorious word: "*almost.*")

But they weren't "bad." All my prospecting calls were great *because I made them*. And because, against every instinct, I found the strength to make *just one more call* (and then just one more, and so on...), I slowly became a person who deserved to hear "yes" — and eventually did. George Washington, whose unshakable faith (and not his generalship) made him immortal, was fond of quoting a line from Joseph Addison's play *Cato*, to the effect that we cannot ensure success, but we can deserve it. You're entitled to the work, but not to the outcome when and how you want it. Live to do the work well, though, and the outcome is eventually assured.

As Zen master Ungo said, "If you want to attain such a thing, you must be such a person." (Of course, he then added, "Since you are such a person, why trouble about such a thing?" Never mind that; *be such a person.*)

(7) START A LIST OF PRINCIPLES YOU WON'T COMPROMISE. This is another tool for becoming the person who deserves success — and for fighting off the temptation to take *any* business from *any* account...because you "need" it. You can't betray yourself for 30 pieces of silver; you can't trade a piece of your core belief system for a sale you think is wrong. Read your Emerson, and don't take blood money; it costs too much.

I'd never sell an investment on the basis of past performance; I'd never take an account who was covertly abusive or disrespectful; I'd never argue in order to make a sale. Those are just three of my basic principles — all learned the hard way, all fired in the forge of pain. Try 'em on; use them as a runway from which your own list can take off. But be assured: all lasting success in this calling is based on principle. And the sooner you start drawing a line in the sand with your sword, the stronger you'll feel about yourself when you're prospecting, and therefore the more prospecting you'll be able to do. And therefore the sooner you'll fill up The Ark.

(8) MAKE FAITH AN INTEGRAL PART OF YOUR WORK. I want to tread very carefully, here, and I'm not talking about your (or my, or anyone's) religion. Rather, I'm talking about your spirituality — about how you see yourself in relation to the universe. (Nonetheless, I would — as gently as possible — wonder how one could be infused with faith inside the walls of a house of worship on Saturday or Sunday, and with despair in the office on Monday.)

"The whole course of things goes to teach us faith," says Emerson, and I believe it. When I look down at the shore on a certain moonlit night, and see the thousands of eggs a turtle lays — and when I look up at the sky on yet another, moonless night, and see a tiny fraction of the uncountable billions of stars — I think (a) there's an intelligence at work here; (b) its law is abundance, and indeed superabundance; and (c) I don't believe it means to exclude me from access to that abundance.

(Even if you have no particular spirituality, and/or see life as random, the reality of American superabundance is a tough nut for a pessimist to crack. Upon what would you base despair? That, amid utter randomness, access to abundance was somehow purposefully denied to *you*? *That* doesn't make much sense.)

My own belief — and this is a psychological rather than a spiritual *or even an economic* theory of mine — is that poverty and want are human creations, which flower out of the toxic root of despair. Financial planning — the thing you propose to deal in, professionally — is the *ultimate* act of faith in the future; is it reasonable to suppose that a successful planning *practice* could ever be based on anything else? And can you ever succeed by inviting people to have more faith in you than you have in yourself?

For in the end, even if you can't muster a belief in anything else, you've simply got to have an abiding faith in yourself — or no one else will, either. And so I say again: make faith — however you define it — an integral part of your work.

You may wish to consider scrolling through a combination of the "I'm a doctor" affirmations on page 35 and these eight attitude adjusters every day before you begin prospecting. It couldn't hurt.

As within, so without. Thus, having effected an attitudinal modification of our *beliefs* about prospecting, we now proceed to a *behavioral* system of altering the way we process the experience of "no."

At the risk of repeating myself (of being redundant, of *saying the same thing over and over again*), what follows is not an attempt to change the statistical incidence of "no." Nor of "yes," for that matter: *assume that can't be done.* If 19 out of 20 people you ask for an appointment before you read this chapter say "no," expect that the same ratio will prevail after you've read it. But know two things, the second of which proceeds from the first:

(1) The effect on you of those 19 "no's" will gradually diminish to the point where you feel no "rejection." Indeed, you will find ways to make a game out of this process.

(2) As your emotional sensitivity to "no" gradually leaves you — as prospecting becomes the game it's supposed to be — you'll be able to prospect more and more over time. (And you'll look and sound better as your prospecting stamina builds up.) The result will be that you'll start getting more (and better) prospects than you ever have — not because statistically fewer people are saying "no," but simply because you're talking — in a positive, enthusiastic way — to *so very many more people*.

Well, good heavens, doesn't that mean that I'm about to set you up to get "rejected" *even more than you do now?* Certainly: "rejected" *and* accepted, both. For the latter is a pure, arithmetic function of the former. That is, if you accept that the incidence of "no" is, beyond a certain point, irreducible, then you must accept that the only way to hear another "yes" is to hear that many more "no's."

Thus, the game of prospecting is, at its most fundamental level, a process of finding out precisely what your own irreducible incidence of "rejection" actually is. Just exactly how many times, over a sample of prospecting approaches large enough to be statistically meaningful, do you personally have to hear "no" in order to hear one "yes"? When you know this, you'll never stop playing the game, because — in a very real sense — you'll have already won it.

I freely admit that the foregoing one-paragraph summary of the prospecting game is a simplification. It's a bit like saying that the game of chess is, at *its* most fundamental level, a process of immobilizing the other guy's king. It surely is, but that reduces the game to a statement of its object, without telling you anything at all about how to play. Fair enough, but there's one critical difference. Even the worst, entry-level chess player knows what the object of the game is. But I doubt that one advisor in 20 who is actively engaged in building a business today knows that the game of prospecting is won as soon as you know how many approaches yield a prospect.

If I looked back at my records from a year of prospecting, and found that I got a solid prospect "only" once in 20 approaches (*never mind how an approach is defined, for the moment*), I'd be all set, wouldn't I? My prospecting life would settle into a joyous, hold-nothing-back attempt to get myself "rejected" as many multiples of 19 as I could...knowing that that multiple is *exactly how many prospects I'm going to get over time.*

I express this iron law by the formula

$$P = \frac{1}{N}$$

which simply states that we get a prospect (P) once in every N number of approaches we make. Thus, we just need to make prospecting a controlled experiment, dispassionately accumulating enough inputs, and recording them with exquisite care, so that the data ultimately yield up a precise value for N. Every advisor's N may be different but — depend upon it — *every advisor has an N.*

How can I be so sure (a) that your N is an objective, real, knowable number and (b) that you cannot fail to discover it, given enough data? That's easy: *because it's not impossible.* And, like anything that isn't impossible, it's inevitable, *as long as you just keep wearing away at it.*

Thomas Edison, the man who invented the twentieth century, had about four months of formal schooling, and was, from adolescence on, virtually deaf. But when, already a famous inventor, he announced that his next project would be an incandescent electric light source, he said it would be ready in about six months. (Modern scholars think it at least possible that even *he* didn't believe this; there's some evidence that he was trying to bluff other talented inventors who were looking for incandescence out of the game.) In the event, it took almost two and a half years, during the course of which Edison performed (and carefully recorded) something like 10,000 separate, different, "failed" experiments.

Now, even people who had much better hearing and a lot more formal education would have given (and indeed, did give) up. They excused their own failure to persist by suggesting that the achievement was beyond the power of mere mortal men. Thus the world's eagerness to call someone like Edison a "genius" is a double-edged sword: it praises him while letting the rest of us off the hook. Which is, I believe, precisely why the man himself was so scornful of the word. He wasn't so much deprecating himself as he was holding the rest of us properly accountable for our lack of persistence when he said, "**Genius is one per cent inspiration and ninety-nine per cent perspiration.**"

I'm not going to ask you for a firm commitment on this until we've agreed on exactly what an "approach" is, but let me just put forth an idea for your consideration. Would you be willing to spend the next two and a half years inventing an incandescent career for yourself? Would you, over those roughly 500 working days, consider taking 10,000 Edisonian licks — about 20 approaches per day — at discovering your N? Is there even the slightest doubt in your mind that, at the end of this experiment — and probably long before that — (a) you'd know exactly what your N is and (b) you'd be well on your way to the inevitable success you deserve?

This is not a rhetorical question. If there *is* a doubt in your mind about your ability to make that level of approaches for that long — and especially if you question the efficacy of doing so — we're not out of bullets, here. Far from it, in fact: we now have an even better insight into the extent to which your anxiety levels may be holding down your capacity to prospect.

Don't beat yourself up. Most normal people seem to feel that the best they can do at the moment is...the best they can do at the moment. But we're not like that, because we're not, in fact, normal. We're exceptionally motivated to be outstandingly successful — remember, we took a job with no salary in exchange for no externally imposed limit on our income. But we're also exceptionally hard on ourselves when we don't measure up to our own very high expectations. This is laudable, up to a point, but beyond that point it just becomes another part of the problem. Take *responsibility* for where you are now — indeed, that's half the battle — but *don't blame yourself.* You are wherever you are in your career: accept it and prepare to move on. You'll never get anywhere until (and unless) you climb down off your own back.

Be assured that, by the end of the very next chapter, you'll be well on your way — regardless of where you're starting (or even re-starting) from.

And in the meantime, hold on to this thought from the Wizard of Menlo Park himself:

> "Results? Why, man, I have gotten lots of results! If I find 10,000 ways something won't work, I haven't failed. I am not discouraged, because every attempt discarded is another step forward. Just because something doesn't do what you planned it to do doesn't mean it's useless. Reverses should prove an incentive to great accomplishment...There are no rules here, *we're just trying to accomplish something.*"

IN SUMMARY

- Prospecting, to the New Financial Advisor, is the act of interviewing large numbers of ultimately unacceptable people, in order to select the 250 households/families who deserve to be saved. *It is heaven's own original numbers game.* The only way in this world ever to hear "yes" is joyously and wholeheartedly to risk hearing "no."

- Literally for years, until you have more referrals than you can possibly handle — *which you will* — you'll have to offer staterooms on The Ark to people who don't know you. Almost (but not quite) everyone will say "no." The few who don't say "no" will, in the fullness of time, be the making of your fortune, and of much of your happiness.

- Anything that isn't impossible is inevitable. It isn't impossible to find 250 qualified passengers for The Ark. Therefore it is inevitable that you *will* find them...provided only that *you don't stop prospecting*.

- "Rejection" — the decision on some poor soul's part to remain on the shore and drown — doesn't hurt you unless you unconsciously allow it to. *You* are manufacturing "the pain of rejection" — *and you can stop doing so*, progressively if not instantly.

- It doesn't matter who you prospect, how you prospect, or what you say: nothing can change the incidence of "no." But you can completely change the way you emotionally experience "no." First you change your beliefs, and then you can change your behavior.

- Eight great attitude adjustments, to be taken daily *or as often as needed*:
    - (1) *Doctor/Noah.* They're all sick. They're all going to drown. Of *course* many are called but few are chosen: *that's the plan*.
    - (2) *Gratitude.* You can do limitlessly well by doing limitless, multigenerational good: clearing — at least financially — a family's path to peace. Where I come from, there's a word for this: *miracle*.

(3) *Crusade.* Don't have a job, or even a career. *Have a calling.*

(4) *The Extra Mile.* Give everything you've got to every interaction — or end the interaction. No good that you do (or even try to do) can ever be lost; it can just be lost on the person you're trying to do it for at the moment. Ka-*ching*! *Another* deposit in the great cosmic bank of compensation.

(5) *Integrity.* "If you have integrity, nothing else matters. And if you don't have integrity, *nothing else matters.*" (OK, so I added the italics.)

(6) *Activity/Outcome.* Disconnect the one you control from the one you don't; revel in the activity — preaching your own special crusade — and the outcome is ultimately inevitable, anyway. The only "bad" prospecting approach *is the one you don't make.*

(7) *Principles.* Make a list of the ones that matter most to you. Don't compromise 'em. Some days they're all you've got. And most days, they're all you need.

(8) *Faith.* Intelligent or random, the law of the universe (in general, and of America in particular) seems to be *abundance.* Yes, even for you. Believe in it; believe, if nothing else, in you.

- When your *beliefs* about prospecting have been repaired, you can start *behaviorally* desensitizing yourself to the (wholly self-induced) "pain of rejection." The inevitable result will be that you can handle a lot more "no" — and will therefore, through the principle of P=1/N, start hearing a lot more "yes."

- You get a prospect (P) once in every N approaches you make. If you knew what your N was, you'd never stop playing the game, because you'd know exactly how often you were going to hit the prospecting jackpot.

- Edison was deaf, had virtually no education, and "failed" to produce incandescence 10,000 times over two and a half years. Didn't seen to bother him. What's *your* excuse?

- Do you think you could make 10,000 prospecting approaches over the next two and a half years, or about 20 per working day? If yes, go in peace. All your problems are solved. If no (or even "I don't know"), (a) don't beat yourself up, and (b) stay tuned. We're going to Plan B.

CALLING THE MANY, CHOOSING THE FEW

THREE

———————•———————

How do I define a prospecting "approach"? If you were at all beguiled by the idea of making 10,000 Edisonian "approaches" in the next 30 months — first to learn your N, then to launch your Ark — what precisely would you be signing up to *do*, some 20 times each working day?

A prospecting approach is any genuine attempt to start a conversation with another human being about financial planning. It could be a phone call to someone, the purpose of which is to invite him to a seminar, or to ask if he'd benefit from a second opinion on his investment portfolio. It could be an "Oh, by the way" when you pick up your dry cleaning, asking the owner if he's heard about the new higher IRA contribution limits in the 2001 tax law. (Dry cleaners, remember, are Stanley's and Danko's archetypal millionaire next door.) It could be stopping by a local attorney's office, just to say hello if she's in, and to drop off a brochure on your firm's financial planning capabilities even if she's not. *An "approach" is simply a spoken attempt to at least begin the process of seeing someone face to face about his financial needs and your ability to meet those needs.*

You may infer from this that a mailing not followed up by a spoken approach is not an "approach." It is a time waster and an avoidance behavior. Even a letter that *is* followed up by a spoken approach is only one "approach." We will get into how far — if at all — a spoken approach has to go to be an official "approach." But no matter how you ultimately decide to keep score, make no mistake about it: *mailings don't count.* You have nice mailing pieces that your firm produces? You have interesting letters you can mail? Send them out to your heart's content, and with my unqualified blessing — *in addition to* whatever number of spoken, and therefore genuine, "approaches" we'll decide you need to make on any given day, as this chapter progresses. Send them out *instead of* any or all of your daily ration of real "approaches," and you're lost. It's an unconditional surrender to your anxiety.

So: we're going to try to start conversations which lead to personal appointments with households/families who meet the general financial and attitudinal guidelines we've established: reasonably affluent, educable, and more or less actively interested in hearing about ways to get their financial lives in better — and perhaps much better — shape. That's quite a bit of information to go on regarding who we're looking for.

We also have a pretty clear idea about who we want to be to — and what we propose to do for — these people when we find them. We offer to become the relationship manager between the household/family and the financial institution which is going to manage all or a great part of that family's affairs pursuant to a formal, comprehensive plan. We will be the family's primary financial advisor, or at the very least an equal member of a team of advisors which will probably include an attorney and an accountant.

We already have a very specific business plan in place: 250 staterooms/$400,000 average assets/one percent fee. And we've decided on an important qualitative criterion, to round out this fairly long list of things we already know: we're only going to work in situations of mutual trust and respect.

One thing we have *not* established yet is the basis on which, if we're asked to do so, we're going to "compete." Hewing to the paradigm of medicine, we refuse to compete on price — great advice isn't a commodity — and we're certainly not going to promise higher returns, or that we can somehow save the family more estate taxes than another planner, or anything along those (essentially quantitative) lines. Better not to compete at all, of course — and I was always most successful when I took the attitude that I didn't really *have* any competition. (Try feeling like that sometime — or at least try *deserving* to feel like that; you'll find its effect on the way you present yourself quite astonishing.) But if you *are* challenged to compete, here's how I'd handle it:

PROSPECT: You're competing with Merrill Lynch, Northwestern Mutual Life, and the trust department of J.P. Morgan Chase.

NEW FINANCIAL ADVISOR: Good heavens; *how?*

P: Sorry?

NFA: *How* am I competing with them? What's the basis for comparison?

P: Well, fees, I guess...how you've performed...

NFA: Gee, I wouldn't dream of competing on that basis — even if we *had* lower fees, or higher past performance, or whatever. Which we *might*, I suppose...for all I know...

P: Then why should we hire you?

NFA: Why should you hire *any* of us in preference to the three others — that's the question *I'd* ask. Look, you're talking to four great firms — the three you mention and mine. Putting aside the quality of the individual representative involved, which can vary quite a lot, you're not going to get a bad plan or a bad portfolio from any of us. But trying to figure out which one is "best" or "cheapest" in some objective way — I don't know how you're going to do that, and I think you're going to end up making yourself nuts. If you were a member of my family, I'd advise you not to try to do it that way.

P: Well, then how in the world *should* we choose?

NFA: Let me try to answer you with a story. Way back in 1957, when Warren Buffett was just starting out, he was referred to a wealthy family in Omaha named Davis. This would be the first really important client he would have outside his family, and so he went over there, and made his presentation, and left — and the Davises didn't know *what* to make of him. He was 27, and kind of odd-looking, and the family just kept talking back and forth, but they couldn't decide what to do. And then Mrs. Davis spoke up, and she just said, *"I like everything about that young man."* And that was that. It may not seem very scientific, but that's the way I'd like to get chosen — or not at all.

Look: my practice is strictly limited to 250 client families. And those people are my life. My commitment to the clients who choose to work with me is simple: I'm going to care more about you, and be more personally devoted to your financial success, than anyone in the world who doesn't have your last name. If somebody else is a little cheaper, or somebody else puts up better numbers for a year or two — I don't think that stuff matters very much in the long run.

The right advisor for you is the one you and your family trust the most, and have the most personal faith in. If that's me, fine. And if it's not me, fine. But the very best advice I can give you, from my heart, is: choose your advisor the way the Davises decided to hire Warren Buffett. You'll sleep sounder, you'll live longer — and you'll make better decisions together.

There are a couple of important things to be learned from that script. The first is to refuse to compete on the basis of any "objective" criteria. He who lives by lower fees and/or higher past "performance" will surely one day die by...you guessed it. To compete on this basis is merely to rent the account until a little bit faster gun than you rides into Dodge, looking to make a name for himself. The whole point of this book's philosophy is to forge unbreakable, fundamentally personal relationships with your clients. Compete on the basis — which can't be objectively verified, and therefore *has* to be trusted — that you're simply going to care about 'em more than any other advisor will. On Doctor Noah's 250-stateroom Ark, *everybody* gets to sit at the captain's table.

The other lesson of the foregoing script is that sometimes a great little story sells better than any rational argument and/or battery of numbers. Stories and analogies — rather than formal argumentation — show that you're relaxed, and truly knowledgeable about how a financial relationship is really supposed to work. The story of Buffett's pivotal meeting with Dr. Edwin Davis and his family is one such terrific vignette; it appears, among other places, in Roger Lowenstein's superb biography *Buffett: The Making of an American Capitalist* (see the bibliography at the end of this book).

(Another striking thing about that conversation is that despite the dollars and the prestige the Davises could potentially bring him, Buffett didn't trim in any way on his standards: he wouldn't disclose his portfolio, wouldn't report results but once a year, and would only let the partners add to or withdraw from their accounts on December 31. "As badly as Buffett wanted the Davises' capital," Lowenstein concludes, "he didn't want it on any terms but his." You and I can't be Buffett, but we can be excellent financial advisors, by *holding fast to our standards*. And who knows? *Maybe that's exactly what Mrs. Davis liked about him!)*

All right, then. Given what we've decided about the types of people we're looking for, and about how we propose to present ourselves to them, three general questions remain to be answered:

(1) Are there any prospecting methods which appear to
    be dictated by our marketing posture, and are there

any methods which seem less likely to succeed?

(2) What shall we say; to whom shall we say it; how many "approaches" can/must we make per day, and how can we build our prospecting stamina up to the necessary levels?

(3) From a standing start, how long ought it reasonably to take us to sell out all the staterooms on The Ark? How long, in other words, must we plan to have to work the program which we derive from the answers to general questions (1) and (2)?

The balance of this chapter is devoted to answering, as objectively as I can, these three questions. Let me preface it, then, with two observations.

You've seen the first of these comments before — and will yet see it again (and again) in this book. I offer it, almost ritually, as the hammer you must use to beat down your anxiety as your highly specialized, multi-year prospecting effort unfolds. To wit: *it doesn't matter how you prospect, nor whom you prospect, nor what you say.* For at least the first couple of years, assume that almost everyone you prospect will either (a) not be qualified, financially or psychologically (or both), (b) not be ready, and/or (c) not recognize you as Doctor Noah. **This has nothing to do with you.** March on, then, in quest of that holiest of grails, your own personal N: the quantification of the golden "almost." For when you find it, "rejection" — i.e. the N-minus-one times you have to hear "no" in order to hear the one inevitable "yes" *which no power on earth can deny you* — becomes a fuel that powers you rather than an acid that corrodes you.

The second observation I'd make, before offering you my answers to the three great questions above, has to do with where to place yourself as you either start or re-start your career on a planning-oriented vector.

If you have the singular good fortune to be just beginning your career in financial services — if, in other words, you are unburdened by the great weight of things the rest of us are having to unlearn — then regardless of your age and previous life experience I'd urge you to get into a group/mentor/apprentice arrangement of some kind. Don't, if at all possible, surround yourself with yourself — not least of all because you may not know, at this very early stage, who that is. God knows I didn't. (Ah, but I was so much older then; I'm younger than that now.)

Look around for an opportunity to insert yourself as the junior member of a group practice. Or see if there isn't some very experienced, much-too-busy senior advisor in your office who might be ready to take on someone just starting up the learning curve. Or simply try to find someone who's willing to mentor you informally. In addition to such a situation (and certainly not instead of it, unless you've absolutely no choice), make common cause with other new advisors in your office and/ or nearby offices. Start a weekly breakfast meeting or conference call with them, to learn from and encourage each other as your careers develop. *Get all the support, structure and wisdom you can find.* Starting off is hard enough, but starting off alone — and you can be alone in an office of 50 advisors — may just prove to be too tough.

If, on the other hand, you are coming to the financial planning paradigm from having operated an advisory practice of some other kind for a time, you have a different set of challenges. Chief among them, I think, is being brutally honest with yourself as to what part of your existing book can be brought aboard The Ark.

The main argument that I hear against doing a fairly radical restructuring of one's business is that it will trigger an insupportable income hit of some duration. If and to the extent that that's true, it's just a testament to how moribund one's existing business already is. If you say, "I'd lose too much of my income if I suddenly started doing business the right way," you've also said, "I currently get far too much of my income from doing it the wrong way (or ways)." The objection answers itself, because it damns itself. How long do you think you can keep your business running the wrong way? Why do Butch and Sundance get their guns in their hands, kick open the barn door and make a run for the horses? *Because it's their only chance.* If you stay in the barn, you're *surely* dead.

And that's assuming the income hit turns out to be as big as you think it will. *It may not.* Consider the case of "George K.," a Merrill Lynch financial consultant whose story is chronicled in a book called *Attract and Retain the Affluent Investor* by Stephen Gresham and Evan Cooper. George finished 1997 with $422,000 in gross production from 631 accounts with $48 million in assets. He had plateaued, was bordering on burnout, and knew he wasn't really functioning as the planning professional he wanted to be. So he started building a series of screens — some quantitative, others qualitative — in an attempt intelligently to thin out his book. In the end, he had a total of 11 screens, the effect of which was *to winnow out all but 33 client relationships* (representing a total of about 100 accounts). The 13 pages of this book which are George's story are absolute "must" reading in every fascinating detail, but for purposes of this present discussion, here's the real epiphany: when George backtested the effect on his previous year's income of washing out over 80 percent of his accounts, he found that his gross production would have declined *just nine percent.* And what a phenomenal release of time, energy and focus attended upon that paltry income give-up!

My bottom line for experienced advisors: it doesn't cost too much to change. **It costs too much not to change.**

In general, there are only two ways of attempting to start a conversation with someone — about financial planning or anything else. One is to try to call him, and the other is to try to see him. (You can also write to someone to tell him you're going to try to call him and/or see him. I can't find any evidence that this reliably changes the outcome often enough to justify your investment of time in it, but it may be an effective way of lowering the reluctance you feel to just jump out of the bushes at people.

If it does, fine. Do whatever makes you feel good, because the better you feel, the more genuine "approaches" you'll be able to make.)

Note, please, that these are the only two ways of making a single "approach." E-mailing without spoken follow-up — trying to get people to contact *you* — is just what it says it is: mailing, albeit electronically. Mailing, instead of trying to call or see people, is an avoidance behavior. It is non-prospecting. (We covered that...right?)

Each of the two methods of attempting to start a conversation has much to recommend it — and also some significant drawbacks.

The telephone lets you try to start the largest number of conversations in the least amount of time with the smallest amount of physical effort and the least risk of personal embarrassment. This is called cold-calling. You can do it from a bought list; you can do it from a professional directory; you can do it from the yellow pages. I've done all three. Indeed, the very thought of cold-calling makes me nostalgic.

It's 1967 again: LBJ is in the White House, John Lindsay is in Gracie Mansion, and the Mets are starting to win ball games. The future mother of my children and I have a beautiful one-bedroom apartment in historic Brooklyn Heights that rents for $200 a month. And this weekend we're going out to the Hamptons — when the Hamptons *were* the Hamptons, before they became the Upper East Side with sand, and before the Montauk Highway became the world's longest, hottest parking lot.

And when I call strangers, "to introduce myself and my firm, and to see if we can compete for a portion of your investment business," I get a fair number of people who say, "Sure; why not?" Because, in two important respects, that's what time it is. (1) *Nobody's* really cold-calling yet, so some people actually find it enterprising and even intriguing, and (2) it's the last full year of the greatest bull market of all time up to that point. Though no one knows it yet — least of all me — next year (1968) the average common stock will begin a 7-year, 70% decline. (As Mets manager Casey Stengel would cheerfully say, "You could look it up.")

That was then. This is now. It's not 1967 anymore. It's a third of a century later. And our society is just about telemarketed to death — so much so that states are beginning to pass laws to protect their citizens who don't actually *want* to be cold-called. Also, through the miracle of modern technology, an advisor has the opportunity to call a couple of hundred people's voicemails in a day, and never speak to a single human being. Moreover, look what I was cold-calling about: just asking your permission to make subsequent calls, in order to pitch you stock ideas.

And, funnily enough, that's what the phone was good for: starting a series of more or less isolated transactions which one hoped would eventually add up to a relationship. But does cold-calling to establish a relationship from the get-go work? These days, I think it's a long row to hoe.

Does that mean you shouldn't prospect via the telephone? No, but it does suggest that perhaps you should be trying to accomplish something fairly specific that's somewhere in between flogging a product and going straight for a meaningful relationship.

RECEPTIONIST: Good morning, Trueheart Storm Door Company.

NEW FINANCIAL ADVISOR: Good morning, this is Doctor Noah Murray from The Ark Financial Planning. Is Mr. Trueheart in?

R: Not at the moment. What is this in reference to?

NFA: I'm calling him up, sort of out of the blue, to invite him to a seminar we're doing at the end of the month on the new tax law. I think he may very well want to come. I didn't expect to catch him this morning, but if you will, please, I'd like to fax *and* mail the invitation. May I have his fax number?

Now, of course, you *might* actually have gotten Mr. Trueheart, in which case the colloquy could have gone something like this:

MR. TRUEHEART: Yes?

NEW FINANCIAL ADVISOR: Mr. Trueheart, Doctor Noah Murray from

	The Ark Financial Planning. Sorry to bother you; I was sure I'd get your assistant. I'm just calling, a bit out of the blue, to invite you or some executive on your staff to the seminar we're doing at the end of this month on the new tax law. I was going to mail you the invitation, although it would be just as easy to drop it off on my way to lunch.
MR. T:	I won't be here.
NFA:	Quite all right; my pleasure. Don't let me keep you...but do, please, look at the invitation. The new tax law is very important to business owners like you, and I can promise you this seminar will be well worth your time.
MR. T:	I'll look at it. No commitment.
NFA:	All we can ask. 'Bye for now.

But now I have a reason to go over there sometime during the day, ask if he's in, give him the invitation and meet him that way if he is, or at least drop it off — and make myself a face, not just a name, with his staff. ("Just dropping off the seminar invitation I promised him. Thanks; have a lovely afternoon.")

The key to all this is that the advisor had a crisp, specific, non-threatening agenda, communicated it briefly and clearly, and fairly quickly gave himself a chance either to hear a fast "no" or to have a reason to go over there. If you're working from a reverse directory, or have the initiative to pay a high school kid $10 an hour plus gas money to go around shooting Polaroids of directories on the ground floor of local office buildings, you can probably cluster a lot of these seminar invitation dropoffs on any given day. (What's a lot? We don't have to know that yet.)

Is this a "better" way to prospect than any other, in that it yields less "no" and more "yes"? Of course not. It's just a way to get you moving, acting, talking to people, and trying to meet the kind of people we want to meet.

Why bother with the phone? Why not just go to 20 offices a day, ask to see the CEO or the CFO (or the doctor, or the attorney, or whoever) and just give her — or leave her — the invitation? I can't think of a single reason — and there, of course, is the *other* way of trying to start a conversation. The first was calling; the second is seeing. Everything else being equal (which it never is, where prospecting anxiety is concerned), why not just...pop in?

RECEPTIONIST: Can I help you?

NEW FINANCIAL ADVISOR: Yes, I'm sure you can. I'm Doctor Noah Murray from The Ark Financial Planning. I'm sort of the new planner in town, and I thought I'd just pop in for a moment and introduce myself to Ms. Trueheart. Is she about?

Same two possible outcomes. You meet Ms. T., you give her the seminar invitation, *ask if there's any particular service you could perform for her today* when you get back to the office — a valuation? a research opinion? — and exit smiling. If you don't meet Ms. T., you entrust the seminar invitation to her assistant, and you still exit smiling. In either case, you're going to call back to see if the prospect is coming to the seminar, and to let *that* conversation lead where it will. At the earliest possible moment, you'll ask for just five minutes — "Really! Time me, and kick me out if I'm still talking after five minutes" — and you'll make your version of the "All you can say" speech on page 16. You can even — and especially — ask for the five minutes if/when the prospect declines to come to the seminar. ("No harm done; there'll be others. As a firm we do crackerjack seminars — *really* helpful to people with significant assets — and I hope we'll do one soon that you'll want to hear. In the meantime, though...")

The downside of just appearing in people's offices is, of course, twofold: (a) it's fairly time-consuming, and no one has any inkling you're coming, so (b) the in-your-face "rejection" may be very cold and hurtful to you, if you haven't built yourself up to it.

So, you tell me: is either of these approaches objectively more likely to "work" better than the other? The operative word in that question being "objectively," my answer is surely no. Now, let's change the question a bit: is either approach likely to work better *for you?* My answer: quite possibly. For that matter, might basing the approach on something other than the seminar invitation dropoff work differently? Sure. Might you just *like* a different approach better? Maybe. But how will you find that out? *Only by trying a lot of approaches and modifying them over time to fit your style.* Let me shorten that sentence for you, so there'll be no doubt in your mind as to what the critical variable is: **only by trying**.

The object of the exercise is eye contact. Transactions can be prospected for on the phone (I guess), and can most economically be done on the phone (or online). But a relationship is to be found only in the mirroring eyes of another human being. People have to see you — even if it's only for a few moments at first — and they need to see you reveling in what you do. I don't mean glad-handing or back-slapping; far from it. I mean letting people see (and feel) what delight you take in offering to do the good that you can do for them. I don't believe they *will* see/feel it unless it's really there; that is, I don't think you can fake it. And they certainly won't sense your love of your craft if the radar of that love is being jammed by negative feelings of prospecting anxiety (much less prospecting despair). This is why it's so important that you find a style of prospecting that you're *personally* comfortable with — and why I can't tell you what that style is: it's as individual as fingerprints. (It's also why, when advisors who've been around for a while ask me "How do you prospect?" I hear them telling me that they don't know who they are, and they don't know what they're selling.)

Granted, the examples I've given you of telephone and/or "pop in" approaches center on one specific idea: come to our seminar. These approaches say: our seminars are great; they're aimed directly at upscale people like you; I'm proud to invite you to one...*I love our seminars; I love my work.*

But suppose your firm has one of those nifty little $250-or-so financial programs that function like an all-day physical examination plus a full set of bitewing dental X-rays. (In other words, it's not a course of treatment, but it very clearly tells you the course of treatment you need.) And suppose you simply *love* that program, and think that no one of the caliber of a true Ark candidate should be safe from hearing about it. ("Heck, these people spend more than $250 in a weekend on greens fees and dinner out!")

Fine: forget about seminar invitations. In fact, forget about everything but that terrific little financial diagnostic. You've found the thing *you* love to show people. This program is great; it's *absurdly* cheap for what it does; you and your family will breathe *so* much easier when you've gone through it — and, hey, you don't even have to implement it through my firm. (In fact you don't have to implement it at all, but that's probably not a good idea; I'm just making the point that doing the diagnostic doesn't obligate you in any way.) The results are yours, to do with what you will...*I love this program; I love my work.*

Or maybe you just love talking about long-term care insurance. You believe, as I do, that to the unsinkable *Titanic* of many affluent families' financial lives, Alzheimer's disease is going to function as the iceberg. With the cost of a year in a nursing home running around $60,000 as a national average (higher, and maybe a lot higher, in nice places where Ark candidates cluster), and rising at about twice the inflation rate, Alzheimer's is a huge — and not at all improbable — threat to clients' financial security. And unless you're so fabulously wealthy that you can self-insure a potential $300,000 - $500,000 five-year hit, then your children will bless you for not letting the burden of putting (and keeping) you in a nursing home befall them.

If one loves, and believes passionately in, long-term care insurance, couldn't one start every conversation with everybody one meets —

butcher, baker, candlestick maker — with this vitally important topic? Is there any doubt in your mind that out of all the people to whom you throw that rope, 250 appropriate clients would grab it, such that you could pull them up to safety in The Ark?

Or maybe your mission is retirement income. We live in a society where even well-to-do people have trouble calculating what their retirement income is actually going to be, and even more trouble figuring out if it's going to be enough. Could you be the Johnny (or Janey) Appleseed of retirement income analysis? Could you just ask every likely person you can put yourself in front of if he'd benefit from having someone who knows her stuff do a no-cost, no-obligation, give-before-you-get, hard-eyed, realistic retirement income analysis?

"Mr. Prospect, if you have your statements on everything you're counting on to provide retirement income, we can eyeball Social Security and probably come up with a pretty good estimate inside half an hour. Even if you *don't* have all your statements, but you know who we need to call — your company's employee benefits people, for example — we can knock it out pretty quick — or I can, and get back to you. If we find there's a shortfall, we can talk about ways to shore it up — or not; your call. If we decide to part friends, you'll have an invaluable piece of information, and I'll have done my good deed for the day. Sounds like all *you're* risking is *my* time, doesn't it? How about over coffee before you start your business day on Tuesday, or is Thursday better for you?" What kind of knuckles-scraping-the-ground troglodyte could say no to *that*? (Answer: almost, but not quite, all of 'em. What else is new? And what does that have to do with *you*, doctor?)

Which one of these programs will "work"? They all will — or none of them will. *Any prospecting program works if you work it long enough.* Or doesn't if you don't. The critical variable isn't in the program/approach. It's in you. All those guys who were working on incandescence around the same time Edison was — you *know* they were all better educated than he was, right? You *know* they could all hear better than he could, right? So how come they didn't invent the light bulb? Simple: *they gave up before he did.* All those college graduates, who could hear a pin drop two blocks away, said things like, "Whew! Two years and 8269 fried filaments — that's enough for me. Put the chairs up on the tables, boys, and the last one who leaves please turn out the gaslights. I believe I'm gonna go work on a horseless carriage, or some damn thing...anything other than this relentless failure." But Edison *couldn't hear them*...and besides, he just couldn't get it out of his uneducated head that *anything that isn't impossible is inevitable.* So, six more months and a couple of thousand additional "failures" later: *Eureka!* That's prospecting. It's not about being smart, or glib, or anything like that. It's about being *relentless*.

What's that? What would *I* do? What method of prospecting would *I* build on if I woke up in Ames, Iowa tomorrow morning, knowing not a soul for 500 miles in any direction, and needing to recruit 250 households/families to *my* Ark? Heck, I'll bet you know even before I tell you. Seminars, of course.

You must have seen that one coming when I couched my scripts/examples of calling and dropping by in terms of delivering a seminar invitation. I love seminars as a business-building tool. Why? For the same reason I love newsletters as a client contact/referral generating/prospecting tool: because I love to do 'em. I love to speak, and I love to write. I don't claim to be objectively very good at either, but that's not what counts. I claim to be able to state complex financial issues in starkly simple human terms that people viscerally grasp, and become motivated to want to learn more (and do something) about, *with me*. The reason it works is that I so clearly (a) believe in what I'm saying, (b) love what I'm doing and (c) genuinely want to help people make better financial decisions. These are human values, and no accumulation of facts, figures, and slides of the efficient frontier (that are illegible more than four rows back in a 40-row hotel ballroom) are ever going to produce the same response. *All great seminars speak into people's hearts.*

Indeed, that very point is the spine of Frank Maselli's immensely helpful book *Seminars: The Emotional Dynamic.* Instead of my doing one chapter on seminars, I strongly recommend that you use Frank's book, which — among its many other attributes — shows you how to organize, build an audience for, and deliver great seminars much better than I could. (And, at 225 pointer-packed pages, in infinitely greater detail.)

Seminars, by the way, are just one more reason that I counseled the newcomer to our profession to get with a lot of structure and support. Until you have the skills (and, even more important, the following) to be able to put at least 50 people in a room every month or six weeks, use group/office seminars to show the few people you *do* draw that you're part of something much larger than you.

Finally: was this me saying that seminars *work better than* calling for appointments, dropping by with or without a call, writing letters and following up with a call/drop-in, or all of the above? Once again: of course not. I said they're what *I'd* do (and indeed have done), and that they worked for me because I loved — and therefore never tired of — doing them.

Plunk me down in Ames, and I'll take my 1975 10-cent Apollo Soyuz postage stamp slide to every Rotary, public library, Communion breakfast, medical and bar association meeting, and radio talk show that'll have me. I'll put on my "Hidden Risks of Retirement Investing" seminar in every town in that 500-mile radius. I'll write a free column for any and every newspaper that'll take it. I'll build a subscriber list for my very accessible, very down-to-earth, straight-talkin', plain-dealin' newsletter. And I'll surely have The Ark full of happy passengers in due time...when I've earned the trust of the good people of Ames and its environs. When will that be? *As long as it takes.*

And so, however discursively, we've answered the first of our three general, procedural questions. Are there prospecting methods that work well in pursuit of — and are there others that mesh poorly with — our relationship-oriented goals? We decided that any approach is to be preferred which gets you out and talking to people face-to-face, so that they can see you doing what you love — and see you loving what you do. Conversely, we concluded that trying to accomplish very much over the telephone would probably not work as well, and that mailing was the last refuge of the prospecting paralytic. Above all, we saw with certainty that the best way to approach our kind of people, and the best thing to approach them with, are those which harmonize with your vision of your calling — the things you most passionately believe in, the needs that you feel people need most desperately to address.

The second question, you'll remember, begins by asking what we'll say, and to whom. But you won't have failed to notice that to a significant extent that's been answered. Say what your heart tells you is most critically important for our people to hear: business owners, corporate executives, members of the professions — *and the centers of influence who advise them.* (One of my other key initiatives, on my first morning there in Ames, will be to start becoming the new professional best friend of every estate attorney in the 500-mile radius. I don't care *what* they need; *I want to be their go-to guy for anything and everything.* Until The Ark sails, every day will be take-an-estate-attorney-to-lunch day.)

The other parts of the second general question have certainly *not* yet been answered, however, and they deserve some extended discussion. How many "approaches" can/must we make each day, and how do we build up our prospecting stamina to the point where we *can* do what we *must* do?

To answer these questions, we have to decide what an "approach" is for scorekeeping/scientific experiment-recording purposes. And it's at this point that I recommend you purchase and listen to Aaron Hemsley's basic behavior modification program, an audiotape set called "The Psychology of Maximum Sales Performance." If I mean Frank Maselli's book to be, in effect, this book's long chapter on how to do seminars, I mean Aaron's audiotape program to be this book's long chapter on desensitizing yourself to "rejection," so that you can joyfully make progressively more anxiety-free "approaches" over time.

My reason for asking that you consult Aaron's work at (and on) this particular point is that you may need to hear someone in addition to me tell you what I'm about to tell you. *An "approach" is whatever you say it is.*

Back in the 1970s, when suddenly everyone was cold-calling, and resistance to it was rising sharply, a great theological debate broke out in the cold-calling community. The issue was whether one should keep score by "dials" or "completions." The adherents of "completion" said, quite reasonably, that it didn't matter how many times you dialed the phone: it only mattered how many people you actually got through to. Because that number drove how many prospects you got, which in turn determined how many accounts you opened.

The "dials" sect held (also quite reasonably) that completions were a variable you couldn't control — that you could cold-call assiduously all day, and some days not get many completions, leading to frustration, anger and self-recrimination. That downward spiral could, in time, take even the most disciplined cold-caller out of the game. Besides, said its religionists, "dials" drive completions in the long run, anyway. So why not keep score by an activity (a) that you could feel in control of and (b) that ultimately ended up in the same place?

If this debate seems silly to you, (1) you've never spent a lot of time cold-calling, and (2) why are you still so worried about what an "approach" is? *My* definition of an "approach," once again, is: **any genuine attempt to start a conversation with another human being.**

NEW FINANCIAL ADVISOR: (Tap-dancing joyfully into estate
　　　　　　attorney's office) Good morning; Doctor Noah Murray, yada

yada, seminar invitation, yada yada, is she about?

RECEPTIONIST: Actually, she just stepped over to the county courthouse to swear out a complaint against you for trespass and harassment.

NFA: Thanks a lot for sharing; have yourself a perfectly lovely day (exits, smiling blissfully).

RECEPTIONIST: (on phone) Good morning, Trueheart Storm Door Company.

NEW FINANCIAL ADVISOR: And a cheerful good morning to you; Doctor Noah Murray here, yada yada, seminar invitation, yada yada, love to drop it off on my way to lunch.

R: I for one sincerely hope you will, because we've instructed our security guards to shoot you down like the dog you are, and to throw your dead, sorry carcass in the dumpster. If you're sure you're coming, I won't take lunch, because I particularly want to see you die.

NFA: (Joyously adding another huge check mark to his "Quest for N" scorecard) I love your honesty! Thanks for sharing, and have a beautiful life!

Those are two genuine "approaches," OK? (If you don't believe that, close this book and put in a call to Aaron Hemsley *right away*. The book and I will be here when you get back.) Oh, and what's that you say? The "rejection" you run into isn't usually *quite* as viciously personal as the two mini-scripts above? Well, then: what's your problem? (And when did you lose your ability to laugh at the silly objections people give you — and to laugh at yourself for getting upset by them?)

How many "approaches" *must* you make a day is a fairly elegant but ultimately secondary question. The real issue — as your courageous conscious desire to succeed battles your unconscious need to avoid the pain of another electric shock — is how many *can* you make. That's all that counts; that's the key behavior we have to modify.

If you're new to the industry, your training department probably told you how many approaches you "should" make — but you may have noticed that those good folks aren't in production anymore, if they ever were. If for no other reason, you have some reason to be suspicious of the practicability of their idea of "should." (That's not to say that they're wrong. It's just to suggest that their idea of what you *should* do and your — albeit unconscious — idea of what you *can* do aren't necessarily going to be identical.)

And you experienced advisors — whose prospecting activity may long since have been beaten down by time, distraction and anxiety — must avoid guilt- and shame-based quasi-religious conversions in which you suddenly see the light and vow to make a zillion approaches a day. That's exactly like jumping up off the couch after 10 sedentary years and saying you're going out and run five miles. You just can't — haven't got the wind, haven't got the legs, haven't got the stamina.

Instead, you need to go out every morning and *train*. Start with an open mind and find out what you can do without killing yourself every day. Soon, you'll feel a little stronger, run a little longer. A couple of weeks more, and you'll find your endurance is even better.

What makes this process successful? Break it down into its component parts:

(1) You tested your endurance, didn't try to be a hero and stayed within your comfort level.

(2) The next day, you did the same thing. No more, but no less either. Then you repeated the process the next day, and the next.

(3) Then, slowly, your endurance started to increase — that's what training is all about. When you felt you

were sustainably at a higher level, you set a new
daily standard.

Prospecting is no different from running, or aerobics, or weight training. The more of it you do, the more of it you can do. (Sadly, the converse is also true: the less...the less.) Just do what you can do — but don't do *less* than you can do, *and do what you can do every day.* (And for those experienced advisors who find "the press of other business" impinging on their prospecting regimen, do what you can do *in the same box of time* every day. Make your prospecting time sacrosanct, and don't let *anything* else leak into it.)

Hemsley — at the risk of terribly oversimplifying him — couches the process in classically behavioral terms.

(1) Spend a week just making "approaches" when you feel like it, non-judgmentally, and stop when you feel your anxiety really kicking in.

(2) Average all the "approaches" you made over the five working days in that week. This average *may be* your "baseline" — the number of perfectly comfortable, anxiety-free "approaches" you're currently capable of sustaining consistently.

(3) Try making that baseline number of calls, but only that number, each day for another week. If you succeed, then try adding one "approach" a day the following week. (If you can't, drop *back* one "approach" a day and see if you can sustain *that* every day for a week. Keep dropping back one a week 'til you hit a sustainable "baseline.")

(4) Advancing one "approach" per day per week when you can, staying steady when you can't sustain an advance for a week, and dropping back one per day per week when you need to, you will — slowly *and* surely — build up over time to any level of prospecting activity you can imagine — and any you could ever need.

(This summary is like describing baseball as a game in which one man tries to throw a ball past another man, and the other man tries to hit it. It's true, and in a certain literal way it gets at some of the essence — but it's not that helpful because it misses so much. Aaron's work is like learning about baseball from Tim McCarver: it shouldn't be missed.)

How long will it take you to build up to — and even surpass — an Edisonian 20 genuine "approaches" a day? I don't know, and you shouldn't care. Because, compared to the beauty of what you're ultimately going to accomplish, it just can't matter. Suppose scholars unearthed new evidence which showed it took Homer 42 years to write *The Iliad* and *The Odyssey*. (Yes, I know: Homer — whoever he was — didn't actually *write* anything, but play along. This is a cool analogy.) Would that make him a bum? Would you say, "The guy must've written nine lines a day and gone to the racetrack; how lazy can a poet be?" I don't think so. You'd say, "The guy produced not one but two of a handful of the greatest works in the canon of early Western literature; it took however long it took; the guy's immortal *and deservedly so.*"

Perhaps even more important — and this is the last of our three great questions — how long should it take us to sell out all 250 staterooms on The Ark? Setting all procedural prospecting issues aside for a moment, how long will the New Financial Advisor, passionately and relentlessly showing the good she can do to the many who are called and the few who are chosen, have to work to secure the 250 $400,000 households/families who deserve her?

My answer is three years at a run and four at a walk. I get there as follows: six months of 10-hour days to fill up the prospect pipeline; 25 qualified accounts (about one a week) in the next six months. In the second year, 75 staterooms. In the third year, under the weight of a surge of referrals — because at that point almost everyone gets you someone else — the dam breaks, and out pour the other 150. (Alternatively, the dam breaks in slow motion, and it takes a fourth year. Are you going someplace? Hey, Homer, who do you like in the third at Delphi?)

Stop for a moment. Take a long, deep breath. Can you think of a lot of professions open to you where you could be running your own business and earning $500,000 to one million dollars in four years... or even less? (And remember: by the time the 250th $400,000 account struggles up the gangplank, there's a lot more than $100 million on The Ark. Because those early accounts grew — and they may have grown a lot.)

And all you had to do to get there was to keep on prospecting. No matter what else you know, or know how to do, it won't matter if you stop prospecting. No matter what else you *don't* know and *can't* do, it won't matter...if you go on prospecting.

"It matters not how far the journey," said Confucius, "so long as you do not stop."

Amen.

IN SUMMARY

- A prospecting "approach" is any genuine attempt to start a conversation with another human being about what you can do for them.
- Don't compete on price. Don't compete on "performance." If at all possible, don't compete at all. But if you must compete, do so on your own terms: that you will genuinely care for and about the family more than any other advisor possibly can.
- Tell stories. Use analogies. Leave left-brain analysis, as much as possible, to people who like numbers more than they like people. *Like people. Stand by your standards.*
- If you're starting out, seek protective/instructive cover. Join a group practice, apprentice yourself, at least get a mentor. Also (not instead), join — or form — a support group of your neophyte peers.
- If you're experienced, be brutally honest with yourself about how few of your current clients may deserve to be on your Ark.
- Leached of all its anxiety and methodology, prospecting is about getting to eye contact. Let people see you doing what you love. Even more important, *let them see you loving what you do.*
- The "best" prospecting method is the one you like most (or dislike least). The "best" thing to prospect with is whatever you're most passionate about. Everything else is mechanics. *Any prospecting program will work if you work it long enough.*
- An "approach" is a genuine attempt to start a conversation; that attempt doesn't have to start a conversation, and usually won't. Keep score by activities that you control, not outcomes you don't.
- Prospecting is like running, aerobics and/or weight training. Find out what you can do. Do what you can do every day, until you can progressively do more. Don't do less. Train, don't strain.
- From a standing start, you should be able to sell out The Ark in three to four years. But if it takes 10, that doesn't make you a bum. Hey,

Homer, who do you like in the third at Delphi?

- You can have anything you want, as long as you keep prospecting. You can't have anything you want if you stop prospecting. Don't stop prospecting.

FINDING YOUR VOICE

chapter four

FOUR

———————●———————

At some point during your three-to-four year quest to fill The Ark with deserving people — and probably sooner than later — you're going to discover what your N is. That is, just by recording all your "approaches," and every 90 days or so dividing the sum of those "approaches" by the number of prospects you got, you'll know how many people you have to make a legitimate attempt to start a conversation with, in order to get one prospect.

Or you won't, because you stopped caring: you got into a prospecting groove; it's working (inevitably); you have growing confidence in yourself and in the prospecting process, and you don't need the crutch of $P = 1/N$. You recognize it for the anxiety management tool it is — a way of making the potentially stressful work of prospecting into a game that you're guaranteed to win every N times you play it.

In any event, whether you've found your N and are joyously pounding away at it, or whether you've outgrown the need for N like the training wheels on your first bicycle, *you now have in place three of the four essential elements you need in order to be wildly — and permanently — successful in building a financial planning practice.* In fact, you've already got all four; you just haven't focused on the last one yet.

Take a moment, now, to review the first three. Then we'll see what that fourth one is, after which we'll proceed to the next major step in the development of your own unique professional self.

(1) YOU HAVE A STRONG, LOGICAL, COHERENT
BELIEF SYSTEM. Either from bitter experience if
you've been around for a while, or by an act of faith
in the earlier chapters of this book if you haven't,

you believe that even monied Americans are eventually doomed without a plan — and a planner. You believe your calling is not necessarily (and certainly not at the outset) to understand exactly what solutions the household/family needs. Rather, your job is simply to establish the facts, the hopes and the fears, and then mediate/translate between the client and the experts. Finally, you believe in yourself as the empathetic and humane healer a family desperately needs.

(2) YOU HAVE AN EXTREMELY DETAILED, RATIONAL AND SOUND BUSINESS PLAN. A hundred million dollars, 250 staterooms, $400,000 average assets, one percent fee, one million dollars of gross income to the practice, half that (before taxes) to you — in three to four years. Let me assure you that definiteness of purpose is simply one of the mightiest forces on earth (faith and persistence are two others), and that not one in 20 advisors ever has — other than in fantasy — so specific a plan. If you truly believe in that plan, and are committed to just wearing away at it for as long as it takes, then in a very real sense you're already in the top five percent of the profession.

(3) HAVING DISCOVERED YOUR N — OR EVEN HAVING TRANSCENDED THE NEED FOR IT — YOU HAVE A PROSPECTING DISCIPLINE THAT IS APPROPRIATE TO THE EXECUTION OF YOUR BUSINESS PLAN IN THE BUDGETED TIME. Moreover, as with all physical and even mental conditioning, the more you do, the more you find you are

able to do. That is, any consistent exercise expands your capacity to perform the exercise — thus potentially shortening even further the time it may take to reach your goal.

Now, the missing piece we need in order to square off this firm foundation to your lifetime's work is:

(4) YOU MUST SET A VALUE ON YOUR TIME — AND THEN STRIVE ALWAYS TO BE WORTH THAT VALUE. And, as I said a moment ago, you've actually already done this, albeit inferentially. The missing variable is just how many hours you have in a working year, in which to produce the gross income you've targeted for your practice. And even in those first three to four years of all-consuming effort, I don't see how that number can possibly be more than about 2,000 hours. So if you propose, at the end of the three-four year process, to be grossing one million dollars, you've set a value on your time of $500 an hour. That is, even by today's standards, a peck of money to be charging in this society — for *anything*. Even doctors doing most forms of surgery, and attorneys litigating all but the largest lawsuits, may not be billing that much. And even I — your biggest fan — don't say you can *price* your time at anything like $500 during the early years. My point is that you have to think in terms of working to *deserve* that much. *And you have to save your staterooms for people willing and even eager to pay it*...because they have the sense to see what a bargain it is!

Remember that we don't have to gross $500 an hour right out of the gate — and we certainly won't — but we have to carry ourselves, and relate to our prospects, in such a way as to deserve it. This precludes things like jumping around trying to prove that our mutual fund will outperform somebody else's mutual fund, or that our net cost of life insurance will be lower than someone else's. A surgeon whose fee works out to roughly $500 an hour doesn't guarantee that you're going to get better, and a $500-an-hour litigator doesn't guarantee that you're going to win your case. What they say — and not even in so many words: they just kind of beam it at you — is that they feel as competent as anyone alive to do what you need done, and that they represent your best chance for success.

And I want precisely that conviction to inform everything you say to all the potential (and, after a while, actual) Ark passengers you're going to speak to for the next four years. Even more important, I want you to let it inform *the way you say* everything you're going to say. Because people may or may not understand what you say, but they respond very powerfully — positively or negatively — to *the way you say what you say*.

So as we begin finding you a voice — a way for you to share the passionate conviction in your heart about how much you can help a prospect household/family, and how much you *want* to help them — let's think in terms of the attitudes (and representations) of the $500-an-hour surgeon and attorney. We'll use them as a platform for what we'll say, and we may be surprised to find that we can go a bit further in what we're able to predict with assurance.

- My firm has the resources, and I have the will, to produce for you and your family a plan which addresses your needs as optimally as can anyone. I don't believe another planner/entity can offer an objectively "better" plan, nor a more appropriate portfolio of investments and insurance to carry that plan out.

- The extra "edge" I believe my clients have is my own unwillingness to be competed with in terms of who will care more for your family. Caring is the basis for my relationships with my clients (just as competence is my firm's basis). If you ever find an advisor more deeply committed to your family's financial success than I — go on his Ark. He deserves you more than I do.

- If you give the plan enough time and enough money — and we can't know for sure what will be enough money, although we can make educated estimates — you'll achieve substantially all the goals we agree on. If you're not given sufficient time, insurance will carry the plan the rest of the way.

The three attitudinal convictions above — felt, if not immediately spoken — carry the "All you can say" speech from page 16 forward; they give it its force and its strength, even as the speech itself comes across as very low-key.

The surgeon doesn't say, "No one can perform this operation better than I." The litigator doesn't say, "No one can make your case and argue it better than I." But the best of them surely believe it, *and what's more you can feel that they do.* They take quiet but very palpable pride in what they can do — and so must you. If you're not convinced that your firm *can* create a plan that's at least as good as anyone's, then clearly you have some decisions to make. But if you *are* convinced, then beam that powerful conviction at your prospects. *And that becomes a substantial part of — indeed, the basis for — your voice.*

Somebody who bills — or will one day soon be effectively capable of billing — $500 an hour doesn't pitch, doesn't "sell," and above all doesn't try to prove anything. The problem — and it's only a temporary problem, easily overcome — is that the millionaire next door may not actually have gotten that memo, in advance of your meeting. So although he's been acculturated not to ask the doctor or the attorney for "proof," there's absolutely nothing in his education, training or experience that would lead him to accord you the same courtesy.

Don't take it personally, and don't try to "overcome" questions that may not even be objections. Use the prospect's skepticism as another opportunity for him to hear your serenely self-confident voice — and for you to find out if he's even capable of hearing it.

PROSPECT: My insurance agent (or: my investment advisor) offered me a financial plan. Why do it with someone I don't know?

NEW FINANCIAL ADVISOR: Did you complete the plan with the person you *do* know?

P: Well, no, but...

NFA: (Smiling, gently) Well, that might be a reason, right there.

P: But why is your plan any better than theirs?

NFA: I'm not sure any really good plan is better than any other really good plan. My basic conviction is that any good plan that you actually put into effect is better than all the plans you don't.

P: I don't really have time for this right now.

NFA: I understand perfectly, and I empathize with you. The demands on the time of someone as successful as you are must be tremendous. That's why I'm happy to work around your schedule. Somewhere there's an hour to do the fact-finding interview, and I'll go wherever and whenever that is. But for what it's worth, I'd almost bet that your return on the investment of that one hour will far exceed that of any other hour you'll put in this year. Are you here at 7:00 a.m.?

P: Not usually, but I guess I could be on Thursday. You'd have to be out of here by 8:00, though. I have a meeting.

NFA: (Smiling) That's not just a start — it's a great start. See you here at 7:00 Thursday morning. How do you take your coffee?

Or, how about steering the discussion directly through the paradigm of medicine:

PROSPECT: How can you demonstrate that your plan is best?

NEW FINANCIAL ADVISOR: I'm not sure I know what "best" means. And I don't know that "best" is a true test of planning. I don't ask my doctor if he's the "best" at anything. I ask if he can cure me, or refer me to someone who can. If I recover, then the doctor was well suited to my needs. Same with financial planning, I think.

P: I still don't see how.

NFA: The test of a financial plan is whether it causes your financial goals to be met, and whether it protects you from the things that can go wrong in your family's financial life. If it does, it's all the plan you need.

P: How do you know in advance that it's going to do those things?

NFA: I'm not sure if I ever really *know* the sun is coming up in the morning. But financial planning isn't like medicine or law, where the issues are so complex normal people can't understand them. When I lay out a financial plan for you and your family, everyone will understand it, sooner or later. I'll make sure of that. That's the really rewarding part of what I do: not just letting people sleep nights, but helping them *understand why* they can sleep nights.

P: What do I have to do?

NFA: You and your spouse, and anyone else in the family you think needs to be there, have to invest an hour in a fact-finding interview. Bring your will, mortgage payment book, bank statements, investment statements, life insurance policies — whatever you've got like that. I'll ask you some questions about what you want to accomplish, and take everything back to my office. We may call you back with some more questions, or seek your permission to call your accountant or attorney with questions. When we know what needs to be done, we'll draw up a basic set of recommendations, and I'll come back and present 'em to you.

P: What if I don't like 'em?

NFA: It'd be hard for you not to like 'em, since all they're going to be are, in our best professional judgment, the most efficient, most economical ways to do what you said you wanted to do. I'm betting that when you understand the plan, you'll like it. If not, all you've got in it is some time and [NOTE: *tell prospect the cost, if any*]. And you get to keep the plan.

P: Are we obligated to do anything more at that point?

NFA: Certainly not. But do you think it's likely that you wouldn't want to start putting a plan into effect, if you and your advisors thought it sound?

P: No; I just don't want to get roped into buying something I didn't know I'd bought.

NFA: (Smiling) You don't know me yet. The fact is, I wouldn't take on a client who wasn't totally in love with the plan my firm and I proposed. Life's too short.

One thing this dialogue points up is that people often aren't that used to the financial planning process. They're accustomed to having salespeople try to sell them life insurance or mutual funds, but planning — real planning, done right — may be something new to them. So a lot of questions that sound challenging (or even adversarial) may just be ways of finding out how the process works — and, as this prospect said, of not getting sold something they didn't quite know they were buying until it was too late.

On the other hand, you don't want to jam a plan on someone, or make him so blissfully comfortable with his absence of further obligation that he's willing to go through the fact-finding process just to get his hands on a plan and then be rid of you. That's why, in this script, the advisor asked if the prospect thought it at least likely that he'd want to put a worthwhile plan into effect. If the prospect were still harboring a flat "no" in him somewhere, that could have been the way to smoke it out.

Another idea I'd have you absorb from this dialogue is that, on balance, I prefer to volunteer my cost at each step of the process, rather than be asked. I know there are two schools of thought on this, but in my school we were taught to stand up very proudly for what we charge. This is, after all, how you earn your living. And pre-emptively announcing your cost is an effective way of communicating to your prospect — and of reminding yourself — that it can't possibly be an objection **since top quality planning advice is always worth untold multiples of what it costs.** This is a theme we'll return to again and again: the absurdly tiny fraction which has the cost of financial planning as its numerator and the benefits/savings/gains of planning as its denominator.

Finally, I'd like you to observe that this colloquy ends with the planner gently making the point that this interview process is going in both directions. That is, the planner suggests that the prospect has to qualify, attitudinally as well as financially, to become a client. The prospect can't just buy your financial plan; *he has to love it.* We're not going to shanghai anyone onto The Ark, or drag him up the gangplank kicking and screaming. Because we know that, human nature being what it is, anyone who gets on The Ark with any significant conflicts or even grave reservations about doing so *is going to go over the side at the first sign of trouble.*

But it isn't enough that *we* know this. The *prospect* has to know it, too — has to hear the confident voice of the New Financial Advisor, gently telling him that *his* suitability for the voyage will have to be established before he'll be allowed on The Ark. Otherwise, the advisor is accepting (unconsciously, and/or out of fear of standing up to the prospect) a one-sided burden of proof. **And this we must never do.** A major part of what your properly trained voice subliminally does is repeatedly to send out the message: you, Mr. Prospect, have to deserve me every bit as much as I have to earn your trust and your business.

Thus we see that there are two major characteristics of a fully developed voice: (1) authenticity and (2) the ability to move people not so much by what you say as by the way that you say it. Some of the worst, most meretricious advice you'll get in your career is to study different personality "types" and to modify yourself in an attempt to harmonize with whatever alleged "type" you think you're talking to at a given moment. This is just the most suicidal thing you could possibly do. Your authenticity, your identity, the beliefs and values that make you uniquely you — those are the very qualities that you must steadfastly nurture in yourself, and broadcast consistently to the rest of the world. *You gotta be who you are.* You don't win lasting client relationships by changing your voice or your tie or anything else — by tricking people into thinking you're fundamentally different from who you are. You win those great relationships by letting people see — and letting the *right* people be attracted to — the real you, the one they learn they can consistently rely on.

That's the reason I would never want you to try to memorize the scripts in this book, or to give back my responses to questions/objections exactly the way I do. If and to the extent that these things appeal to you, please realize that it's only because they're written in *my* authentic voice — in what I said to prospects and clients *the way I said it.* Be assured that *your* authentic voice, as you perfect it, will turn out to be better than mine is — *for you.* Because, of course, it's genuinely yours. **Just as your behav-**

iors flow out of your beliefs, your voice has to flow out of your own genuineness. No one has ever been able to help people in exactly the way you can, and no one ever will. Guard the integrity of your true self, literally with your life. **You gotta be who you are.**

Having said all that, I do think there are a few things you can consistently do to train your voice — to organize your general approach to what you say about financial planning, and the way you say it. To name five:

(1) Talk as much as possible in terms of the stark simplicity of human financial needs, and indicate clearly how deeply you empathize with those needs. Talk as little as possible about the technical complexities of a plan's solution to those needs.

(2) Stress, over and over again, every chance you get, *that it is going to be all right* — that with enough time and enough money (and enough insurance against not having enough time), and most of all with enough faith in the plan, your clients will get the outcomes they want. Talk as little as possible, unless you are asked, or unless it's absolutely critical to the client's understanding, about *how* it is going to be all right.

(3) Strive always to make it clear, without in the least puffing yourself up, that the critical variable in the long-term success of the plan will be *you.* Your laser-like focus on the family's deepest hopes, dreams and fears — together with your ability to ride herd on the "experts" to make sure that the clients are getting what they need and deserve — are the things that make all the wheels turn. Make it *very* clear

that you are the client's advocate vis-à-vis the rest of the world — and not, among other things, your firm's advocate vis-à-vis the client.

(4) Never stop asking questions. In particular, every time you make a major point *about anything*, ask if the client is OK with it. Don't sow the seeds of deal-killing objections that you never even know are there because you didn't ask. Don't call in an air strike on your own position.

(5) As often as you possibly can — even when it may not be strictly accurate — say, *"I don't know."* A lot of what people very humanly want to know (which mutual funds will perform best) isn't knowable, and a lot just doesn't matter. "I don't know" is a nice, non-confrontational way of bringing a flurry of Q&A back down to earth, and of reminding prospects of an important truth: you fly 'em. You don't build 'em.

Let's see if we might not easily find opportunities to work all these aspects of your clear, coherent, consistent voice into the very average preliminary conversation we were listening to a few pages ago.

PROSPECT: What's involved in financial planning? What does it entail?

NEW FINANCIAL ADVISOR: On its most fundamental level, planning acts to eliminate your financial fears: what would happen if you became unemployed, became disabled, or passed away? Planning can't prevent those things from happening, but it can, within certain tolerances, prevent them from turning into financial disaster. On the upside, I think planning gives you the best possible chance to grow and protect your earnings and assets so that you can live, as nearly as possible, financially worry-free. And so that you can do the things you want for the people you care about, both during your life and after it.

P: I meant technically. Do you have to set up trusts, or change your insurance? Do you give up control of your investments?

NFA: Technically, we won't know anything until we've been all through the fact-finding process. But let me tell you that the technical aspects of planning are never that important; they're just ways of doing whatever you decide you want to do. Philosophically, in planning, you do as little as you can possibly do to accomplish what you want to accomplish. You don't have brain surgery to fix a sprained wrist, and you don't do hugely complex trust and estate work on simple inheritances. Finally, and above all, you don't do anything you don't genuinely want to do. You're in control of the process. I'm your advisor. We don't like what we see, we send the experts back to the drawing board. Or we walk.

P: Where do you fit into all this?

NFA: As I said, I'm your advisor. I put all my professional energy into thoroughly understanding your situation. Then I put it all into finding the least complicated, most effective ways of accomplishing what you want to accomplish. Lots of times, I end up talking to your attorney or accountant — but only with your approval — to make sure everybody's on the same page — and that it's still the right page. Along the way, your family and I get a pretty good idea about whether we want to work together or not. That's just human chemistry. When I'm satisfied that the plan is as good as it can be, I present it to you and to your advisors. If everybody's happy, we go with it. If everybody isn't happy, at least you learned a heck of a lot about your financial situation, and I spun my wheels in a good cause. When the plan's in place, I'm kind of a coach, or a repairman, or both. Keep it running smoothly, keep everybody informed, replace a part when it needs replacing. Things like that. Not sure how much detail you want me to get into. Conceptually, at least, are you comfortable with that?

P: Yes, that seems logical. But your card says Gronsky Mutual Life/Gronsky Securities. Who do you represent?

NFA: The short answer is: I represent you. And the long answer is: I represent you. My allegiance is to my clients, of whom I never want more than about 250. I sit on your side of the table. If you suddenly weren't there one day, I'd sit with your family on their side of the table. If you ever see — or even *think* you see — me sitting on the *other* side of the table...you have my permission to get up and walk away from the table.

P: How do you get paid?

NFA: It depends on what you need done. [*Describe what, if anything, you charge for the plan itself.*] If it turns out you need some form of insurance, and you want me to place it for you, I'd be paid a commission, same as any insurance agent. Investments are managed on a fee basis — usually something in the neighborhood of one percent of the assets. We'll know the specific answer to your question when we see the plan; the general answer is: about what any high quality, reputable planner charges for similar services. Again, though, it all depends on what you need done, and what you decide you *want* done. Does that make sense to you?

P: Until I see the actual numbers, it does.

CHAPTER FOUR: FINDING YOUR VOICE | 119

NFA:	Fair enough. Anything particularly bothering you, financially?
P:	I worry a lot about running out of money in retirement.
NFA:	Is that something you think might actually happen to you?
P:	I just don't know. I can't figure out how to get my arms around it. That must be why I'm talking to you at all.
NFA:	Well, you're in luck, because retirement income analysis is a huge part of the basic financial planning process. In the meantime, I wouldn't worry about it.
P:	Why not?
NFA:	Because you have some time, and you have options. Maybe we can figure out a way for you to invest more. Maybe we can figure out a way to invest for better returns. Maybe we can figure out ways to control your expenses in retirement. It's going to be all right.
P:	What do you think of hedge funds?
NFA:	Don't really know much about 'em. Do you own any hedge funds?
P:	No, but...well, I read about a couple that were really shooting the lights out.
NFA:	In my experience, a lot of things that shoot the lights out for a while end up getting shot. I still haven't figured out what's wrong with getting rich slowly. I'll be happy to look into them, though, if you like.
P:	No, never mind. Think we'll ever get privatized Social Security accounts?
NFA:	I sure hope so, for our kids' sakes. Probably a little late to mean that much to you and me, though.
P:	Well, I'll give you this: you don't say much, but you're reassuring to talk to. Although I'm not sure *why*, exactly.
NFA:	Thanks. I take that as a great compliment. I'm looking

forward to our fact-finding meeting on Thursday.

P: Oddly enough, so am I.

I think you'll agree that what we saw here was the prospect asking every pointed question you might expect, hearing a lot of self-possessed and highly reassuring answers, and getting progressively more relaxed with the New Financial Advisor...who, as the prospect perceptively observed, hadn't really said much. But he'd said everything he *could* say, everything he *chose* to say — and, as it turned out, everything he *needed* to say, in order to get the job done. The advisor just kept putting out a steady (if deliberately non-specific) beam of tremendous confidence in the planning process, as well as in himself. And this time, it worked.

In this conversation, the advisor did three specific things that are particularly noteworthy, and that you will especially want to work on mastering. First, since the prospect evinced a very high degree of uncertainty over how the planning process works, and of the advisor's role in it, the planner kept reinforcing the idea of how totally in control of the process the prospect would be, and how he could stop it at any point. Second, the advisor didn't bat an eyelash over the compensation issue. He didn't tense up, or overexplain his compensation, or even mount an argument in justification of it. *He answered only the question he was asked,* in itself a priceless skill. Above all, the advisor made it clear that the prospect would only pay for whatever he — the prospect — consciously decided he wanted done.

The third and most important point the advisor made — and one that people need to be told in so many words, because they don't intuitively assume it to be true — is that he is working for the prospect/client. ("The short answer is: I represent you. And the long answer is: I represent you.") In the script, the prospect gave the advisor the perfect opening to do this, by asking exactly the question that calls forth this all-important answer. In real life, you may not always be so lucky. So even —

and especially — when the question isn't asked, you have to make your version of this point very clearly. The prospect needs to hear — and believe — your heartfelt assertion that it's *you and he against the world.*

You may find it very useful to copy out on a 3x5 card the five voice-training suggestions you read a few moments ago, and review them before you go into every face-to-face prospect/client interaction — until they become second nature, and you can throw the card away.

It has thus far gone without saying that the one indispensable precondition to starting a financial planning practice is to do (and/or to have done) a comprehensive plan on yourself. This is simply the most efficient, and by far the most intense, professional learning experience you'll ever have. Moreover, how can you possibly persuade people to do something you haven't had the courage or the discipline to do for yourself and the people *you* care about? Finally, you will be amazed at the number and variety of opportunities you'll get to refer back to your own plan when you're talking to prospects about theirs — especially when handling questions and objections.

MATURE PROSPECT: You can recommend anything you want, but I don't want to buy any more life insurance. I just want to keep building my investments.

NEW FINANCIAL ADVISOR: That's *exactly* what I said!

MP: Beg your pardon?

NFA: I went into my last major round of estate planning saying exactly what *you* just said: I have enough insurance; I can invest whatever I need to invest from now on. (Silence)

MP: And?

NFA: And quickly became convinced that just about every dollar I invested at this point in my life — and all the earnings thereon, for however much time I have left — would ultimately be estate-taxed at 55 cents on the dollar. So I felt that just investing, no matter how successful it might be, was creating an estate tax nightmare for the kids. Made no sense. (Silence)

MP: So what did you do?

NFA: (Almost as an afterthought) Oh, well, I...listen, please understand, I'm not making a recommendation, here. We're nowhere near to being far enough along in the process for me to do that. But what *I* did was buy a pretty substantial investment-based life insurance policy, and I put it in something called an insurance trust. I'm vectoring a lot of my investments in there, because they grow on a tax-protected basis. The trust is outside my estate. And when my wife and I are both gone, the insurance should knock out the estate tax liability that comes due on the second death. Turned out to be the cheapest way to vaporize the estate tax. So I did it. (Smiles contentedly)

MP: So is this you saying *I* should buy this kind of life insurance?

NFA: (Heartily) Not at *all*! This is me saying (a) keep an open mind, and (b) realize that we're going to come back to you with what we believe is the most efficient, least expensive, least complicated way to accomplish what you tell us you want to accomplish. I neither know nor care what that solution is — and, as a friend and advisor, I don't think you should, either.

Your own feelings — the way you wrestled with your own issues during the formulation of your plan — serve to make you much more *real* to your prospects. Because, at the end of the day, the most powerful force in the financial advisory profession — more powerful, in my experience, than all the other forces combined — is **empathy**. There's a tremendous closing of the emotional distance between advisor and prospect that takes place when you let them see that, even for a professional, some decisions are a struggle. Yes, it's important and helpful to be able to share with your prospects the technical/intellectual things you've learned in your personal planning. But it's *infinitely* more effective — and may be downright decisive — when you let them see what went on in your heart. For these and a hundred other reasons, your own plan — a formal, written, comprehensive financial, investment and estate plan — is *sine qua non*.

When I started out in the stockbrokerage business, I was so afraid of talking to wealthy strangers about their money — and so unsure of my own grasp of the key factors affecting the stocks I wanted those strangers to buy — that I literally wrote down, word for word, my presentations. And then I'd practice those presentations on my wife, to see if they made sense *and* sounded deeply felt. (I didn't know much in those early days, but I'd already realized that *when I believed, I was believed.*) And the fact is that the book you're reading, as did its half-dozen predecessors, flows out of those painstakingly crafted, oft-rehearsed sales presentations. I mentioned earlier that today I love to write, but back then I certainly wasn't writing out my presentations for any but the most basic anxiety management/effective selling reasons. And it's on that basis that I strongly recommend that you *write out everything you propose to say to people about financial planning, through every step of the process.*

Planning is so multifaceted and complex — there are so many things that you *could* try to talk about — that it defies, even for the most glib among us, all attempts to just wing it. Add to that fact the absolutely wild dispersion of issues that prospects unfamiliar with the process may conjure out of thin air, and you'll see why, within the limits of your power to control it, every conversation you have with people about planning should be fairly formally structured in your mind. Your emotional intelligence may be more evolved than mine was (indeed, whose isn't?), such that you don't need to go word for word, but at the very least I think you'll be well served by an outline of what you're trying to accomplish — of how you want the conversation to go, and where you want it to end up. That way, when the interview threatens to go crashing off into the bushes chasing some tertiary issue, you'll be both quicker and more adept at getting it back on the high road. (Do, however, make at least a mental note to keep an eye out for that tertiary issue if it reappears, because it may be a proxy for something larger and more ominous — something the prospect as yet can't/won't articulate.)

In addition to outlining/writing your agenda — and possibly in the same notebook, if that works for you — keep a journal of each important face-to-face interview, at least for your first couple of years. Write down who you saw, what the setting for the interview was, what you hoped/expected to accomplish, and what the outcome was. Most particularly — and I think this is the key benefit of an interview journal — *record in some detail the questions/objections/stalls you hear.*

Personally, as a right-brain/empathetic/heart-on-my-sleeve, I-fly 'em-I-don't-build-'em guy, I was never particularly bothered by questions I couldn't answer. I just had to learn ways to keep those questions from derailing the process, and I did. First, I'd say, "There has to be a compelling answer to that, or else the technical people wouldn't have crafted the plan exactly this way. Is this very important to you, or can we just keep going, and I'll get you that answer tomorrow?"

A fair amount of the time (not *all* the time, certainly, but plenty often enough to make it a worthwhile tactic), the questioner would say, "Never mind; it probably isn't important." Or, "I wouldn't mind knowing at some point, but let's go on." Or even, "Let's keep going, but I couldn't make a final decision without knowing that answer." (I *told* you you could get an awful lot of mileage out of "I don't know," but you didn't want to believe me.)

Sometimes, though, a prospect — or far more often his accountant or attorney, trying to be a hero — would say, "No, stop right here, because this is in the nature of a dealbuster unless we can get comfort on it right quick." And at that point, of course, I'd be stuck.

So I ended up developing a kind of lifeline system. I wouldn't schedule an appointment where there was any real chance I'd get asked a question I couldn't answer *unless and until I had arranged to have a backup person standing by to take my call if/when I got in trouble.*

So when we got to the "I'm stumped/Well, too bad, 'cause that's a dealbuster" stage, I just said, "No problem; I know the senior person in our firm who worked on your plan. If you have a speakerphone, I'm sure we can ring right through to her, and get the answer." And that was the end of that — especially when I'd come back in at the end, and ask, since we had Ms. Expert on the line, if they thought they saw any other issues that would keep them from making a decision *at this point.* (This is just another indication, if you still needed one, of why you don't initially — and may never — have to have a whole lot of technical expertise.)

Questions and objections, however, aren't necessarily the same thing. Questions I learned to handle — by *not* handling them, as you just saw; by suddenly unleashing my trained attack experts on the questioner(s) at exactly the moment they thought they had me run to earth. Objections can be, and often are, a different kettle of fish.

Technical objections are just like questions you can't answer, only more so. Let's say your firm comes back with a recommendation that a family put its closely held business into a family limited partnership. But the prospect's attorney says that there isn't enough case law on family limited partnerships yet, or that the case law is too ambiguous. That's a situation you want no part of; just make emotional common cause with the family (you and me against the world; we shall overcome...even our own Larry Lightbulbs) and let the "experts" go in a room and fight it out. You can't win this one, but of course you can't lose it, either. If the particular solution your firm recommended isn't acceptable...the family still has the problem, still has the need for planning — and, most important of all, still has you. Send the experts back to the drawing board to tell you what Plan B is. No harm done. Beam constantly at the family: *this has nothing to do with us.* We'll get through this the way we'll get through everything: together.

But *non*-technical objections — the soft, murky, human kind — are something else. If you doubt this, I anticipate a deeply religious experience for you when you lay out a whole plan for an obviously upscale prospect, and he turns to you and says, "We don't have any money." You shouldn't ever get to that point, of course; in time you'll learn (albeit the hard way, the same way we learn *everything* important) to flush this kind of deeply conflicted prospect much earlier in the process. But once in a while you may sense that an oddball objection like that is merely a proxy for another, far darker issue. And you may want to spend some time and effort trying to bring it up into the light. Start by listening to what the objection *doesn't* say — what points in the negotiations it's not arguing with.

"We have no money," for example, doesn't say, "We don't need a plan." And it doesn't even say, "This is a bad plan." You may just be dealing with a normal, flawed human being, looking at what it will cost to do what he wants to do, and choking on his own feelings of inadequacy.

NEW FINANCIAL ADVISOR: (Looking around prospect's well-
    appointed office/house) Not quite sure I'm following you
    on that one.

PROSPECT: A $35,000 insurance premium? *Plus* $4000 a month in
    this investment program you've laid out? *Plus* long-term
    care insurance? *Plus your fee for the plan?* Forget it. I've
    got tuition, I've got orthodontia...

NFA: (Smiling) You've got sticker shock. Don't worry about it.
    It happens to us all — and (gesturing to himself) I do mean
    us. We start thinking in terms of all the things we'd *ideally*
    like to accomplish — and I still believe that's the right way

to start. But then financial planning (like everything else in our economic lives) becomes a series of choices. The next step is deciding what we *need to have* and what would just be *nice to have*. I *need to have* a nice, safe, roomy car. It'd be *nice to have* — I mean, I guess it would be nice to have — a Rolls Royce. But I don't *need* a Rolls Royce, and buying one would be a bad economic choice for me and my family.

Let's go through the plan again, and separate *need to have* from *nice to have*. And, although you may not have a lot of *cash* right now — and I agree that you don't — you've got a lot of the three next best things.

P: (Brightening) What are those?

NFA: Income, assets and — if necessary — borrowing power. Now, shall we start through the plan again?

P: Let's do it.

A lot of boxing is learning how to get hit. And a lot of building a financial planning practice is learning how hard even good people will at times resist doing the right thing. As your voice develops — as you worry less about what you're going to say, and just learn to say it — you'll find people not just understanding you, and not just respecting you, but *liking* you. And that's when they accept you and your plan.

Will your voice be perfectly formed in the first month, or even the first year? Surely not. Will it be fully — authentically, uniquely — developed in four years? *I guarantee it.*

IN SUMMARY

- You have to put a value on your time — and, without realizing it, you may already have. Any way you slice it, a 250-family/$400,000 average assets/one percent fee Ark means Doctor Noah bills $500 an hour.

- What does a $500-an-hour professional sound like? What does he — and especially what *doesn't* he — promise/guarantee? Start training your voice to that persona. This will help you train yourself to be that kind of professional. You have to deserve it before you can earn it.

- Most people — even most monied people — haven't been through a formal financial planning process before. So they may have a lot of questions. Take 'em in stride; questions aren't objections until proven guilty.

- Stress that a plan is never going to be any more or less than *what the prospects themselves said they wanted.*

- Explain how you get paid, before you're asked. Don't *overexplain* how (or why) you get paid.

- Two most important aspects of your voice: (1) authenticity and (2) the ability to move people not so much by what you say as by the way you say it. *You gotta be who you are.*

- Five voice-training exercises:
    - (1) Talk as much as possible about the prospect's needs and your empathy therewith. Talk as little as possible about the technical aspects of the solutions.
    - (2) Tell them it's going to be all right. Don't, unless asked, spend a lot of energy telling them *how.*
    - (3) Make it crystal clear that you are the client's advocate — that your first and only allegiance is to him and his family.

(4) Keep asking questions. Get agreement at every important point.

(5) Say "I don't know" as often as you can. *You fly 'em. You don't build 'em.*

- Get your own comprehensive plan done; it will make you infinitely stronger technically *and empathetically.*

- Write out what you're going to say. Keep a journal of your interviews, particularly as a growing compendium of answers to questions and objections.

- Let people hear you. Help them like what they hear.

SPEAKING IN YOUR VOICE

chapter five

FIVE

———————•———————

At some point you'll actually be sitting in a room somewhere — in the prospects' home, or in their office, or yours — and you'll start into the process of discovering who they really are, financially. At that point, as well, it will be incumbent on you to let them begin to learn who *you* really are.

Because, remember, this isn't just about selling staterooms on The Ark to anybody who can afford one. It's *at least as much* about establishing — in your own quiet but very clear voice — your expectations regarding the conduct of those few households/families you'll choose to save from the flood. (Bear in mind — always — Buffett and the Davises.) **They have to deserve you every bit as much as you have to deserve them.**

Otherwise, it won't be a relationship, which I define in this context as *a fair sharing of rights and responsibilities in pursuit of a common goal.* Nobody can get on The Ark just because they have a lot of money and don't want to drown. The voyage of The Ark isn't a pleasure cruise, and you certainly aren't there to make the passengers nice and comfy, nor to indulge their whims. This voyage is a life-or-death mission, on which the clients' long-term financial fate depends. The passengers have their own roster of duties — some of which will turn out to be fairly arduous — and it isn't totally inconceivable that you might have to put one or two of them off The Ark from time to time. *None of this can come as a surprise to them later on;* full (though gentle and diplomatic) disclosure of the passengers' duty roster is both your right *and* a grave responsibility on your part.

So the qualitative aspects of the first real interview you have with the household/family become even more important — indeed, much more important — than the so-called fact-finding process itself. Yes, you have to establish, at some point, how much credit card debt they have, and who the beneficiary is on their employee group life insurance, and what the asset allocation is in their 401(k) account. But these are relatively minor issues. As you begin exploring the values, attitudes, family dynamics, hopes, fears, preconceptions, misconceptions, biases and blind spots that everyone brings to this process, you need to try to get as clear a sense as you can of *what's really going on here:*

- How do these people seem to feel about each other, and about the world in general? What are they trying to use their money to do? In reasonably functional families, money is — in a very real sense — love, and financial planning becomes an expression of love, of concern and caring. In dysfunctional families, money has a way of turning into a weapon. When people start asking you about ways to put a financial stake through an ex-spouse's heart, or they tell you to forget about estate planning because they don't want their rotten kids ever to see any of their money, it's time to suddenly and vocally remember a pressing appointment back on Planet Earth, and to exit stage left. Because even if you want to — and you shouldn't want to — become a non-combatant advisor to one side or another in a family financial/psychic shoot-out, I guarantee you'll sooner or later get caught in the crossfire.

- Have they got an agenda, and if so are you pretty sure you know what it is? Are they, at the moment, just trying to scratch a particular financial itch, or are they already open to the larger issue of comprehensive planning? What do they think this meeting is about, and does that mesh pretty well with what you think it's about? *Are you both on the same page?*

- How are you feeling about these people, and how do they seem to be feeling about you? Are they open and forthcoming in response to your questions? Or are they defensive? If they seem uncomfortable, is there something you could be doing to help them relax, or do you just keep peppering them with questions? Are you being sufficiently sensitive to their legitimate concerns? Are they responding properly to you, or do they seem to be digging in? *Don't try to muscle your way through the vibes,* because sooner or later they'll take you down from behind. Slow down, so the people can calm down. If nothing you say or do seems to calm them down, stop and turn the meeting completely over to them. If they still can't or won't articulate what seems to be troubling them, ask yourself why you're still there — and make yourself come up with a *real* good answer. Once more: respect the vibes. In financial planning, *emotions are to facts as 19 is to one.* You ignore this iron law at your extreme peril.

- Are you gently but firmly establishing and maintaining your position as a peer? You may neither make nor have as much money as these prospects do — *yet* — but, as with the $500-an-hour surgeon or litigator, these people are on your turf now. It is, at the end of the day, your Ark, and the folks are applying for a place on it. Don't let them think — even unconsciously — that they can order Doctor Noah around The Ark. Be exquisitely respectful, *but never the least bit servile.*

So the mission of the New Financial Advisor, in this crucial first real interview, is to:

(1) give the conversation some meaningful structure;

(2) ask the questions which will get at the prospects' most cherished goals *and* deepest fears;

(3) ask those questions in the tone, and with the feeling, of a genuinely empathetic therapist, so as to help the prospects open up fully to you;

(4) listen as closely to what isn't being said as to what is;

(5) allow both parties to begin to form a sound judgment as to whether the basis for a pleasant as well as productive relationship exists here.

If the analogy of a therapist surprises you in any way, it's at least possible that you may be thinking about our profession in the wrong terms. We're not just accountants; the financial planning process mustn't (and can't) be reduced to a set of numbers. Financial planning is an intensely therapeutic (and, on occasion, even cathartic) process. It would be nice to think of what we do simply as helping people become wealthy, but first it's helping them become *functional* — that is, able to think and act openly and rationally about the difficult and sometimes painful economic choices we all have to make in life. Wills and trusts may be tools in planning, but we're really talking about issues like love and death. Sibling rivalry, feelings of regret and inadequacy, having to say goodbye to some dreams even as others can be realized — these are the real coin and currency of financial planning. Money is never *just* money, and it's usually not even *mostly* money; it's something else as well, and the New Financial Advisor has to find out what that is, if she's truly going to help the family *and* gain a long-term Ark stateroom occupant.

The straightest path into the darkness, it seems to me, is an inquiry into the seven key issues whose successful resolution produces The Seven Glorious Outcomes we talked about earlier. This will allow us to raise the financial issues we believe are usually most important. Our prospects' responses — confirming which issues matter more to them, and which less or not at all — will give us both a financial and psychographic profile of the family. And we'll learn — by stepping on it, because there's no other way — which if any of these issues is a land mine in the life of the prospect household. So put your laptop away, get as visibly comfortable as the physical setting allows, and take out a yellow legal pad and a pen (or, better still, a pencil; what could be less threatening than a pencil?). And so — gently, gently — we begin.

(1) DO YOU KNOW EXACTLY WHAT WOULD HAPPEN TO YOUR FAMILY IF YOU DIDN'T WAKE UP TOMORROW? (Or: "if you woke up sitting on a cloud, learning to play the long version of 'Stairway to Heaven' on the harp?" Find your own nice, personal way of stating the obvious issue, while — if at all possible — avoiding the "D" word.)

This is actually a very smart question, and it may take the prospects a moment to realize just what it's really asking. Note that we don't ask if they have life insurance (they do, but it's not enough; moreover it's titled in the wrong name, and the wrong person/entity is the beneficiary). And we don't ask how much life insurance they have (they know or they don't, but in the absence of any other data at this point, what meaning would the number have?). *We don't even ask them to tell us* what would happen to them financially if etc., etc. We simply ask the very best, most perceptive question of all: **do you *know?***

Knowing what would happen is actually different from what would happen (very different, in fact), and *knowing* — not getting surprised, *having a plan* — is what this process is all about. Thus, our very first question announces our most noble intention — not to re-engineer their whole financial lives, and certainly not to "sell" them more life insurance (or anything else), but to **help them know.** Because mostly, being human, they don't.

PROSPECT: Well, I have a lot of life insurance. I've got three times my annual earnings in group insurance at my company. And a million-dollar term insurance policy I bought myself a few years back. And some odds and ends...but it adds up to a lot.

NEW FINANCIAL ADVISOR: I'm sure it does, and good for you. I was asking a slightly different question, though. (Silence)

P: Mind asking it again, then?

NFA: Not at all. *Do you know exactly what would happen to your family financially* if those polices all became payable tomorrow? Would part of it be used to pay off your home mortgage? Is part of it earmarked for education? *Is there a plan* for where the insurance proceeds would go, and is everyone very clear on what that plan is?

MRS. P: I certainly don't know what the plan is, and I'm the one who'd need to know, aren't I?

P: (To NFA) Yes, when you put it that way, I think the answer would have to be no: we *don't* know exactly what would happen. Maybe I've been thinking of it as a bridge we'd cross when I didn't come to it...

NFA: (Making a note on his yellow pad) Fine. This is not a problem. (Reassuringly) *None of this is a problem.* It's just something we need to know, and don't quite know yet. That's what I'm here for. I'll just ask you to throw all your policies in my trusty burlap bag, here, and to get from your office the description of your employee coverage. We'll get to the bottom of this in no time. (Pause) Realize, though, that we can't go too much further into the planning process until this issue gets bolted down pretty tight. Planning *for* the things that can go right in your life is a luxury you have after you've planned *against* the one big thing that can go wrong. Yes?

P: I guess so.

MRS. P: Does that mean we have to stop talking?

NFA: On the contrary. It's just my way of establishing priorities.

	There are a lot of other things we can make a start on

There are a lot of other things we can make a start on tonight — just nothing more important than this, or even *as* important as this. *I'll get to the bottom of this,* because that's what I do. But for instance, when we start dealing with investments, which are actually very pleasant to think about, realize that that stuff is contingent on our getting a lot of comfort on this make-or-break financial issue.

P: Sure; that makes sense.

Let's pause, here, and look at the volumes of information that became available through this very innocuous, straightforward-sounding colloquy, which I assure you took less than three minutes.

First, one great lesson: no matter how sure you are of what the household/family dynamic is, *be prepared to get surprised.* I don't care how impressed you may have been with your primary contact, the accomplished entrepreneurial/executive Mr. P.; it wasn't more than about a minute into this interview that we found out who it is who's really hell-bent on moving the planning process forward. (Hint: it ain't him.) And, at the risk of taking all the suspense out of the rest of the story, this particular "sale" is already "closed."

(I'm hoping your instincts were good enough that you spotted that right away. An old poker-player's maxim holds that if you can't tell who the patsy is in the first half-hour of the game, it's because you're the patsy. My corollary is that if you can't spot the decision-maker well within the first half-hour of the financial planning interview, either there *is* no decision-maker, or he/she has already gone silent because he/she doesn't like you. In either case, you're going home empty-handed.)

In this particular (and not terribly subtle) example, Mrs. P. saw her husband's somewhat macho chest-pounding about how much insurance he had for what it was, and grabbed onto the advisor's rephrased question for dear life. Short of whupping the husband upside the head with a tire iron, she could not have more clearly said, "I don't know what the plan is *because there is no (expletive deleted) plan;* so let's stop posturing and get on with it, shall we?"

Does a surprise this salutary happen most of the time, or even a lot of the time? Of course not. Sometimes you'll prospect St. George (of one or the other gender), and get into the interview to find that the decision-maker is actually the dragon. And sometimes, halfway through the interview, St. George turns *into* the dragon. I'm merely trying to illustrate the point that I now repeat: when, in the interview process, the family dynamic really gets cranking, *be prepared to get surprised.*

I would also invite you to observe how, even before Mrs. P. suddenly appeared in his corner, the advisor slipped the prospect's first punch. Mr. P. said, in effect, "I think I have enough insurance; don't try to sell me any more." The advisor didn't respond or even engage; he just kept asking — as this question is deliberately formulated to do — what the plan for the insurance proceeds was...betting, as you can very safely always bet, that *the prospect didn't have one.* This established three things. (1) The one overriding issue on the table isn't insurance (or investments, or trusts); it's *planning.* (2) The advisor has a (very healthy) agenda, and proposes — gently but firmly — to stick to it. (3) The prospect's insurance program can now be reviewed by the advisor without his having to even question its adequacy — without, in other words, even an implied criticism of the prospect.

Life insurance is something nobody wants to think about, and nobody wants to admit he needs more of. Yet it is the threshold financial planning issue. The challenge is to raise that issue both pointedly and (relatively) painlessly; my solution, again, is to question not the coverage but the plan for its proceeds.

Of *course* he's underinsured. *Everybody* is. Why, the accretion of real household wealth in this country since the beginning of history's greatest bull market in 1982 dwarfs anything in previous human experience.

Whether to maintain a family's unprecedentedly affluent lifestyle, to fund soaring education costs, or to defray estate taxes on their greatly appreciated net worth — if a family hasn't completely re-done its life insurance in the last five years, chances are their coverage is woefully inadequate, as well as inefficiently owned. (And even if they *did* look closely at their insurance within these five years, they didn't especially care for the agent they did it with. Because if they had, *you'd have never gotten this interview in the first place.*)

Sorry; what's that? You're an investment advisor, not an insurance expert? You don't have any background in this stuff? Well, so be it. Welcome to financial planning: death is the first and last planning issue, and *life insurance is the spine of financial planning.* (I'm terribly distressed that this isn't convenient for you, but I'm sure I'll get over it somehow.) *Suck it up.* Remember: you have a financial planning department *and* an insurance department. And you have hordes of insurance wholesalers all over you (and the aforementioned departments), *pleading* for the opportunity to review your prospects' insurance program, and to help whip it into shape. Somewhere along the line (with the 50th family who comes aboard, or maybe the 100th), you may actually bestir yourself to learn something about insurance. *But not unless and until you want to.* In the meantime, just (a) ask the right question the right way, (b) decline to get sidetracked, (c) get the policies in your burlap bag, and (d) take 'em back to someone who's trained to know what to do with them. Let us proceed, then, to the second question, which is the same as the first, except that it concerns disability rather than death.

(2) DO YOU KNOW EXACTLY WHAT WOULD HAPPEN TO YOUR FAMILY FINANCIALLY IF YOU BECAME DISABLED, AND COULD NO LONGER WORK?

PROSPECT: Guess you don't want to hear me tell you we have

long-term disability insurance at the office, right?

NEW FINANCIAL ADVISOR: No, I *do* want to hear that, and I'm delighted to — just as I was happy to hear that you have a good bit of life insurance. (Silence)

P: But it doesn't answer your question.

NFA: (Gently) Right.

P: So you need to look at the policy.

NFA: I certainly need *someone* to look at the policy — somebody on our staff who's really an expert. Because disability insurance, like disability itself, is very, very tricky.

P: How so?

NFA: Is it long-term or short-term? How long do you have to live on your savings until benefits start? How long do the benefits last? Do you get paid if you can't do your usual work? Or do you get paid only if you can't do *any* gainful work? Do you get paid *on top of* Social Security, or does Social Security offset your insurance benefits? *Very* tricky. Has to be looked at by someone who specializes in this field, which isn't me. But I know who it is.

P: Good, because I have to tell you, I don't know what *any* of those answers are, and I don't even remember the questions being asked.

We should probably stop here, and ritually note that, if both the people you're talking to worked, you would simply amend these first two questions to read, "Do you know yada yada if *either of you* yada yada?" I'm not forcing the interview (much less your practice) into mode Ozzie and Harriet; I just need a track to run on, and tend to go running home to Stanley's and Danko's *The Millionaire Next Door* (as well as to my own personal experience; as Satchmo said, "You blows what you is").

The advisor also used this opportunity to make a point to which

you'll want to return fairly frequently: that he's not the universal expert —
that he's backed up by a lot of narrowly but deeply focused specialists
who can be relied on to understand the most sinuous and complex issues
right down to the ground.

This is yet another reason why, if at all possible, you should try to
do major interviews with prospects in your own office, where they can
see, or at least sense, the depth of the human and technological resources
that support you. When they know you better — when they've come to
rely on you, and don't care who attends to the details — the meeting
venue may become much less important (and then again may not). But
particularly in the early going, when prospects are still trying to get a
handle on who you are and what (if anything) you represent, use every
available means to impress upon them the immense support that you
command.

Finally, although in this brief script it went by awfully fast, you
saw a glancing reference to an emergency savings fund of some kind, to
bridge the waiting period between the onset of disability and the com-
mencement of long-term disability benefits. Such a war chest doubles as
a rainy-day fund in the event of loss of employment, as well. And it may
also help people insulate themselves psychologically against temporary declines in the market values of their long-term investments. ("So
what if the market's down for a season or two; it's not as if I need the
money to live on.")

These are three reasons why I think it's usually a good idea to
have about a year's living expenses parked in a money market fund, and
why that's a fundamental building block of financial planning, to me.
Such an arrangement is not without its opportunity costs, to be sure,
but the emotional comfort that it gives people, and the number of different things it guards them against, are usually worth it. In the context
of this very first real interview, though, I think you can let it slide by.
Recommending an emergency cash reserve is, after all, a little bit like

shaving and showering every day: if you don't do it you're a bum, but nobody gives you credit for it.

(3) WHO WILL YOU NEED TO, OR JUST WANT TO HELP, EDUCATE? WHEN? AND DO YOU HAVE YOUR ARMS AROUND WHAT IT WILL COST?

It is at this point, I think, that we begin getting a more nuanced sense of what a family's financial/emotional dynamics are. That's because different people have very different attitudes toward their education funding responsibilities, and about the extent to which those responsibilities are really their children's — and even their grandchildren's. Moreover, you may find the attitudes of some of your prospective clients to be in conflict with yours...and then you may have some decisions to make.

I have never actually heard a baby ask to be born, so when one is, I think it comes with certain birthrights — one of which is the best education for which it can qualify. Many people feel that their kids should work summers and after school to earn part of the money for their education; I'm very OK with that. Some people also feel that their kids should get student loans, and pay them off out of the increased earnings they get from a good education. I'm very, very not OK with that.

Every parent has a minimum of 18 years' warning that his/her child may qualify to go to college; no one actually gets *surprised* when college rolls around. So, with a little discipline and a lot of compounding, I don't immediately see why any family that could get anywhere *near* The Ark would plan — that's the operative word in all this, right? — *plan* to let most of the burden of their kids' higher education fall on them.

You may disagree with this. Even more to the point, a prospect family may *quite vehemently* disagree with this. They are entitled to their beliefs. My only point is: *they ain't gettin' on my Ark.*

The foregoing disquisition — and you may as well hear this from me — has really nothing whatever to do with financial planning. It does not even suggest — though you may find this a bit harder to swallow — that student loans are either "wrong," or just not "right," or susceptible to any such value judgment at all. It just says that I don't believe in student loans, that I don't like student loans, and especially that I don't care much for people of reasonable means — our kinds of prospects — who would let the bulk of the burden of education fall on their children.

In the long run, we are only going to be able to survive a long journey on The Ark with people we like, or at least whose values we respect. I could not like nor respect people with the values I've just described. (If you can, take them on *your* Ark, with my most sincere and unconflicted blessings on you both.) *You gotta be who you are* — and you gotta sail with people you respect. Now can we go back to talking about financial planning?

Not too long ago, Putnam Investments conducted a survey which documented an eerie disconnect between people's great avowed seriousness about saving for education — and how little money they were actually putting away. The New Financial Advisor can be of inestimable help to her client families by gently getting them to face the truly awesome cost of modern quality education. Further, she can help them meet this responsibility — and expand her own influence across the family's generations, in the process — by urging the parents to react appropriately to their developing educational emergency by turning in the 529 alarm: break glass, call grandparents.

My belief has been for some time that the next generation of our prospect families which is coming into the world today will be educated largely by its grandparents. And with the advent of the new, improved (by the 2001 tax law) Section 529 provisions, one would have to wonder: *why not?*

If grandparents are thinking of leaving — or even of ultimately giving — their grandchildren any money at all, the new 529 (with its gifting ability of up to $50,000 in one shot per grandparent or whoever, removal from the estate, tax-protected buildup *and now tax-free payouts for qualified educational expenses*) has simply got to be one of the best ways to do it — if not *the* best. So, to the three questions which begin this discussion, one could consider adding, when the moment feels right: WOULD YOUR PARENTS WANT TO HELP?

Stanley and Danko found that the habitually frugal millionaire next door was nonetheless a prodigious investor in his children's education. To which I can only add: he — and his parents — will have to be. You can help — by forcefully pursuing this third of the seven great questions.

(4) HOW AND WHEN DO YOU SEE YOURSELF RETIRING? WHAT WILL YOU DO, AND WHAT WILL IT COST TO DO IT — NOT JUST THE DAY AFTER YOU RETIRE, BUT 10, 20 AND EVEN 30 YEARS LATER?

This question goes to the pivot point of multigenerational financial planning. And its stinger, as I hope you'll have noticed, is in its tail: what will it cost to be retired in the style you've become accustomed to *after 10, 20 and even 30 years of rising living costs?*

People tend to see retirement planning in terms of one number — how much income will I need in order to retire in reasonable comfort — as if that one number, once known and achieved, would stand still. It won't. If history is any guide — and it's the only guide I'll ever have — the amount of retirement income we'll need *just to maintain the same standard of living* will not merely rise but compound. And as life expectancy continues dramatically to lengthen, the effect of this compounding becomes the decisive factor in the economic life of a family headed by retirees.

Specifically, the joint life expectancy of a non-smoking husband and wife who are both 62 — which is roughly the average retirement age in the U.S. today — is 30 years. (That is, the second death will occur at age 92.) And these are, I caution you, statistics for the population as a whole. Our kind of clients — who may very well have enjoyed better education, better healthcare, more comfortable working environments and healthier lifestyles than the average person — are probably retiring even sooner and living even longer. So if the average two-person retirement is pushing 30 years, my guess — and I freely concede that it's only a guess — is that you can tack on another five years for Ark candidates as a group. At the long-term U.S. inflation rate (1926-2000) of about three percent, these people are looking at a tripling of their living costs in retirement...easy.

Thus the great risk which must be addressed in retirement financial planning becomes not so much a function of principal — losing one's money — but rather of income: **outliving one's money.** If one's nominal income — the number of dollars coming in every year — fails to rise at least as much as one's cost of living goes up, then one's *real income* is inexorably declining — *and one's standard of living along with it.*

Nor are the effects of this problem confined merely to the current (retired) generation of the family — its shadows fall across the lives of the succeeding generations. Because when the retirees' income lags far enough behind their inflating living costs, they will have to begin invading principal to close the gap. This becomes a financial death spiral: the more principal we draw down this year, the less income we will have next year, the even greater amount of principal we'll have to draw down next year...and on, and on. The retirees' golden years turn into a race between destitution and death.

The retirees' dreams (and their childrens' hopes) of a meaningful legacy turn to sand. And in the last five years of their lives, *they must still face nearly half of their entire lifetime healthcare expenditures* — with diminishing, or even vanished, resources. Thus, far from inheriting their parents' wealth, the adult children may have to shoulder a financial burden which their parents can no longer bear. This, in turn, may impinge on *their* ability to provide for their children's education, on *their* retirements, on *their* capacity to create a legacy...and so the damage spreads, down through the generations.

In a later chapter, we will fully explore the tragic cultural disconnect between what Americans *want* from their retirement investments
(fixed income from fixed-value debt securities) and what they really *need*
(income and capital values capable of rising far in excess of the cost of
living, from equities). This chapter isn't about answers; it's about questions. Specifically, it's about helping people get seven critically important
questions framed in the right terms. For the moment, I would just have
you intuit (until I can prove it to you, which I faithfully promise to do)
that **if life insurance is the spine of financial planning, equities are its
brain.**

I suggested in the Foreword to this book that multigenerational
wealth — wealth like a river, that grows in size and power as it flows
down through the generations — is available pursuant to only one investment philosophy. Now you may begin to see at least the outlines of what
this philosophy must be: that equities accrete real wealth over time, and
that bonds destroy it. If I have not yet attempted to demonstrate the
inevitability of equities, at least let me have caused you to infer the un-
thinkability of bonds. *You can't fight a war against 30 years of rising living
costs armed only with a fixed-income weapon.* Bonds are, as Yeager said
about trying to punch out of a malfunctioning aircraft at supersonic speeds,
"committing suicide to keep from getting killed."

Most people will have little or no trouble accepting the idea that
equities are necessary, and even highly desirable, in the quest to accumulate a sufficient pool of capital — a retirement "nest egg" — *before* they
retire. It is the deeply countercultural notion of equities *after* they retire
that we'll need to get across to them. And — I say again — we will.

But in the narrow context of this chapter, we are just trying to give
you an interrogatory track to run on: seven carefully phrased, highly intelligent, deeply empathetic, critically important questions whose goal is
nothing less than to set the financial and emotional agenda for the rest of
your and the prospects' relationship with each other. *Don't get ahead of*

yourself, or get sidetracked into offering a particular (nor even a general) solution to any of the seven issues — not until you get all the way through them, and the prospects glimpse your truly awesome grasp of the big picture.

Suffice it, in asking this question, to accomplish two things: first, to raise the fairly obvious issue of the need for retirement planning, and second, to plant the seeds of the not-at-all-obvious imperative to keep retirement income growing dynamically to offset decades of inflation.

PROSPECT: Are you saying you want us to own *stocks* in
    retirement?

NEW FINANCIAL ADVISOR: I don't want anything, except that you
    be as happy and as independent in retirement as you want
    to be. I want what you want. I know — or at least I'm
    pretty sure — that if you're blessed with a long retirement,
    you'll want your income to grow at least as much as your
    cost of living grows, so you can maintain your standard of
    living without running down your capital. How you do
    that is a subject for another day. Maybe the investments
    you've got now will be fine. I don't know; I haven't even
    seen 'em. All I care about right now is: what's important to
    you in retirement, and what will that cost...through the
    years. Is that fair?

P: Yes, yes. I see what you're doing. I was trying to look
    ahead to the solution.

NFA: And I'm still trying to make sure we all agree on the nature
    and scope of the challenge.

P: Fair enough; please go on.

You're allowed to brush people back once in a while, and — human nature being what it is — you will not infrequently have to. Doing so calmly, effectively and without giving offense is an acquired skill, but it's easier if you stay focused on what you're trying to accomplish — which is, at the moment, just getting an understanding of what *they're* trying to accomplish. Take your eye off that agenda, and virtually any prospect interview has the potential to degenerate into a group primal-scream therapy session. Keep the interview running on a track, and you have a real opportunity to earn the trust and respect — and maybe even the affection — of your prospects.

(5) ARE YOUR PARENTS LIVING, AND IF SO WILL YOU BE EXPECTED TO CONTRIBUTE TO THEIR SUPPORT AT SOME POINT? AND HAVE YOU MADE ANY PROVISION FOR THE POSSIBILITY THAT *YOU* MAY NEED NURSING HOME OR OTHER CARE, LATE IN YOUR OWN LIVES?

If your prospects are going to have to assume responsibility for the care of their parents some day, that has to be factored into whatever plan you and your firm eventually come up with. If, on the other hand, you discover the existence of living parents, and the prospect says that he and his siblings will *never* have to support them, then chances are you've stumbled on some fairly affluent parents. So you will, when your interview progresses to the point of counting up the assets, want to take particular care to discover what if any legacies the prospects are expecting.

The larger issue, of course, is what provision the prospects have made for their own old age. And here we find that reality has outrun people's emotional (and financial) ability to keep up with it.

In 1900, the life expectancy of the American population had still not reached 50. In 2000, nearly 30% of the millions of American 50-year-olds — the baby boomers, the largest generation ever — reported having at least one living parent. In a sense, then, there are not one but two whole generations walking around in America today who (a) barely existed 100 years ago, and (b) control virtually the entirety of this country's personally held net worth.

Moreover, in the context of the planning question we're asking, we need to be particularly aware of *how* life expectancy took this unprecedented leap forward. Is there something about the nature of medical progress in the twentieth century that is important to the inquiry we're conducting? I believe there surely is.

You see, I think we can summarize the history of medicine in the last century — glibly, but not inaccurately — in one sentence: we conquered everything that used to kill people quickly. In 1918, 500,000 Americans (and 22 million people worldwide) died in the flu epidemic. One of them was my father's older sister. In 1951, when I was in the third grade, one of my classmates went home on a Friday afternoon and was dead by Sunday night — of a particularly virulent strain of polio that simply shut down her lungs. Is there one person reading this book who hasn't been cured, by an antibiotic, of a fever or respiratory infection that, prior to World War II, would have carried you off in a week?

It's possible that today in America, no one will die of the flu, or polio, or common pneumonia. And this is spectacular — nay, miraculous — progress. But it is progress of a very specific kind, and it has been nowhere near as dramatic in pathologies — the cancers, cardiovascular disease — that wear people away slowly, painfully...and very expensively. The phenomenon of long, wasting illness in the later years has led to the situation in which Americans can now expect to spend *one-half of their total lifetime medical expenses in the last five years of life.*

And seemingly overshadowing all health concerns of the very old is the specter of Alzheimer's disease. Today, the number of 85-year-olds in the U.S. is growing *five times faster* than the population as a whole. *One in two American 85-year-olds already has Alzheimer's disease.* Please note that I didn't say half these people would eventually get this dread illness. I said, and now say again, half the 85-year-olds *already have it,* in some stage of its progression. (For confirmation, and a wealth of other information, go to the Alzheimer's Association website, www.alz.org.)

Here again, we're making strides in the treatment of the disease. We can slow its progress in some cases; we can keep some of its victims alive longer, with proper care. *But we can, as yet, neither prevent it nor cure it.* And so its sufferers live on, year after year — having to be watched over and cared for around the clock, in a nursing facility or at home, at horrific cost. (Ronald Reagan, who does not know that he was once President of the United States, was diagnosed in the autumn of 1994 — and is still alive as these words are written, seven years later.)

A year in a decent nursing home probably costs upwards of $60,000, if there's really such a thing as a national average; three-shift-a-day home care might cost a little less, but not much. And in upscale enclaves around the country, the cost can be nearly twice the "average." Moreover, the upward pressure on these costs is likely to make a mockery of the trendline Consumer Price Index. It's not just that there aren't enough beds, it's that the caregiver population is about to plummet relative to the burgeoning population in need of care. The resulting wage-and-benefit spiral is not going to be pretty — especially in a country whose overall structural unemployment seems to have reached historic lows.

In light of all these trends, it seems clear that, for all but the wealthiest clients, long-term care insurance has become an essential building block of a financial plan. To self-insure a potential exposure in six and even seven figures is a reckless decision even in risks which are highly improbable — your house burning down, for example. But when you can look at mom and dad, and think that chances are *one* of them's going to get it, you want to run, not walk, to someplace where you can pool that risk.

(6) HOW IMPORTANT IS IT TO YOU TO BE ABLE TO INTERVENE IN THE FINANCIAL LIVES OF YOUR CHILDREN AND GRAND-CHILDREN — WHILE YOU'RE STILL HERE, AS LEGACIES, OR

BOTH? HOW DO YOU PLAN TO DO IT?

There's one overriding financial issue here, but a whole mess of emotional ones, and they intersect at critical points.

The financial issue, of course, is the potential tension between the parents wanting to take good care of themselves and their wanting to do as much as they can for their heirs. And simply stated, bonds intensify this tension, while equities relieve it. Clearly, if in retirement the parents invest in bonds — and even if the fixed income does keep them afloat, which I say again it won't — the kids are going to inherit wallpaper. (And quite brutally taxed wallpaper, at that.)

Let's say you've got a retiring couple with five million dollars. (That's five million in today's dollars, which is, *ipso facto,* five million in today's purchasing power.) And, even though the cost of living triples during their retirement, make believe the fixed income is still enough. Parents die in 30 years; kids get a one million dollar exemption on the estate of five million, pay half the rest, end up with three million — *which is one million dollars in then-current purchasing power!* Think of it — an 80% net diminution of purchasing power, after inflation and taxes...so mom and dad could feel "safe." (While in the last 30 years, to pick a not-necessarily-good example, the five million invested in the S&P 500 would have become nearly $50 million, even *after* the bear market of 2000-2001; forget the exemption, make it $25 million in estate taxes, which *leaves* $25 million; which is...give it the same inflation haircut and call it eight million dollars in current purchasing power: a 60% net *increase*. And this is ignoring the fact that, during their retired lifetimes, the parents' cash dividends *quintupled!*)

The financial (if not emotional) bottom line is: we want this generation's retirement income to grow over time, offsetting inflating living costs. But if we don't want to do this on the backs of the heirs — and I'm assuming that we don't — then we also want the patrimony to continue to keep growing for the succeeding generations. Which brings us right back to equities as the only financial asset class that serves both generations' needs (or, if you prefer, *all* the generations' needs), *and not at each other's expense.*

The emotional issues implicit in this sixth question revolve around what, if anything, parents think they *should* do for the succeeding generations — which is a different question entirely. (Unless it really isn't. "I don't want to spoil the kids with a lot of wealth they didn't work for" could be — and I think often is — a proxy and/or a justification for "I don't care what anybody says; I'm too scared to hold anything but bonds in retirement." That is, it could just be a "valid" excuse for leaving the kids wallpaper.)

You have to make your own business decisions, but I would counsel you to think long and hard about taking accounts who have bitterly dysfunctional relationships with their own children. People who want to deny their money to their children in order to hurt them are often (if not always) very disturbed individuals. Which isn't to say that the kids aren't, or even that the kids are right and the parents wrong. It's just that very disturbed people will usually find a way, at some point, to take that disturbance out on you — to beat you up in a way that they can't beat the kids up (other than spitefully to deny them the inheritance). If a nice, sad, semi-functional couple says, "We can't leave money to our 35-year-old son because he's a cocaine addict, and he'd just put it all up his nose as fast as he could, and die that much quicker" — OK. *I'm* convinced. But if you hear, "Those ingrates yada yada after all we did for them yada yada never come to visit, etc." — well, boys and girls, you've got some decisions to make.

Of course, this is always assuming there *are* kids. What do you do with childless — and even totally heirless — people? They have financial planning needs, too, even if those needs essentially come down to not using up all their money before they use up all their heartbeats. Question is, do you really want to allot one of the precious staterooms on your Ark to an account that's essentially going to get liquidated on your watch? And that's a very serious question, indeed.

Also, in fairness, even heirless clients may be investing for some larger purpose. Wake Forest University recently got the seven million dollar estate — the largest single gift ever given the school — of a frugal bachelor alumnus who owned a barbecue restaurant. Now, that fellow would've gotten on my Ark in a New York (or even a North Carolina) minute — even if I *did* know that one day the whole account was going to go over the side. But, as heirless accounts go, I think you'd have to say that he was the exception to the rule that proves the rule. The rule is: wealth that isn't multigenerational isn't really wealth, and therefore there's a very finite limit to what you can do for it.

It probably wouldn't hurt, though, even when you're talking to people *with* heirs, to consider slipping in at this point a kind of Question (6)(a): IS THERE AN INSTITUTION THAT YOU CARE DEEPLY ABOUT — A CHURCH, CHARITY OR SCHOOL, FOR EXAMPLE — TO WHICH YOU WOULD WISH TO LEAVE A MEANINGFUL LEGACY, ASSUMING WE COULD CREATE A HIGHLY TAX-EFFICIENT WAY FOR YOU TO DO SO? (Did somebody say "charitable remainder trust"?)

In summary, this inquiry about what people want to leave behind, and to whom, (a) is essential to the planning process, and (b) has investment implications that may not immediately be obvious. But most of all (c), if there's a howling, screaming Tasmanian devil of a transgenerational family dysfunction hiding anywhere around here, this is the most likely place for it to jump out of the bushes at you and try to tear open your throat. Be vigilant. Ain't no tellin' what that devil might do, if he gets aboard your Ark.

(7) ASSUMING, AS WE HAVE TO DO, THAT WHEN YOU'RE BOTH GONE, UP TO HALF YOUR ESTATE WILL GET TAXED AWAY, HOW DO YOU WANT THE TAX TO BE PAID? IF YOU WANT THE KIDS TO

JUST PAY THE HALF, MIGHT THEY BE FORCED TO SELL SOME-
THING YOU REALLY WOULDN'T WANT THEM TO HAVE TO SELL?

This seventh and final question goes to the heart of the issue in all substantial estates — an issue that even many smart people haven't faced, because they so much don't want to face it.

Something like 70% of all the privately held net worth in this country is first generation. That is, it's still owned by the people who sweated and saved to accumulate it. And to those people our society says: thanks for working so hard, saving so assiduously, risking your capital to invest in productive businesses, and paying up to half your income in taxes as you went along. And congratulations: you succeeded. You built something from nothing. And your reward is that when you die, in "fairness" the society is going to tax away half what you managed to accumulate.

The best shot we've ever had to repeal this "philosophy" came and went in 2001 — and it was the dud heard 'round the world. So now it's time to go back and re-double our efforts to protect what our clients have accumulated. You have a lot of great ways to do this — and until you know which particular ones work best in each individual case, let your experts figure it out. But help people face the issue. And help them see that, in estate planning as much as or more than in any other area, *the value of expert planning is orders of magnitude greater than the cost.*

Before you go on to the next chapter, please consider transcribing these seven questions, without any commentary, on a sheet of paper or a big index card. Then make a recording of yourself asking those seven questions — slowly, confidently, empathetically — and play that recording back to yourself, over and over, every chance you get. Listen to your own authentic voice. Listen to what your prospects are going to hear. Listen to what a glorious new career you've just embarked upon.

IN SUMMARY

- The first long interview you have with your prospects has to go far beyond fact-finding. It's your opportunity to examine the household/family dynamic, to show people who you really are — and to begin to decide if these people deserve you.

- In financial planning, emotions are to facts as 19 is to one. Amateurs think money is money. The New Financial Advisor knows that *money is love.* And planning, when it's done right, is a form of therapy.

- Ask seven great questions, in order to discover which of The Seven Glorious Outcomes the household/family is — or ought to be — most concerned about. Don't get drawn into talking about solutions. This interview isn't about getting answers. It's about making absolutely sure you have the really important questions framed in the most productive way.

(1) DO YOU KNOW EXACTLY WHAT WOULD HAPPEN TO YOUR FAMILY IF YOU (OR: ONE OF YOU) DIDN'T WAKE UP TOMORROW? Nobody has enough life insurance, or the right kind, or has it titled right. Never mind that. Slide into this threshold issue sideways, via the question of what the plan is for the deployment of the current insurance coverage. (Hint: there is no plan.) *Life insurance is the spine of financial planning.*

(2) Ditto disability (DO YOU KNOW EXACTLY...). You might use this issue to put in a plug for the technical expertise you've got behind you, and/or to refer glancingly to the need for an emergency cash-equivalent fund of some kind.

(3) WHO WILL YOU NEED TO, OR JUST WANT TO HELP, EDUCATE? WHEN? AND DO YOU HAVE YOUR ARMS AROUND WHAT IT WILL COST? A financial planning question, to be sure, but also a potentially revealing insight into the family dynamic. Also, for many affluent grandparents, 529 has aspects of a potential no-brainer, so

this may be a way for you to draw them into the planning process.

(4) HOW AND WHEN DO YOU SEE YOURSELF RETIRING? WHAT WILL YOU DO, AND WHAT WILL IT COST TO DO IT — NOT JUST THE DAY AFTER YOU RETIRE, BUT 10, 20 AND EVEN 30 YEARS LATER? The great risk of modern retirement — to the heirs every bit as much as to the retirees themselves — is that they'll run out of purchasing power. Which — if they buy nothing but "safe," "conservative" bonds, CDs, etc. — they surely will. Equities are the water of life; bonds are the sands of death. Stay tuned. But for the moment, know that *if life insurance is the spine of financial planning, equities are its brain.*

(5) ARE YOUR PARENTS LIVING, AND IF SO WILL YOU BE EXPECTED TO CONTRIBUTE TO THEIR SUPPORT AT SOME POINT? AND HAVE YOU MADE ANY PROVISION FOR THE POSSIBILITY THAT *YOU* MAY NEED NURSING HOME OR OTHER CARE, LATE IN YOUR OWN LIVES? Alzheimer's is to our world what AIDS is to the third world: the Black Plague. Unless you're richer than Yoko Ono, you *gotta* have long-term care insurance.

(6) HOW IMPORTANT IS IT TO YOU TO BE ABLE TO INTERVENE IN THE FINANCIAL LIVES OF YOUR CHILDREN AND GRANDCHIL-DREN — WHILE YOU'RE STILL HERE, AS LEGACIES, OR BOTH? HOW DO YOU PLAN TO DO IT? At the end of the day, the prospects' attitude toward legacies is the acid test of the family dynamic. Also, if you want meaningful legacies — denominated in real purchasing power, not wallpaper — repeat after me: equities, life; bonds, death. Also, heirs or no, consider Question (6)(a): IS THERE AN INSTITU-TION THAT YOU CARE DEEPLY ABOUT — A CHURCH, CHARITY OR SCHOOL, FOR EXAMPLE — TO WHICH YOU WOULD WISH TO LEAVE A MEANINGFUL LEGACY, ASSUMING WE COULD CREATE A HIGHLY TAX-EFFICIENT WAY FOR YOU TO DO SO?

(7) ASSUMING, AS WE HAVE TO DO, THAT WHEN YOU'RE BOTH

GONE, UP TO HALF YOUR ESTATE WILL GET TAXED AWAY, HOW DO YOU WANT THE TAX TO BE PAID? IF YOU WANT THE KIDS TO JUST PAY THE HALF, MIGHT THEY BE FORCED TO SELL SOMETHING YOU REALLY WOULDN'T WANT THEM TO HAVE TO SELL? A smart estate plan can't make anybody's fortune, but it can keep the one you spent your whole life building from getting broken. Don't be surprised if, just as a financial plan begins with life insurance, it ends with the estate tax liability being insured.

- Transcribe these questions. Record them (and re-record them) in your own voice. Listen to what the folks are going to hear. *Listen to your glorious new career.*

THE
BRAIN
OF
FINANCIAL
PLANNING

chapter six

●

SIX

———●———

Even in the cursory, non-technical, and even back-of-an-envelope view of the building blocks of a financial plan that we've taken thus far, the purest neophyte may find some comfort in the specificity of what we can already infer.

- The household/family should probably have an emergency fund equal to about a year's living expenses, in a money market fund appropriate to the clients' tax bracket.

- Large, predictable future liabilities (tuition, a mortgage balance) should be insured against a/the breadwinner's premature death. His/her/their future income streams should also be covered by life insurance, to the extent that their cessation would seriously compromise the family's lifestyle. In calculating coverage of something like future tuition expense, inflation must be accounted for, e.g. $100,000 in today's tuition is probably something like $180,000 in 10 years. Also, assuming that one wanted the breadwinner's income to continue indefinitely, it would have to be insured at some capitalized function. For instance, $200,000 of income must, at a six percent withdrawal rate, be insured for $3.3 million.

- Integrating with whatever coverage is provided by the employer(s), the income of a/the breadwinner should be insured against long-term and even permanent disability. Life insurance premiums should probably also be protected by disability waiver of premium.

- A program of appropriately inflation-indexed tuition savings should be underway. Parents *and* grandparents should be invited to consider the most tax-efficient methods of doing this. Tuition savings earmarked for expenditure within five years should be invested in debt of comparable maturity (or in pools thereof). Expenditures scheduled more than five years out — although this is getting just the teeniest bit ahead of ourselves — should be invested preponderantly if not entirely in equities.

- The current generation of the household/family should be investing systematically on a schedule which, assuming some rate of return, would give it a pool of capital from which a six percent withdrawal would produce their first-year retirement income needs, net of Social Security and corporate/401(k) benefits. (Where did six percent come from? It's the 75-year average total return of high-quality corporate bonds...and it's something else as well, as we'll see when we start taking about systematic withdrawal from equities.) These investments should be *entirely* in equities.

- After retirement, the preponderance if not the totality of the capital must remain in equities, if both this generation's income and the succeeding generations' patrimony are to stay ahead of inflation (i.e. are to earn *any* real rate of return).

- All the adults who are unable or unwilling to self-insure six- and perhaps even seven-figure nursing home/home health care exposure should have long-term care insurance.

- Because the wealth of the household/family will continue to grow, even during the retirement of the generation that currently owns it, particular vigilance must be exercised with respect to the estate tax liability. Especially if a large part of the estate is dear to the heirs and/or illiquid, the tax liability should probably be insured against the second death.

Advanced planners may shudder at the plethora of nuance this summary misses. Every case has its unique circumstance — a child with special needs, a breadwinner whose insurability is already impaired, and on and on. And what's the interaction of the life insurance and the equities (to cite just one of a hundred issues of implementation)? Shouldn't the latter be held inside the former, in many situations?

My answer is that these issues are well beyond the scope of what we've established so far, and may ultimately be beyond the scope of this whole book. I seek, by means of the foregoing summary, merely to focus your attention on the enormity of what you can already know about financial planning from these hundred-odd pages, and about how far into the planning process this knowledge can take you. And I think we were able to get to this happy state by three relatively simple steps.

(1) *We began with the end in mind.* We asked: what might an affluent household/family want to accomplish financially — or what *should* it want to accomplish — for the balance of this generation, and on into succeeding generations? When we framed the essential question just this way (which had the effect of blinding us to counterproductive distractions like the economy and the markets), we were more or less instantly able to formulate The Seven Glorious Outcomes.

(2) *We were then able, in Chapter Five, to back into an exceptionally focused and effective initial prospect interview,* simply by turning The Seven Glorious Outcomes into an extended interrogatory: *which of these goals would you accomplish if you could?*

(3) *We used a little bit of financial common sense* (e.g. you insure against a known future expense dollar-for-dollar, but you'd have to capitalize an ongoing income need). We added a *very* little bit of *very* basic insurance knowledge (e.g. disability insurance isn't just an amount; it's a set of other — easily knowable — variables such as how disability is defined). And we finished up with a *very* basic notion of how the capital markets work (equities have historically produced a multiple of the real return of debt; particularly if you spend the interest, bonds leave your capital totally exposed to inflation; the longer your time horizon, the less stock market volatility affects you, and therefore the more irrational bonds become).

Everything in the foregoing is easily knowable; none of it has to —

or even should — be discussed in depth in the first, essentially interrogatory, interview. When the experts decide how these issues should play out in your prospects' case, they'll explain the details to you and/or directly to your prospects (depending on how you structure the presentation of the plan). Yet again — and not for the last time — I invite you to marvel at the straightforwardness and simplicity of your role in this process.

You're essentially on a reconnaissance mission. No one is asking you to do anything but (1) find the prospective client household/family, (2) discover its general intentions (is it or is it not open to the idea of securing a financial plan soon?), (3) gather as much information about its present situation as possible, (4) deposit that information in your real or metaphorical burlap bag, and (5) hightail it back to your own lines. This is a not inconsiderable set of skills, but — and here is the whole point — *those skills have virtually nothing to do with the complexities of financial planning.*

It isn't until you go back to the household/family with the completed plan — or, ideally, until the prospects come to your office to have you (and whoever else you need) present it — that, as Ricky always said to Lucy, you got some 'splaining to do.

For the moment — and, mostly, for good — let me put aside a lot of what you have to explain about a plan on the simple grounds that so much of it speaks for itself. (Or, as my tenth grade Latin teacher always said, just before whacking me in the head with a ruler, "*res ipsa loquitur.*")

Your plan is going to recommend an amount of life insurance appropriate to the goals your prospects enunciated; that's going to look to them like an awful lot of insurance; what else is new? You'll recommend an adequate type and amount of disability insurance, and the premium is going to seem like a lot of money to your prospects, because good disability coverage isn't cheap; what else is new? If you find that the most efficient way to deal with estate taxation is to insure the second death through an insurance trust, some prospects are going to struggle with control issues; what else is new? *Res ipsa loquitur:* this is the least complex/most efficient/least costly way to do what you, dear prospects, said you wanted to do.

The exception to this rule, of course, is equities. Equities in general — and, heaven knows, equities as the only truly "safe" retirement investment — most assuredly do *not* speak for themselves. (They *should*, and perhaps one day they will, but they certainly don't yet — even to the baby boomer generation, and that's mostly whom you're going to be talking to for the next 20 years.) Once again, the great financial conundrum of our time: in this first, greatest capitalist democracy, the idea of holding equities throughout the entirety of one's life is countercultural. (And the idea of holding equities for the production of income is downright counter-intuitive.) Yet equities are quite simply the brain of financial planning: a multigenerational investment program *not* based on equities is a dead thing. It makes no sense, because it *has* no sense, because it cannot reason, *because it has no brain.*

So this seems like as good a place as any to stop and make sure that you, the New Financial Advisor, have a clear understanding and an impregnable conviction as to where equities fit in a very long-term/multigenerational plan. Because the challenge to you is not merely to get people to accept an equity-based investment plan as they come up the gangplank of The Ark. It's to keep them from throwing themselves overboard in a stock market storm, *of which there will be many before the voyage is over.* Better to leave the timorous prospect on the shore to drown than to suffer the pain of seeing him drown himself on your watch, and then having to replace him and start all over again with someone new.

A very few of your clients will die prematurely, and life insurance will take care of that. A very few will become disabled, and insurance will cover that, too. But the great preponderance of your clients will live on for decades of productive life and active retirement, hoping to die in the knowledge that they endowed their children and grandchildren. And if you can only believe one thing that you read in this book, I beg you to let it be this: *only equities can take care of that*. Only equities, in other words, can grow the real income of one long-lived generation *and* grow the real patrimony of the next, and the next. I love equities, and I always tried to help my clients love them, too. But you don't *have* to love equities; you just have to understand and accept that you can never achieve, preserve or bequeath real wealth over time without them. We can't say of equities *res ipsa loquitur;* that is, they don't speak for themselves. But we can and we must say that equities are *sine qua non*. **Without them — in the long run — nothing.**

What follows, then, is my fundamental way of framing the case for equities. You will find that this presentation, in effect, "wraps around" my book for your clients, *Simple Wealth, Inevitable Wealth: How you and your financial advisor can grow your fortune in stock mutual funds*. That is, I'm about to make the same case to you, in what I'd call professional terms, that *SWIW* makes to your clients in layman's terms.

(Let me offer three asides, at this point, and then we'll plunge on. (1) *SWIW* isn't about equity mutual funds at all — or at least not *just* mutual funds — but about *all* managed and/or pooled equity arrangements, including wrap accounts and the sub-accounts of variable life insurance and variable annuities. I just needed to warn the potential reader off the misapprehension that I was going to tell him how to pick individual stocks, God forbid. (2) *SWIW* makes not one but two — albeit related — arguments to which you may very well wish to expose your prospects/clients. The first is that they're not going to make it without equities. The second is that they're not going to be able to hold equities in the long run without an advisor: that the alternating current of euphoria and then panic which stocks induce will surely electrocute investors if they're not grounded in the steady wisdom of an empathetic coach. (3) If you need further clarification of, or more comfort with, the case for equities after reading the following discussion and the one in *SWIW,* I urgently recommend Jeremy Siegel's classic book *Stocks for the Long Run.* For that matter, even if you've got all the clarification and comfort you'd ever need, read Siegel anyway. He'll turn you into the Robocop — or the Bionic Woman — of equities.)

We begin with one stark, simple, incontrovertible truth, with which — other than during bear markets, when it's fashionable not to "believe" in equities — most people don't quarrel much:

(1) **THE REAL LONG-TERM RETURN OF EQUITIES IS MUCH GREATER THAN THAT OF BONDS.** Ibbotson Associates, Inc., publishes an annually updated analysis of the returns of certain asset classes, based on a landmark study by Roger Ibbotson and Rex Sinquefield, that begins with the year 1926. It measures average annual compound rates of total return (i.e. with income reinvested). In a simplified form, and including Consumer Price Index inflation, this is what it looked like at year-end 2000.

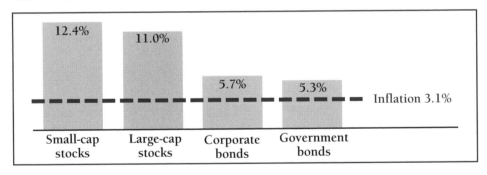

Source: *Stocks, Bonds, Bills and Inflation®️ 2001 Yearbook,* © 2001 Ibbotson Associates, Inc. Based on copyrighted works by Ibbotson and Sinquefield. All rights reserved. Used with permission.

Now, this is a potentially very interesting period of time, and not just because it's long. It contains just about every extreme of political, economic and financial market behavior in history, lending this time clip a lot of credibility in the sense of its having no real biases to it.

This period includes mankind's most terrible world war (1939-

45), plus 30 more years of global thermonuclear overhang, during which mankind could, and on one occasion in 1962 almost did, obliterate itself. But it's also got (since 1989) something very much like world peace — excepting only chronic pockets of ethnic slaughter, and a brief confrontation in the Persian Gulf during which the U.S. and Russia were on the same side.

We've seen periods of deflation (1930-32, when the Consumer Price Index went down 24%) and, at least by our standards, hyperinflation (1979-81). I remember a day in 1968 when the dollar was unredeemable in Paris; today it is the reserve currency of the planet. I've seen an auction of 90-day U.S. Treasury bills bring 15%; in the autumn of 1939, when all Europe's wealth turned into flight capital, the effective interest rate at a similar auction was zero. The marginal tax rate on dividends and interest in this country has been from 25% to over 90% and back down to the top rate on earned income, currently about 39%. Long-term capital gains taxes have been, somewhat less dramatically, from 15% to 40% and down to the current 20% — albeit unindexed for inflation, which of course makes them higher.

The period 1926-2000 also encompasses the two greatest stock market crashes in the nation's history, as well as its longest-lasting economic depression. But it also covers, starting after World War II, the greatest economic expansion and the longest, strongest bull market in common stocks the world has ever known. Vietnam, OPEC, *two* impeachments — you name it, this period's got it — *in unprecedented extremes of good and bad.* And therefore, as you watch the above chart's long-term pattern emerging from all that chaos, you have my permission to pay a whole lot of attention to it, because it just may be trying to tell you something.

At first glance, it may look as if the chart is trying to tell you that — over this potentially very meaningful three quarters of a century — stocks (at 12.4% for small-cap and 11% for large-cap) returned twice what bonds did (at 5.7% for corporates and 5.3% for governments). And that would be plenty impressive enough, because remember, we're talking about *compound* rates of return, and therefore gigantic differentials in the dollars accumulated.

But that isn't what the chart *really* says, is it? Because nominal returns don't — or shouldn't — mean much to the long-term investor (and nothing at all to the multigenerational investor). What *really* counts is one's *real* rate of return, net of inflation. Don't tell me what my nominal return was; tell me what part of that return wasn't confiscated from me as soon as I bought another box of Cheerios, or paid my next light bill, or got another haircut, or replaced my Ford. (If you'd paid $3000 for a Galaxie 500 in 1968 and $30,000 for an Explorer in 1998 — as I did — you'd know exactly what I mean. Of course, if it took you that long to figure this out, you'd probably already be in a peck of trouble.)

So, since you didn't just roll into town on no turnip truck, you would cannily return to those four nominal rates of return, back the 3.1% inflation number out of each of them, and see what you got. And what you'd find is this:

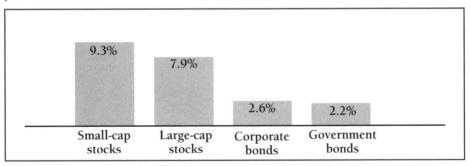

Source: *Stocks, Bonds, Bills and Inflation® 2001 Yearbook,* © 2001 Ibbotson Associates, Inc. Based on copyrighted works by Ibbotson and Sinquefield. All rights reserved. Used with permission.

In real, inflation-adjusted terms — the only ones that count — these 75 years didn't see the stockholder earn twice what the bondholder earned at all. The owner actually earned *over three times* what the loaner did — and, even more importantly, *got to compound the difference.*

(Just to make sure I'm not sandbagging you with some arbitrary period that's slanted in a way not immediately obvious, look at Jeremy Siegel's book, which examines returns back to 1802. From then through 1997, Siegel found that stocks returned 8.4%, that long-term government bonds did 4.8%, and that inflation was 1.3%. This would suggest a real long-term return for stocks two times that of bonds — but Siegel quickly points out that bonds put up their big numbers in the wild and wooly nineteenth century, when the U.S. was the mother of all emerging markets. With Ibbotson and Sinquefield, Siegel found that real bond returns in the twentieth century — both absolutely, and especially relative to equities — came down like a rock.)

OK, so equities in the United States have a very long history of producing much, much higher real returns than bonds. Let's take that as a given. And, speaking of givens, here's another one: there's no free lunch. So, even as we accept the idea of a more or less constant long-term equity premium return, the question has to be forming in our minds (as you can be sure it's forming in the client's): *what's the catch?*

(2) IN AN EFFICIENT MARKET, THE INCREMENTAL REAL RETURN OF EQUITIES MUST BE DISCOUNTING *SOMETHING* BAD. WE JUST HAVE TO MAKE SURE WE KNOW WHAT IT IS. From 1926 through 2000, the market paid the holders of large-company common stocks three times the real return it paid the holders of long-term, high quality corporate bonds. Same country, same time frame, and in many cases *same companies.* (In even more cases, same *kinds* of companies.) Now, why on earth would it do that?

Let's remember that the market (or perhaps I should say The Market) is, above all else, *efficient.* That's the most beautiful thing about it. Our system didn't triumph over Communism because we were good and the Russians were evil. It wasn't politics, it was economics: free-market capitalism is an infinitely more efficient allocator of resources than is any form of centrally mandated economy. (The victory wasn't even one of democracy over socialism. As the Chinese are currently demonstrating to a fare-thee-well, capitalism doesn't need democracy in order to flourish.) The Market won. *Efficiency* won.

And here comes The Market, paying stockholders three times the real return it paid bondholders *for 75 years!* It isn't doing that because stockholders are better human beings (we are, but that's not the operative variable). Stockholders must have to suffer with something — struggle with something — that doesn't afflict bondholders. The incremental return can only be an efficient market's way of pricing into the equation (i.e. of demanding adequate compensation for) some very significant incremental pain that is uniquely the lot of the stockholder. That's self-evident. (It isn't good; it isn't bad. It's merely self-evident.) So the first thing we have to do is make absolutely sure we understand what that added cost really is (and what it isn't). Then, and only then, we can help our clients decide whether the premium return is worth its incremental price.

Ask 100 American investors the question "Why do stocks have so much higher returns than bonds?" and you will get the same response 100 times: *much higher risk.* This is such a good, plain, common-sensical kind of answer that — without a gifted advisor to give them guidance on this issue — people will never notice either of two critically important things: (1) what they call risk isn't really risk at all, but merely volatility, and (2) they don't know what the great financial risk of the rest of their lives really is. (Hence the deep wisdom in Buffett's gnomic observation, "Risk is not knowing what you're doing.")

In the first of these two fundamental misperceptions of risk — the inability to distinguish between it and mere volatility — people mistake temporary declines in the *price* of their investments for permanent losses in their *value.* But, in a well-diversified portfolio, temporary price declines have not historically turned into permanent losses in value. In fact, quite the contrary: major cyclical declines in stock prices have been followed by advances which erase the decline and carry prices to significantly higher levels. "The upward movement of stock values over time," as Jeremy Siegel writes, "overwhelms the short-term fluctuations in the market."

In the "new era" madness of the late 1990s — when, as all revolutionary new technologies do, the Internet spawned arguably the greatest financial bubble in history — investors lost sight of the fact that significant temporary declines in stock prices are quite common, and always will be. Here, at a glance, are all the declines of roughly 20% or more (from peak to trough) in the S&P 500 since the end of World War II — for purposes of this discussion, the modern era.

Bull Market Top	Bear Market Bottom	# Days Duration	% Decline in S&P 500
05/29/46	05/17/47	353	-23.2%
04/06/56	10/22/57	564	-19.4%
12/13/61	06/26/62	195	-27.1%
02/09/66	10/07/66	240	-25.2%
120/3/68	05/26/70	539	-35.9%
01/11/73	12/06/74	694	-45.1%
09/21/76	02/28/78	525	-26.9%
04/27/81	08/12/82	472	-24.1%
08/25/87	12/04/87	101	-33.5%
07/16/90	10/11/90	87	-21.2%
07/17/98	08/31/98	45	-19.3%
03/24/00	09/21/01	546	-36.8% *
			*at this writing

We may sum these data roughly as follows: since WWII ended, the broad stock market has declined an average of nearly 30% a dozen times (about every five years, say). And these declines have gone on, from peak to trough, for an average of about a year.

But the most remarkable thing about these data is something they *don't* tell you. To wit, that at its bull market top in May of 1946 — just prior to the first of these dozen cataclysms — the S&P 500 stood at 20. (No, that's not a misprint; there's no digit missing: *20.*) Near its 2001 trough the S&P 500 was about 1000...*50 times higher than it was 55 years — and 12 bear markets — earlier.* What did the master say? "The upward movement of stock values over time overwhelms the short-term fluctuations in the market."

And yet, since the greatest bull market in history got under way after the August 1982 lows, equity mutual funds in the U.S. have only been in net liquidation four times — all of these episodes corresponding, as we noted earlier, with the market lows of 1987, 1990, 1998 and 2001.

Why did Americans capitulate? Why did people who had years and years of investing yet to do, who should have welcomed a bear market as a big sale on the quality investments they needed to own more of, instead liquidate their holdings at panic prices? Siegel again: "Fear has a greater grasp on human action than does the impressive weight of historical evidence."

Real risk is not inherent in normal, cyclical and above all temporary price declines. Risk is that people will read into those declines something that isn't there, and that having done so, they will panic, and sell. The issue here is **fear**: not what the market does, but *how people react to what the market does.*

This is almost indescribably good news for the New Financial Advisor. Because not only does it begin to free her from her *own* worries about the vagaries of the stock market, it also tells her how critically important her calm, perspective-restoring counsel will be in the financial life of her client households/families.

An advisor's job is not to predict which mutual funds will "outperform" which others, or to get clients into and out of the market at bottoms and tops — things which absolutely no one can reliably do. (Buffett, at Berkshire Hathaway's 1987 annual meeting: "I have never met a man who could forecast the market.") Rather, the advisor's job — once a plan is in place, and has been funded with an appropriate portfolio — is to prevent clients from making The Big Mistake. And panic — the supremely irrational act of liquidating a long-term portfolio because of short- to intermediate-term concerns — is one of the classic Big Mistakes. So when it comes to assessing the worth of an advisor, *perspective* is the ultimate value added.

The foregoing is not meant to be an encyclopedic look at the pattern of the stock market (which, like the economy it mirrors, is one of permanent advance punctuated by temporary declines). It does not address such issues as how long the market may take to recover, or how the returns of stocks compare to those of bonds over shorter time periods than 75 (much less 200) years.

During bear markets, for instance — and the most recent one was no exception — it becomes suddenly quite fashionable to cite the factoids that stock prices did not regain their 1929 highs until 1954, and that the Dow in 1982 stood exactly where it had in 1966...as if, somehow, this proved anything.

In fact, the dividend yield of the Dow from 1930 through 1954 averaged 5.37%, while the interest on 10-year Treasury bonds averaged 2.64%. (The dividend yield of stocks didn't fall below that of bonds until 1958 — at which point yet another generation of permabears became convinced that the end of the world was at hand.) With income reinvested, and adjusting for inflation, Siegel found that $100 invested at the 1929 stock market top had earned $565 30 years later, vs. $141 for an equivalent investment in bonds on the same day. Even from the 1966 peak, using the same methodology, stocks still returned twice what bonds did in the next 30 years.

Time, finally, is the equity investor's greatest ally — and time is what the multigenerational investor has the most of. Though stocks beat bonds "only" about three out of every five years, over 10-year horizons stocks have outperformed about 80% of the time; for 20 years, it's over 90%. And the last 30-year period in which bonds provided greater returns than stocks ended in 1861, with the outbreak of the Civil War. Moreover, the longest it's ever taken for stocks to break even (with dividends reinvested) is 17 years — predictably, after the 1929 top. And following the greatest stock market cataclysm of most of our adult lives — 1973-74, the century's second-worst — time to breakeven with dividends reinvested was a mere three and a half years.

I do not mean to beat this issue into the ground like some great, statistical tomato stake. I wish only to establish — authoritatively if anecdotally — one transcendent truth: that the *permanent* incremental returns of equities have historically been available in return for one's ability to endure *temporary* price declines. *The benefit was permanent, the cost was temporary,* assuming always that one maintained a properly diversified portfolio (about which more later).

Assuming that stocks will continue to be more volatile — subject to sharper and more sudden price fluctuations around their trendlines — than will bonds, one must also assume a premium equity return of some magnitude. Whether that premium, net of inflation, is 2x, as it seems to have been for the last 200 years, or 3x, as it's been for the last 75, is both unpredictable and, finally, immaterial. (Suppose, for the next 30 years, the equity premium was only 1.5x. (A) That would surely mean equity volatility had declined concomitantly, which would probably help people feel a bit more comfortable with stocks. (B) You'd still be compounding your wealth at half again the rate of bonds, which may not be up to the historical norm, but is still orders of magnitude better than a poke in the eye with a sharp stick.)

Temporary declines in price have historically driven permanent incremental returns. (That is all ye know, as the poet says, and all ye need to know.) Do not fear volatility; embrace it (a) because it never lasts and (b) because it's what causes an efficient market to demand higher returns *for those who can keep the faith.* And for those who can't, there is — thank heaven — Doctor Noah.

I leave this discussion with my own all-time favorite personal temporary volatility/permanent return story, concerning the events which befell the greatest stock investor who ever lived on the single worst day in American stock market history.

On Monday, October 19, 1987, Berkshire Hathaway common stock declined in price from its previous close of $3,890 per share to $3,180. This caused the value of the shares owned by the company's chairman, Warren Buffett, to fall by some $342,000,000. Now, how much money do you think Warren Buffett lost on October 19, 1987?

If you said, "He didn't lose anything, because he didn't sell," there is good reason to hope that you truly apprehend the difference between temporary decline and permanent loss (without which understanding, the only place you're taking The Ark is to Davy Jones's locker). In fact, he *didn't* lose anything, because — and only because — he *didn't* sell. And at this writing, the price of each share of Berkshire Hathaway that Warren Buffett didn't sell on October 19, 1987 is about $60,000. (He "lost" $6.2 *billion* in 45 days in the global meltdown of 1998. And, strictly speaking, he hasn't quite made that all back yet. *But he will.*)

(3) IF YOU CAN'T TIME THE MARKET — AND YOU CAN'T — YOU NEVER HAVE TO WATCH IT ANYMORE. EVEN MORE IMPORTANT: NEITHER DO YOUR CLIENTS. It may occur to you at some point to wonder why one has to sit through even temporary declines. Why not just stay in the markets during advancing phases, and step out when they're starting to get (however temporarily) massacred?

Timing the stock market — selling equities at the onset of an important decline, and repurchasing them near the end of that decline — is, to the modern world, what alchemy was to Europe in the first half of the last millennium. It is the vectoring of the time and energy of many of the world's best minds in pursuit of an illusion.

Alchemy — the search for the philosopher's stone that would turn base metal into gold — was probably the greatest single obstacle to real scientific progress (with the arguable exception of religious orthodoxy) in the West for 500 years. It diverted the world's finest intellects into a fool's errand, generation after generation.

Market timing is the financial equivalent of alchemy. In the half a century since the invention of the mainframe computer, generations of scholars in Wall Street and in academia have been washing every recorded financial transaction back to the Babylonians and the Sumerians through their increasingly powerful, ever-more-subtle computing capability, searching for the modern philosopher's stone. And finding nothing, because there's nothing there to find.

Listen: a person of reasonable intelligence, using very good common sense, is much smarter than the smartest guy in the world, banging his head against a wall over and over again. Use your good common sense: 50 years and a gazillion gigabytes later, if there were a pattern that reliably predicted market tops and bottoms, *somebody would have found it already,* and would currently be in the process of taking away the chips of everyone else in the game. Don't rely on Buffett, or Peter Lynch, or Jeremy Siegel, or Vanguard's John Bogle, or even me, telling you that you can't time the market; *rely on your own good common sense.* A consistent way to time the markets has not been found because it doesn't exist. *The pattern is that there is no pattern.* There: isn't that a tremendous load off your mind?

That was not at all a rhetorical question. If you can't time the market — if the only way to capture every day of the permanent advance of equities is to be stoically (if not joyfully) prepared to accept every day of their temporary declines — *then why would you ever need to watch the market again?*

Moreover, the only real reason to spend any energy and time on an economic outlook is to infer, from your take on the economy, a market outlook. But the only reason even to *want* a market outlook is so that you can determine advantageous entry and exit points: when to put money in or take it out; when to hold new money back, waiting for better prices. *But we just concluded that this is impossible.*

Now come at this issue the other way. We've established that, historically, the longer your investment time horizon, the less "risky" stocks become, both absolutely and especially relative to bonds. We've decided that, since cyclical declines are always temporary anyway, the urgency to be out of them — to "protect" capital that's not at much long-term risk to begin with — isn't very great. (We have *not* mentioned — so this would be the pluperfect place to do so — that historically half the gains in the first three years of a new bull market come in the six months immediately following the trough. This means that the opportunity cost of being out of the market when it turns is quite horrific.) And now we conclude that, even if you wanted to, you couldn't consistently augment your return by moving in and out.

It seems to me that, no matter how you reason this out, you ultimately arrive at the same conclusions:

- You always win, if you stay in.
- You *have* to stay in, in order to win, because you can't consistently identify advantageous entry and exit points.
- The only clearly "right" time to buy equities, then, is when you have the money to invest.
- The only "right" time to sell equities, by the same logic, is when you need to take money out.
- If your decisions to purchase (or sell) equities are based solely on your personal ability to invest (or your personal need to withdraw) capital, there's nothing to be gained from watching the market.
- If you're not going to watch the market, why watch the macroeconomy? The only practical reason to do the latter would be to obtain some timing advantage with respect to the former, a timing

advantage which, we're now sure, does not — because it cannot — exist.

In the bad old transaction-based, commission-driven days, advisors invested a lot of time and energy in the economy and the market, because that whole business was based on the illusion of the potential for advantageous timing: *when* to be in or out of the market; *when* to lengthen or shorten maturities; *when* to go short and *when* to cover; *when* to move out of big-cap into small-cap, or out of the U.S. into Europe; *when to sell X and buy Y* — thereby *possibly* yielding the client a return advantage, but *certainly* yielding the advisor a commission — or two. And even today, the agendas of the meetings I speak at are littered with economists and portfolio managers, all professing some insight into the economy and/or the markets which would lead you to conclude that *this is a good time* to put some more money with them.

Of course, in the great speculative bubble/national stock market mania of the late 1990s, the most avid purveyors of the timing illusion — the people who refined it into a drug — were the Internet trading croupiers and their bought dogs in financial journalism. Before the inevitable crash, these people corrupted investing into speculation, and then into a video game. And they still don't learn — because they have no incentive to learn.

There's no percentage in CNBC telling you the truth. Because the truth is that your best chance for success is a diversified, long-term, low-turnover managed/pooled equity portfolio that's goal-focused rather than market-driven. In other words, one of the best things you can ever do for your portfolio (and your life, and your soul) is to turn off CNBC. You can't expect drug dealers and bartenders to warn you off drugs and alcohol, and you can't expect CNBC (or its ilk) to do anything but ask each talking head who appears there what his short-term market outlook is, and what three stocks he's buying right now.

But I digress. There is an immense release of energy which attends upon abandoning a market viewpoint, and you suddenly find a big empty box of potentially productive time which need no longer be wasted reading economic and financial tea leaves. But by far the most valuable benefit of having no outlook is the extent to which it can purify your interactions with your clients.

Tom Seaver swears that he once asked Yogi Berra what time it was, and that Berra replied, "You mean now?" This may sound funny to you, but that's how you can very quickly re-set the agenda against all manner of going-nowhere market questions:

CLIENT: What do you think of the market?

NEW FINANCIAL ADVISOR: You mean now? Or 20 years from now?

C: Huh? What are you talking about?

NFA: I mean, what do I think of the market *when*?

C: Now, of course.

NFA: I haven't looked at it in a while. What's it doing?

C: Are you, my financial advisor, seriously asking *me* what the market is doing?

NFA: I'm not really *that* serious. I'm just trying to hold up my end of the conversation, until I can figure out how to help you. You know that all I really care about is helping you, right?

C: Let's start over again. The market has been going down a lot lately. You do know *that*, right?

NFA: Sure. I mean, I guess so.

C: Well, what do you think we should do?

NFA: Have your long-term goals changed?

C: No, of course not.

NFA: Then what would you want to do?

C: Wait a minute. I'm the client. You're the advisor. What do *you* want me to do?

NFA: Stand by your plan. Do you have any new money?

C: As a matter of fact, I think we're going to be able to start funding this year's pension plan contribution about three months ahead of schedule.

NFA: That's terrific. Really. Just please send it along when you can.

C: And what will you *do* with it?

NFA: Invest it in the portfolio of equity mutual funds we've been buying all along. That's the plan, right?

C: *When* will you invest it?

NFA: Soon as I get it. Why?

C: Don't you want to wait to see if the market goes lower?

NFA: Heck, no. Bad odds. Not my game at all.

C: What on earth are you talking about?

NFA: Do you remember that chart of all the bear markets since WWII that I gave you when we set up your plan?

C: Couldn't possibly forget it. *Great* piece. Got it right here in my desk drawer.

NFA: Thanks. You know how it shows that, about every five years, the market went down a fair amount?

C: Yes. That's my point.

NFA: What do you think the market's done the *other* four out of five years?

C: Gone up, I suppose.

NFA: Gone up a whole bunch. Like, 50 times in 55 years, net of the dozen bear markets. Remember?

C: Vividly. It's how you got me so heavily into equities in the first place.

NFA: Exactly. So if I get your pension contribution and sit on it, waiting for lower prices, I'm *giving* four-to-one odds, yes? I'm playing Russian roulette with one empty chamber and

	four bullets, in a real sense, am I not?
C:	Gulp.
NFA:	Didn't quite hear you.
C:	I said, "Gulp." Do you think I could get you to forget that we ever had this conversation?
NFA:	What conversation?
C:	Thank you. One last thing. What was that you said about thinking of the market 20 years from now?
NFA:	I'm a long-term planner, so I'm a long-term investor. I've trained myself to think about what things will be like for my clients 20 years from now. For instance, you'll be 78, retired 16 years. Your granddaughter who was born last year, she'll be a senior in college. I think about getting you both ready for that.
C:	Where do you think the market will be?
NFA:	A whole lot higher than it is today, would be my guess. Went up close to 10 times in the *last* 20 years, even after the big bear market of 2000-2001. Can't imagine it'll do anywhere near that well, of course.
C:	How can you be sure?
NFA:	You're starting to sound like me. When do you think you might be sending me that pension contribution?
C:	Think I might just walk it over there in the morning.
NFA:	I look forward to seeing you.

You can't have an argument with someone who refuses to argue with you, and you can never be drawn into a conversation that centers on market prognostication if you steadfastly refuse to have a market viewpoint. And what on earth would a long-term/multigenerational financial planner *want* with a market viewpoint, anyway? Planning is first and foremost about getting your head out of today, and nothing pushes your face right back into today as hard as does "the current market" — which won't matter at all 20 years from now, and may not matter *two* years from now. (And 20 years from now, I can just about guarantee that you'll wish you'd put every dime you ever had into equities *today*.) *Today is always the hardest day to invest — and the only day we'll ever have.*

This chapter has talked mostly about equities, and about what the risk of equities appears to be, but really isn't. (The next chapter will talk about what risk really is, and how to explain it to people.) We've looked at some of the not-very-bright things people do to try to protect themselves from the historically nonexistent long-term principal risk of holding equities, with particular attention to market timing — about which we concluded (a) you can't and (b) why bother? But no discussion of the great lengths people will go to in order to meliorate the essentially illusory "risk" of equity volatility would be complete without a word or two about asset allocation.

I want to be as gentle as I can on the subject of asset allocation, because I know that many of your firms are strong believers in it, and actively encourage you to practice it. (Let me suggest very quietly, however, that the enthusiasm of many firms for asset allocation may ultimately be less about seeking the best returns for the clients than it is about mounting the best defense in a lawsuit.)

Asset allocation, broadly defined, is a philosophy of building portfolios using different asset classes — typically stocks, bonds and cash, but sometimes extending to international stocks and bonds, and sometimes to real estate, as well. For clarity and simplicity, let's just assume it's stocks, bonds and cash. The theory is that mixing these asset classes spreads the risk of investing in any one of them, reduces the overall volatility of a portfolio, and captures a blended, weighted average sort of return. And it certainly does all those things.

My problem with asset allocation in very long-term (and even multigenerational) portfolios is that it trades off some of the incremental *permanent* return of equities in order to defend against equities' incremental *temporary* volatility. And ultimately, that logic is lost on me: giving up a permanent benefit to avoid paying a temporary cost isn't something I would ever do, or recommend to a household/family whose most cherished goal is true multigenerational wealth.

I don't say *you* shouldn't ever do asset allocation, nor that it is in some way an intrinsically invalid strategy. I know there are households/families who are just never going to be able to handle complete exposure to equity volatility, no matter what their stated long-term needs and goals are.

But asset allocation is no panacea, either. It's a nice, straightforward, middle-of-the-road strategy. But you owe it to your clients to ask them — and ask yourself — whether they can ever hope to get where they need to go by driving down the middle of the road.

IN SUMMARY

- The great bulk of everything you ever need to know about financial planning is the mechanics of securing The Seven Glorious Outcomes. Aside from adequate savings and insurance, and getting all the assets titled most efficiently, most of the rest of long-term planning is buying and holding equities.

- Equities are the only major building block of financial planning that isn't intuitively obvious, and to which people bring large and complex accumulations of misconception. Educating people about equities turns out, therefore, to be a process of helping them unlearn things which they think are true, but which aren't.

- The real long-term return of equities (net of inflation) puts all other financial assets in the shade. Equities' real, compound return has been twice that of bonds for the last 200 years, and three times for the last 75. And there's a lot of credibility in those last 75.

- In an efficient market, incremental returns of that magnitude *must* come at a price. Most Americans call that price *risk,* but it turns out to be just volatility — and very temporary volatility, at that.

- There've been 12 devastating bear markets in U.S. stocks since the end of WWII. Near the trough of the last one, stock prices were 50 times higher than they were at the top of the first one. The real risk of *that* asset class was *being out of it.*

- Without guidance, Americans can't distinguish between temporary declines in the price of their investments and permanent losses in their value. Mistaking the former for the latter, they panic, and sell. You were sent into the world to stop this.

- Time is the equity investor's greatest ally. And time is what the multigenerational client family has the most of.

- If you can't time the market — and you can't — there isn't much point in watching it. The right time to buy equities is when you have the money; the right time to sell them is when you need the money. You just have to stay in it to win it. Everything else is voodoo, alchemy or — even worse — journalism.

- Today is always the hardest day to invest — and the only day we have.

- Asset allocation seems as American as apple pie, mom, the flag and baseball — until you realize that it trades away some of the permanent return of equities in order to secure relief from some of the temporary volatility. Are you absolutely convinced that that's a good long-term strategy?

DOCTOR NOAH'S Rx FOR *REAL* SAFETY AND INCOME

chapter seven

SEVEN

———————•———————

In the last chapter, I suggested that most people you'll come in contact with misperceive the risk of equity investing in two important ways. First, as we've seen, people greatly overestimate the potential long-term risk to their capital of holding equities — a risk which, historically at least, does not exist. (And even the *opportunity* risk of equities — the possibility that bonds will do better, somehow — has all but disappeared over time horizons out past 20 years.)

Granted, the short- to intermediate-term *volatility* of equities — the historical probability that, one year in five, an average of 30% of your equities' market value will suddenly but temporarily disappear — remains always with us. And we accumulators of real wealth must thank heaven that it does, because we know that, in an efficient market, volatility is the cause of the premium return. (If the volatility of stocks drifted down to where it wasn't much greater than that of bonds, God forbid, the return of stocks would inevitably drift down...to where *it* wasn't much more than that of bonds.) And besides, in a properly diversified portfolio, volatility isn't risk, it's just...volatility. If my investments decline in price by 20% to 30% — which they've done four times just since 1987 — and then come back, and then become worth much more than they ever were before...well, they were certainly volatile, but I don't accept that they were, in any real sense, risky. The only two ways that volatility can turn into risk are:

> (1) You need to withdraw the capital. That's easily handled: don't put capital you will *probably* need to withdraw within five years into equities. What's magic about five years? Well, no guarantees, but — with dividends reinvested — large-company stocks

have produced positive returns in over 93% of all the rolling five-year periods (a new one of which starts every month) since 1926. Now, 93% isn't 100%, but I believe the other seven percent is a risk worth booking.

(2) *You panic; you sell.* This is the preferred way to turn volatility into risk — or, more accurately, to turn temporary decline into permanent loss. What did the master say? "Fear has a greater grasp on human action than does the impressive weight of historical evidence." People look right at those dozen postwar bear claws hanging off a trendline that goes up 50 times in 55 years. Then they leap up onto the gunwale of The Ark, sing the four-word death song of the North American investor — "This time, it's different!" — and plunge forever into the raging sea. (How do you, Doctor Noah, prevent this panic-induced self-destruction? Well, more about that in a little while, but the single most efficient way is not to let panic-prone people on The Ark in the first place. *And don't tell me you don't know who they are.*)

We turn now to the *other* fatal misperception of risk which is pandemic among even our better-educated, more affluent prospective Ark passengers. One, we said, was overestimating the risk of holding equities. The other, far more insidious mistake is *underestimating the risk of not holding them.* **The real long-term risk of equities is not owning them.**

For most people, the idea that what you don't own *can* hurt you is counterintuitive. Naturally distrustful of equities, especially in retirement, people reason as follows: "I may not earn as high a return in bonds, CDs and fixed annuities, but *if I don't own stocks at all, at least I'm safe.*" The truth is, if you don't own stocks at all, you're dead.

If you're thinking in terms of anything like a 30-year retirement, and *if* you want your income to *at least* keep pace with your living costs so you can *at least* maintain your standard of living, and *if* you want to grow your heirs' patrimony even as your own income grows...and *if* — hey, *especially if* — history is any guide at all:

> "Although it might appear to be riskier to hold stocks than bonds, precisely the opposite is true: the safest long-term investment for the preservation of pur-chasing power has clearly been stocks, not bonds."

Wait a minute; *I* didn't say that. (I *would* have said it — gladly — but I just got a vibe that maybe my relentless equity zealotry might be wearing a little thin, so I called for backup: *Jeremy Siegel said that.* **"The safest long-term investment for the preservation of purchasing power has clearly been stocks, not bonds."**

Gentle reader, you are surrounded by people who believe — fer-vently, deeply, even passionately — that, especially in retirement, stocks are risky and bonds are safe. Gentle reader — would that there were some softer, easier way to tell you this — *it's the other way around.* In the long run — and the quest for multigenerational *real* wealth is the pure essence of a long-run enterprise — it is stocks that are safe, and bonds that are risky.

Please note that we're not talking about return anymore. We're no longer saying — or no longer *just* saying — equities have historically pro-duced a much higher return than bonds. *We're saying that equities are safer.* But to understand that, you have to understand what "safety" really is. Americans don't. To understand "safety," in turn, you have to under-stand what "risk" really is. Americans don't. And above all, to under-stand what "risk" *and* "safety" really are, *you have to understand what "money" really is.* Americans — heaven bless and keep them — don't, and never will, until it's much too late...*unless you consent to save them.*

To help you comprehend all this — so you can help *them* comprehend all this — I'd like to perform a couple of simple exercises with you...just the way I did with my own clients, and just the way I hope you'll do with your Ark candidates.

First, go into your pocket or wallet, and pull out one American greenback. The denomination isn't important; just take out one official green portrait of a dead president (not to slight Ben Franklin or Alexander Hamilton); hold one end of the bill in each hand, and look at it — giving it your full, undivided attention — for 10 seconds. Now: describe the thing you are holding in your hand, *using only one word.*

I'd bet just about anything that you said the one word **money.** That was your first mistake. It's *everybody's* first mistake, so don't feel bad about it.

What you're holding in your hand is *currency.* And currency is a wonderful thing. Why, it's the most efficient medium of exchange ever invented. Without it, we'd be standing around bartering with each other all day — how many bushels of oranges do you want for that Buick? — and our economy would be low, slow and very inefficient. Yes, currency is a lot of great things — but a store of value isn't one of them.

Currency loses a tiny bit of its value just about every day. Over time, that loss of value compounds. Every four weeks or so in this country, the government publishes a statistic: at what annual rate did the Consumer Price Index go up last month? Turn that question around, in this context, and you'll see what it's really asking: *at what compound annual rate did the U.S. currency lose its value last month?* From 1926 through 2000, as we've seen, the Consumer Price Index went up — meaning the value of the currency, in terms of what it would buy, went down — at a 3.1% compound annual rate. At that rate, the currency loses about half its value in 20 years, and two-thirds of its value in 30 years. More to the point, **after 30 years of 3.1% inflation, it will take about three dollars to buy what one dollar buys today.**

When I was a kid, my mother used an expression to indicate something she was absolutely sure of. She said, "I'll bet you dollars to doughnuts that..." Mom meant that she was so certain, she'd be willing to give somebody very long odds to bet on it with her — probably about 20-to-one odds, if you stopped to think about it, because a doughnut in those days cost about a nickel.

These days, in some of the gourmet coffee shops around New York, wagering a dollar to a doughnut would probably be like flipping a coin — an even-money bet. (And in some of these joints, I wonder if you can even *get* one doughnut for a dollar.)

All of our lives are filled with similar vignettes — little things we remember from our own experience that bring home to us with perfect clarity the awesome extent to which the currency loses its value over time. I've already mentioned that in 1967, my wife and I had a beautiful one-bedroom apartment in Brooklyn Heights, New York that rented for $200 a month. Another one-bedroom apartment in that building rented, in 2001, for $2,200, and you can't get a monthly space in a parking garage anywhere in the Brooklyn Heights historic district for $200 a month. I also contrasted my $3000 '68 Ford Galaxie 500 with my daughter's $30,000 '98 Ford Explorer — and they probably weighed about the same. Finally, when I was in college in 1962 — and John F. Kennedy was a president, not an airport — I quite vividly remember buying a summer suit for $50. That's about what I'd expect to pay for a good dress shirt today — if not more.

Before we do our second exercise on this subject — please keep your item of currency out where you can still see it — I'd like you to just grab a sheet of paper and jot down the three things in your own life experience that most readily convey *to you* the slow but ultimately precipitous decline in the dollar's purchasing power. *This is important.* Take all the time you need; I'll wait here.

Welcome back. Remarkable, isn't it? All of your life experience —
encapsulated in the three things you've just written down — tells you that
the currency is, over the long haul, a fiction, and not a terribly amusing
fiction at that. It tells you that long-term investing whose goal is to fix the
number of units of the currency you own — and, even worse, to fix your
income in terms of a set number of units of the currency that you're "guar-
anteed" to receive each year — is, indeed, "committing suicide to keep
from getting killed."

And yet older Americans — *whose life experience has not been one
whit different from yours and mine, in this regard* — invest as if the greenback dollar were a shaving from the True Cross (or whatever your personal idea of a sacred relic is). **Their concept of investment safety is
completely disconnected from their common sense** — and from a lifetime of observing the consistent behavior of the prices of virtually everything they live in, drive, wear, consume and use. As Satchel Paige observed, "It's not what you don't know that hurts you, it's what you know
that just ain't so."

Mystifying though this may be, it should serve as a source of some
comfort to you, as you think ahead to how you're going to convince people
that, in the long run, **the only sane definition of "money" is "purchasing
power."** If you had to get clients to understand something entirely new
and totally alien to them, that might be a very long row to hoe. But it's
not, because the essential challenge is simply *to reconnect their approach to
investing with all of their common-sense life experience.* We will do that —
or at least begin the process of doing it — by giving people who are trying
desperately to understand us new and better definitions of three key concepts: "money," "risk," and "safety." (I say again, and not for the last time:
we will help people understand *who are trying to understand.* We will not
argue, we will not "sell," and we will not play dueling definitions.)

We accomplish this not with charts, graphs, scattergrams, erudite
academic treatises, or perambulations along the efficient frontier (what-

ever that is). You can lead a horse to water, but you can't make him think, much less stop rolling over his cancerous CDs. No, if the basic problem is that people have lost contact with the one great financial lesson of their entire life experience, then one bright, clarifying glimpse of that life experience is how — if at all — we will help them recover it.

At the moment of truth, I'd like you to hand your prospect, *face down,* one of your business cards — one, that is, for every person in the room. So that they can see, laminated to the back of each card, this startlingly clear, virtually unmistakable message — not from you, but from their own life experience.

1975 · ARBOR DAY · 10¢

Have you hugged a tree today?

This, of course, is a make-believe stamp (which you and they will also find in Chapter Four of *SWIW*), because the U.S. Postal Service — America's leading producer of postage stamps — gets extremely testy if you duplicate any of their actual stamps. On the other hand, two important aspects of this otherwise imaginary stamp *are* real. And therein lies the value of this second exercise.

The mind-boggling, heart-stopping, illusion-of-safety-shattering message of this humble postage stamp is implicit in the juxtaposition of the date and the price: **1975/10 cents.**

My personal favorite 1975 10-cent stamp commemorates the first linkup of an American with a Russian spacecraft: the Apollo Soyuz Space

Test Project, as it was officially called, which took place on July 17, 1975. Space buffs of a certain age have a soft spot in their hearts for this mission, because it was commanded by the last of the original seven Mercury astronauts to go into space: the late Donald K. "Deke" Slayton. The stamp is number 1569 in the U.S. Postal Service's stamp catalog — and it's a real beauty.

Along with stories and analogies, *symbols* are a very powerful yet non-argumentative way of communicating important ideas to people. And I've always found this postage stamp (or any postage stamp that's less than one normal retired lifetime old) to be the ultimate proxy for the insidiousness of inflation in real life — the slow, inexorable and ultimately quite terrifying erosion of the dollar's purchasing power over time.

I think that a good many people who retired in 1975 are still alive, just as I think at least one of the two people in a couple retiring today is going to be alive 30 years from now. American history back to 1802 tells me not to worry about equities — either absolutely or relative to bonds — over 30-year periods. But the stamp very eloquently tells me (and you, and especially your prospective clients) to be worried — very, *very* worried — about bonds. Here's how the exercise plays out (with or without, at your discretion, the additional symbol of a shiny new 25-cent piece).

NEW FINANCIAL ADVISOR: I'd like you to imagine that you retired in 1975, right around the time this stamp was issued. And let's say your entire cost of living — the only thing you needed to buy every year — was one first-class postage stamp. Now, I don't want to influence your thinking unduly — I want you to make up your own mind — but I need to remind you that, in 1975, the stock market was just starting to recover from its worst decline in the second half of the twentieth century: in 1973-74, with OPEC, Watergate and Vietnam, it went down about 45% over two years. In 1975, that would still have been pretty fresh in your mind, don't you think?

PROSPECT: Good heavens, yes.

NFA: So you probably might not have been jumping up and down to invest your retirement nest egg in equities to begin with. And then, let's say that, with interest rates where they were in '75, you found that you could very easily invest your retirement savings in good quality bonds and CDs, and get an annual income of [NOTE: this is where you brandish that shiny new quarter — or not, as you choose] 25 cents. Have I made the issues clear so far?

P: All we need to buy is a stamp, which then costs 10 cents, and we can get a safe, secure income of 25 cents. Right?

NFA: Exactly right.

P: (Looking at the stamp — or from the stamp to the quarter and back again, over and over) Why am I getting such a bad feeling about this?

NFA: Because you're already ahead of me. Just let me ask you one question, while I try to catch up. OK?

P: Shoot.

NFA: Knowing what you knew then, what percentage of your retirement nest egg would you have invested in equities as you went into your 1975 retirement, and what percentage would you have put in bonds and CDs?

P: You have to know the answer to that already. We'd have put it *all* in bonds and CDs.

NFA: (Gently) Yes, I think so, too. (Silence)

P: So then what happened?

NFA: (Very gently) Would it be OK if I asked you to sort of think it through?

P: If I'm following you, which I'm afraid I am, the price of our

	one stamp kept going up every year...
MRS. P.	...and our income stayed the same.
NFA:	(Giving just the slightest hint that the truth is even worse) Well, that's *about* right...
P:	Wait a minute, is this legitimate? Are you saying that, in real life, the cost of living is up like three and a half times since 1975?
NFA:	(To Mrs. P.) What do *you* think?
MRS. P:	At *least*. I'd have guessed more.
NFA:	No, three and a half times is right in the ballpark. (Silence)
P:	I know I'm going to be sorry I asked you this, but when did the price of a stamp get to 25 cents?
NFA:	In 1988. And then in 1991 it went to 29 cents.
P:	What did we do then?
NFA:	(Looking from one to the other) Well, I assume you started cutting back on your lifestyle. Fewer vacations...maybe moved to a smaller house. Things like that, I would think. (Very quietly) And then, of course, interest rates started to *really* come down...
MRS. P:	You mean we're not even getting the 25 cents anymore?
NFA:	I wouldn't think so, no.
P:	You know, I think that's right. I remember nine, 10 percent CD rates in the '70s. Don't get those anymore.
NFA:	That's right. (Silence)
P:	So what were we supposed to have done: invest it in *stocks*?
NFA:	Well, actually...yes. Of course, instead of 25 cents in interest income, you'd have probably started off with dividends of about...a dime.
P:	Barely enough for the stamp!
NFA:	(Serenely) Right.
P:	And we'd have run out of income *even sooner!*

NFA: (Very reluctantly springing the trap) Well...no, actually. You see, a dime in dividends in 1975 is about 45 cents today. Maybe a *tad* more...

P: (Blowing a head gasket) Wait a minute! Wait a minute! What stock raised its dividend four and a half times since 1975?!?

NFA: (*Very* quietly) Well...on average, in a sense, they *all* did. The cash dividend of the S&P 500 is up...just about four and a half times since '75. Maybe a *tad* more...

MRS. P: Let me make sure I understand this. Are you seriously telling us that, since 1975, the cost of living is up three and a half times, and the dividend of the stock averages is up *four* and a half times?

NFA: Round numbers...sure.

P: This is a fluke, right? The last 25 years or so has been some kind of golden age?

NFA: (With feeling) Not for dividends, it hasn't!

P: Are you trying to tell us it *usually* works like this?

NFA: (Calmly) Well, over long periods of time...like your retirement...sure. I mean, dividends didn't go up as much as companies' *earnings* went up — they haven't for a while — but they've gone up a heck of a lot more than the cost of living.

MRS. P: No one ever told us this before.

NFA: (With perfect equanimity) I'm sorry to hear that. (Silence)

P: (Remaining incredulous) I still think somehow we're not getting the whole picture, here.

NFA: (*Very* reluctantly) Well...not the *whole* picture, no...

P: I knew it! What haven't you told us?!?

NFA: (Letting P. drag it out of him) Well...your principal, you see...it's...it's gone up a lot. I don't know if you want to

	focus on that yet, though; I'm just trying to help you think through the issue of retirement *income*.
MRS. P:	(Who is — get used to this, because it happens a lot — actually a lot smarter than you-know-who) I think we're strong enough to handle whatever you have to tell us.
NFA:	Well, your principal — the retirement nest egg you invested in stocks in 1975 — it's up about 10 times since then...
P:	Ten times!? Our capital's grown *10 times?*
NFA:	All right, maybe it's closer to 12...
MRS. P:	*Who cares?* If our income keeps growing more than our cost of living does, *who cares* what the capital does?
NFA:	(Very reasonably) I would think...your children and grand-children. I'll bet if we asked them...they'd probably care quite a bit.
MRS. P:	Oh, my gosh. Of course...that's right.
NFA:	(Sits back contentedly, folds hands, looks happy, says nothing)
MRS. P:	(Abandoning any pretense that she's not the decision-maker) OK, let me see if I've got this straight. (Note non-use of the word "we") I always thought that in retirement you were supposed to buy bonds and CDs for a safe, predictable, steady income.
NFA:	Yes; I guess most people *do* think that.
MRS. P:	But if our cost of living keeps going up, that income might not be enough.
NFA:	Sooner or later...it wouldn't be enough.
MRS. P:	But if we invest in equities, even though the dividend in-come starts *out* lower, it grows, in the long run, more than our cost of living grows, so we stay ahead of inflation.
NFA:	Well, that's the way it's always worked in the past, and I'd certainly expect...
MRS. P:	(Interrupting) OK, OK: nothing's guaranteed.

NFA: Precisely.

MRS. P: And, as our dividends grow, our capital could be growing, too...for the kids.

NFA: Yes. Dividends rise when companies' earnings rise. And if earnings are rising, sooner or later stock prices tag along.

MRS. P: Right. (Stands, takes NFA's coffee cup) Would you like some more coffee?

NFA: Very much, thanks. It's *terrific* coffee. (Mrs. P exits)

P: (Feebly) Wait...I don't...what did we buy?

VOICE FROM KITCHEN: Explain it to him.

Look, I don't want to be sexist, here, even if it's sexism in reverse. Maybe it's *he* who "gets it" with instant, crystal clarity — and she starts crying, says that if he puts their retirement money in the stock market she'll leave him, and runs screaming from the room. That happens. (And I have to be honest with you: it's not usually a good sign.) But that stamp, that quarter and that hypothetical 1975 retirement story are an acid test of your prospects' *educability* — which, you'll remember, is one of the key characteristics of people we're going to allow onto The Ark. And I guarantee you that, 10 minutes after the stamp hits their coffee table, you'll know with virtual certainty whether you've got real prospects or not. (You may not *like* the outcome, but at least you won't have to wait long for it. And the faster you flush marginal or problem prospects, the sooner The Ark will be booked full.)

But when the stamp/quarter/story gambit works — and I know from joyful personal experience that it works *a lot* — your prospects get up from the table, consciously or unconsciously, with a new definition of "money." Once more, with feeling:

In the long run, the only sane

definition of "money" is

"purchasing power."

Now let's just take a quick time-out, and have a pop quiz, to see how you yourself are progressing on this critical, countercultural issue. *Please fill in the blank:*

> Chicken Little kept his money in greenback dollars, where it would be "safe." One day, Chicken Little took one greenback dollar to the post office, and used it to buy 10 first-class postage stamps. A very few years later, Chicken Little took another green-back dollar to the post office, but this time the nice man would only give him five first-class postage stamps. Chicken Little was very sad, because he had lost half his _____.

Now, if you said "purchasing power," you're not necessarily wrong, but you still may not be right, either. If you thought "purchasing power" was the right answer *and that "money" was the wrong answer,* it's a sign that you're still struggling with this whole idea. *The only unequivocally correct answer is "money."* If Chicken Little maintained his number of greenback dollars, and his cost of living doubled, then Chicken Little did well and truly lose half his *money.* Because — say it with me, please, out loud — in the long run, the only sane definition of "money" is "purchasing power."

In turn, then, we need new definitions of "risk" and "safety." When we equated money with greenback dollars, we said that risk was implicit in anything which threatened the number of greenback dollars we had. Laboring under a corollary misapprehension — that a diversified portfo-lio of quality stocks could and often did cause a permanent decrease in the number of greenback dollars we had — we called stocks "risky." By the same logic — that safety was implicit in anything that fixed and guar-anteed the number of greenback dollars we had — we called bonds "safe." To summarize: if currency is money, bonds are safe and stocks are risky.

When we recover from this toxic delusion, we see that money is not currency, but purchasing power. Risk is therefore inherent in that which threatens to diminish purchasing power, and safety inures to that which preserves and even accretes purchasing power. Equities — even if you're spending the dividend income, rather than letting it compound — have a brilliant long-term record of preserving and even accreting purchasing power. Bonds, virtually all of whose total return is interest income, barely keep ahead of inflation, and *only* do so if you compound the income. If you're *spending* the interest — *fahgeddaboudit!* Then the question becomes not *if* bonds are eroding your purchasing power, but *how quickly.* To summarize: since purchasing power is money, stocks are safe and bonds are risky. And so we say, "the *safest* long-term investment for the preservation of purchasing power has clearly been stocks, not bonds."

Although it's nowhere near as elegant or simple as the starkly eloquent 1975 10-cent stamp, I do have another way of expressing the long-term mutation of risk from principal to purchasing power. You can do it on a yellow legal pad across someone's desk, or in a seminar situation, and within five minutes make your point.

First draw a simple graph; make the north-south axis *RISK* and the east-west axis *TIME*, thus:

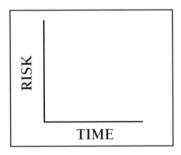

Then start by graphing the progress of the obvious "risk," which is principal loss. I think we would all agree that over very short periods of time the principal risk of equities is astronomical. Why, one day not so very long ago the American stock market lost 23% of its value between sunup and sunset. And that was an *average*. So we're talking huge short-term risk.

As I say this, I make a big dot on the chart, as follows. You see that, because it's very low on the *TIME* axis, the dot is very high on the *RISK* axis.

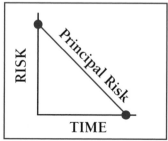

But almost immediately a funny thing happens. With the passage of time, the risk of holding equities historically declines, quite literally to zero. Jeremy Siegel says there's never been a 17-year period in history in which stocks (with dividends reinvested) have produced a negative real return.

Now, there's nothing sacred about 17 years (any more than your potential short-term loss is limited to 23% — or any other number). So the graph is illustrating a concept (indeed, as you'll see, two concepts); it's not predicting or calibrating the future.

The concept is simply that, over some period of time, the risk of holding equities falls all the way to zero...and stops there, because it can't go any lower. (This last point may seem so obvious that it needn't be mentioned, but it's about to become very important. Just watch.)

I illustrate the decline of principal risk to zero as follows, and then label the resulting bar:

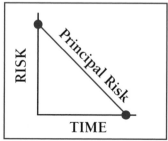

Now, I say, let's look at the *other* risk of your economic life — the risk that does *not* decline but only keeps rising, without limit, for as long as you live (and then goes on rising throughout the lives of your heirs). That is the risk of the loss of your purchasing power — the risk that your cost of living will outrun your income.

In the short run, purchasing power risk is exactly the opposite of principal risk, in this sense: while short-term principal risk is astronomical, short-term risk of purchasing power is virtually nonexistent.

What is the chance that you'll walk into the supermarket tomorrow and find that a diversified basket of your household needs is markedly more expensive than it was today? I would say that risk is close to zero. So let's start graphing this risk literally at zero, by putting our starting dot right where the axes meet:

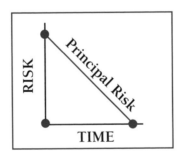

Here, though, we find that with each passing day the risk of losing our purchasing power — through the slow, steady increase in the prices of nearly all the goods and services we consume — *rises* over time. But unlike principal loss risk, *it has no finite limit*, other than the days allotted to us and to the loved ones who will survive us.

So when we graph the progress of purchasing power risk — which is the last step in this visual presentation — our chart ends up looking like this:

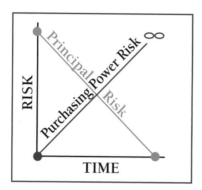

Forgive me; I couldn't resist putting that little "infinity" sign at the top of the "purchasing power risk" curve. It's slightly hyperbolic, I admit, but in a just cause. And overall, I still think the point is fairly made: that principal risk, even if you *can't* distinguish it from volatility, has nowhere to go but down over time, as it mutates into purchasing power risk (or, more accurately, loss), which marches inexorably upward through the years, without limit.

Samuel Johnson said that patriotism is the last refuge of a scoundrel. But in the context of this chapter, it's yield.

Our countrymen, as we've seen, are all too willing to sail into a 30-year retirement — during which, at their 75-year trendline rate, consumer prices will triple — armed only with a fixed-income investment strategy. And will consider themselves not merely rational but prudent to do so. Right up until they notice they're beginning to run out of money — by which time it's too late — these folks call themselves **conservative investors**. When in fact, with the arguable exception of the Internet day trader of the late '90s, the fixed-income retirement investor is about as reckless as anyone could possibly be.

"Conservative," like "risky" and "safe," is one of those words whose meaning is tied to one's definition of "money." The threshold question is: *what are you trying to conserve?* The self-styled "conservative" investor will respond somewhat snappishly (because isn't it obvious?) that, of course, he's conserving his "money." But in fact, he's doing just the opposite. He's squandering his money (i.e. purchasing power) in the act of conserving the number of units of the currency he has — *fatally mistaking greenback dollars for money.*

It is we equity investors who are truly "conservative." We're diligently investing to conserve our purchasing power (i.e. money), *and even to enhance it over time,* since equities are the financial embodiment of the eternal truth that the best defense is a good offense. Someone who can look for more than 30 seconds at a 1975 postage stamp next to a current one, and then turn right around and put his retirement capital into bonds, not only isn't conservative, he isn't an investor. Heck, he's not even a speculator, because intelligent speculation pays off *sometimes.* A bond buyer with a 30-year time horizon is nothing more than a gambler, sitting at a great cosmic poker table, trying to draw to the mother of all inside straights.

Yet even as he watches the dealer slowly but inexorably taking away all the chips he worked a lifetime to accumulate, the bond buyer still clings to one last rationalization:

"I need the income."

The unspoken corollary of this seemingly reasonable plea is, of course, "And bonds yield more than stocks do." The straight-faced, single-minded irrationality of this mental accounting reminds me of nothing so much as the story Woody Allen tells in voice-over at the end of *Annie Hall.* Guy goes to a psychiatrist for help in dealing with his brother. Seems the brother is driving this guy crazy by constantly insisting that he's a chicken. Psychiatrist asks if the patient has thought of sitting down with his brother and trying gently to convince him that he's *not* a chicken. Guy says, "I can't do that. I need the eggs."

"I need the yield" is the financial equivalent of "I need the eggs." It says, in effect, "There is a good and compelling and ultimately decisive reason for me to cling to an investment strategy which all my life experience tells me is insane." (We don't go out anymore, and I had to sell my boat, and my 10-year-old car has bald tires I can't afford to replace, and I'm looking into taking a job at McDonald's...but at least our investments are safe, and besides, I need the yield. *Dingalingalingaling!*)

The current cash distribution of an asset expressed as a percentage of its price — its *current yield*, in other words — is arguably the dumbest method ever devised to analyze and compare investments. If current yield were the determining factor, everyone would own bonds and no one would own stocks. And they'd all be right, because bonds would return more than stocks...*which is the opposite of reality.* Am I getting through to you on this?

Using current yield as a key (never mind *the* key) investment criterion will cause you to prefer asset classes with lower long-term total returns, and to shun asset classes with higher long-term total returns. There is a word which, however colloquially, describes the process of avoiding higher long-term total returns in order to secure lower long-term total returns. This word is *crazy*. Investing primarily for high current yield is...*crazy*. Believe me, brother — even if you can't understand me yet — *you don't need the eggs.*

The 75-year average total return of large-company common stocks (denominated, in modern times, as the S&P 500) is, as we've had many occasions to observe, 11%. About three percent of the total return of 11% has been contributed by the cash dividends, and the other eight percent by long-term capital appreciation. The average total return for high quality corporate bonds during the same period has been a bit less than six percent — virtually all of which has come from current interest payments, because bond prices neither appreciate nor depreciate in the long run: they finish up right about where they started out. That's what bonds are for.

Stocks, in other words, have had about half the current cash return of bonds, and about twice the total return. The converse is also true, but let's spell it out just the same: bonds have produced around twice the current cash return of stocks, and about half the total return. Without in any way trying to predict what these relationships might be in the *next* 75 years, we may at least observe that **an asset class's current cash return and its long-term total return are inversely related.**

And this is critical, because *the one and only rational test of an investment's income-producing capacity is its total return.* If a bond's total return over some period of time is six percent a year, all of which is current interest, I can withdraw up to six percent a year without invading my original principal. If a stock's return over the same period is a combination of three percent in dividends and eight percent appreciation, *I can withdraw up to 11% a year without invading my original principal.* So if I decided that my current income needs in retirement were, let's say, six percent of my capital, I'd have to ask myself just one question: *do I feel lucky?* (Well, *do* ya, punk?) No, no; wait. Sorry; wrong movie.

The one question — although it's a two-part question — that a rational investor seeking six percent current income should ask is, of course:

> Do I want to try to recover six percent a year from
> an asset class whose total return has historically
> been six percent a year? Or do I want to try to
> recover six percent a year from an asset class whose
> total return has historically been 11% a year?

The investor who equates income with current yield doesn't merely ignore appreciation; he assumes that it isn't there. That is, he unconsciously holds all asset values constant over time, which is — forgive me, but I still can't think of a more accurately descriptive word for it — *crazy.* It's the same as looking at the well in your backyard, and saying: I can safely draw out only the water that got into the well from snowfall. If I try to draw out the water from rainfall, I risk depleting the well to the point of its running dry.

Snowfall, rainfall; it's all water once it gets into the well. And as long as you're drawing out less water than nature puts in, you'll be fine.

If your plan is to take six percent income from an asset class whose total return has been six percent (let's call this asset class "bonds"), you'll tend to find the landscape all around you littered with rocks and hard places:

(1) You have no margin for error of any kind.

(2) You'd better pray that inflation doesn't raise your cost of living anytime soon, because your income is capped, at least until your current bond portfolio starts to mature and you can reinvest at higher rates.

(3) While you're at it, better pray that inflation doesn't *fall* much, either. Because your interest income will eventually follow inflation down, but your living costs will, at best, just level off. Even zero inflation isn't deflation, and I've got *no* picture of the Postal Service *lowering* the price of stamps.

If, on the other hand, you thought you'd try getting six percent a year from an asset class whose total return has been 11% (let's call it "stocks"), you'd find yourself virtually besieged by elegant outcomes:

(1) You have a very large going-in margin for error/ margin of safety.

(2) Your dividend income can (and will) continue to grow over time as good companies go on raising their dividends.

(3) The balance of your total return — historically, the remaining five percent or so a year — can be left to compound, allowing you to (a) increase your withdrawals later on as inflation warrants and/or (b) grow your heirs' patrimony.

Of course, there are going to be years — one in five, historically —

where it never rains, and it never snows...and in which you still get just about as thirsty, just about as often, as you usually do. In bear markets, your "water table" will be falling, and you'll deplete it even further with your regular withdrawals. Mightn't this cause you to run out of money (by both definitions)?

The short answer is: yes, it might. Never say never, (a) because you can't be sure it's true, and (b) because doing so puts you, albeit by default, in the position of guaranteeing something, which the New Financial Advisor's principles forbid her ever to do. But although you can't eliminate the risk of the well running dry, you *can* reduce it to the point where an educable household/family will accept it as a risk worth booking...particularly when they consider the alternative: bonds. You do this in two complementary ways:

- *Limit your withdrawal rate to a maximum of six percent a year.* From the end of WWII to the present, there's no entry point in the S&P 500 where six percent would have tapped you out; the same can't be said for seven percent. There are, of course, particular mutual funds that couldn't stand up to six percent, just as there are more than a few that could have handled seven percent. But in terms of a credible average, six percent — while still no guarantee — has a lot of torque.

- *Lay in a couple of years' supply of bottled water.* If, with respect to systematic withdrawal from equities, six percent has functioned in the nature of a belt, two years' living expenses in a money market fund may be regarded as a pair of suspenders. When, in response to financial constraint or psychological need — or both — you're able simply to shut your withdrawal program down for a while, you hugely

increase your chances of survival...financial, or psychological, or both. On balance, this is more an
anxiety management device than an essential ele-
ment of financial strategy. And predictability —
knowing what's going to happen, not getting surprised — is the key to managing anxiety. So your
clients should know exactly where (down 20%, or
25%, or whatever) or when (if the account is still
making new lows a year after the previous peak, for
example), the withdrawal program will "automatically" shut down. Equally important, establish a pre-
arranged signal that will "officially" mark the passing of the crisis and the resumption of withdrawals
(50% recovery from the trough, six months without
a new low in the market, or some other objective
signal that seems both comfortable and reasonable).

When all is said and done, as in every other aspect of Doctor Noah's
client relationships, the folks who make it onto The Ark will trust in the
concept of systematic withdrawal about as wholeheartedly as you do...and
no more. (When you believe, you'll be believed.) Moreover, although the
passengers should ideally have blind, untutored faith in you, your own
faith *that* systematic withdrawal works will have to be grounded in a firm
understanding of *how* it works. There's nothing riding on systematic withdrawal except whether or not your clients run out of money in retirement,
and whether or not they can endow their children and grandchildren. So you
have my permission to invest some significant time and energy making absolutely sure you understand it, believe it, and can clearly (and warmly) explain
it. To that end, let's take a hard look at one real-life example.

Massachusetts Investors Trust (MIT) is America's very first mutual
fund; it was started in 1924 by the company now called MFS, and its
investment objective is reasonable current income and long-term growth

of capital. Since the end of World War II, the absolute worst time you could have started a systematic withdrawal plan from MIT was right at the beginning of 1973 — the cusp of the longest, deepest bear market *by far* in this period (and the second worst, after 1929-32, in the twentieth century).

In this illustration, you put one million dollars in MIT on the first of January 1973, and then — with the market already dropping like a stone, as you can see — withdrew your six percent, or $60,000, at year-end. Each year-end thereafter, you increased your withdrawal three

Period End	Invest	Withdraw	Income	Capital Gains	Reinvest	Market Value
01/01/73	$1,000,000	$0	$0	$0	$0	$1,000,000
12/31/73		$60,000	$30,480	$12,042	$42,522	$814,235
12/31/74		$61,800	$31,217	$0	$31,217	$542,817
12/31/75		$63,654	$26,367	$12,461	$38,828	$658,643
12/31/76		$65,564	$25,081	$15,428	$40,510	$749,015
12/31/77		$67,531	$28,291	$10,779	$39,071	$599,054
12/31/78		$69,556	$28,950	$10,309	$39,259	$578,593
12/31/79		$71,643	$31,035	$20,830	$51,865	$634,853
12/31/80		$73,792	$33,130	$52,262	$85,392	$754,417
12/31/81		$76,006	$34,895	$52,318	$87,213	$641,556
12/31/82		$78,286	$34,724	$58,910	$93,634	$684,479
12/31/83		$80,635	$29,300	$80,774	$110,074	$746,788
12/31/84		$83,054	$30,126	$29,837	$59,963	$685,660
12/31/85		$85,546	$29,239	$70,056	$99,295	$768,518
12/31/86		$88,112	$25,638	$113,466	$139,105	$812,656
12/31/87		$90,755	$26,811	$95,084	$121,895	$782,540
12/31/88		$93,478	$27,445	$57,548	$84,993	$770,311
12/31/89		$96,282	$31,452	$86,215	$117,666	$952,279
12/31/90		$99,171	$30,229	$59,203	$89,432	$852,168
12/31/91		$102,146	$27,178	$95,886	$123,064	$985,800
12/31/92		$105,210	$24,396	$161,742	$186,138	$953,382
12/31/93		$108,367	$30,246	$131,096	$161,342	$940,620
12/31/94		$111,618	$20,278	$88,823	$109,101	$819,421
12/31/95		$114,966	$38,115	$67,946	$106,062	$1,026,839
12/31/96		$118,415	$16,553	$108,134	$124,687	$1,174,364
12/31/97		$121,968	$18,630	$100,408	$119,038	$1,424,572
12/31/98		$125,627	$13,029	$86,716	$99,745	$1,625,891
12/31/99		$129,395	$7,939	$46,798	$54,737	$1,609,584
12/31/00		$133,277	$2,787	$63,271	$66,057	$1,470,818
TOTAL	$1,000,000	$2,575,855	$733,561	$1,788,342	$2,521,903	

Total ending amount: $1,470,818 Copyright© 1993-2000 by Wiesenberger®, a Thomson Financial Co.

percent to combat inflation. Meanwhile, whenever the fund made income or capital gains distributions to shareholders, you reinvested them.

You paid no sales charge on your million dollar investment (as you wouldn't today), nor any charge to make withdrawals. MFS currently pays its dealers a 35-basis-point trail, so that's been applied each year in this illustration. You're assumed to have paid taxes out of your withdrawals and/or from another source.

Get a load of your account value at year-end 1974, right after you made that year's withdrawal (and just three weeks or so after the market made its historic bottom, as we saw on page 170). That's right: $542,817, or roughly a 46% decline in your original investment. *But that was the worst of it.*

By 1990, your withdrawals neared $100,000 a year, even though your capital was still below the original million. At year-end 2000, halfway through the deepest bear market in 13 years (and the longest since 1973-74), you took over $133,000 from an investment that was still worth almost half again what you paid for it. (And can you even imagine where you'd be if you'd shut down your withdrawal program when your capital had declined 20% or 25%, and lived off your cash reserve for even a year? Or if you'd started this program in 1975 instead of 1973?)

Please understand that I'm not making any representation about the future performance of Massachusetts Investors Trust, the equity market, or anything else. Past performance is no guarantee of future results, and it may not even be an indication. I'm not saying that this is the worst that *can* happen, but merely that this is the worst that *did* happen, in this fund during this period.

I simply ask two unrelated but critically important questions. (1) What are the chances of starting a systematic withdrawal program within a few trading days of the biggest bear market in half a century? (2) Can you imagine a bond-based strategy in which you would have more than doubled your income in a similar length of time?

IN SUMMARY

- Americans wildly overestimate the long-term risk of holding equities — which is historically nonexistent — and totally underestimate the long-term risk of *not* holding them — which is historically fatal.

- In a properly diversified portfolio, the only way to turn temporary decline into permanent loss is precipitously to withdraw the capital, either due to poor planning or to panic.

- The only sane long-term definition of "money" isn't currency but **purchasing power.** Those investments are "safe" which accrete purchasing power, even after the current dividend income is spent. Those investments are "risky" which deplete purchasing power, especially after the current interest income is spent. "The safest long-term investment for the preservation of purchasing power has clearly been stocks, not bonds" — Jeremy Siegel.

- The price of a postage stamp has risen three and a half times since 1975; interest rates since then have meaningfully declined. Meanwhile, the dividend of the S&P 500 is up about four and a half times; the index itself — even after the worst bear market in nearly 30 years — is up about 10 times. The next quarter century won't be exactly like the last — but can you seriously think it'll be the *opposite?*

- Current yield is no way to judge an asset class; long-term total return is. The two are inversely related.

- The investor needing current income is best advised, on the evidence of the last three quarters of a century, to ask one question:

  > Do I want to try to recover six percent a year from an asset class whose total return has historically been six percent a year? Or do I want to try to recover six percent a year from an asset class whose total return has historically been 11% a year?

- Snowfall, rainfall: *it's all water.*

- Best to keep a couple of years' income in cash equivalents when you're doing systematic withdrawal, primarily as an anxiety management device. Pre-establish, and communicate clearly to clients, where systematic withdrawal will shut off automatically, and where it will turn on again.

- Clients will believe in systematic withdrawal about as much as you do — and no more. But you also have to understand it, right down to the ground. If Doctor Noah loses *his* nerve in a typhoon, *everybody* drowns.

- If they don't believe in systematic withdrawal, they probably don't believe in equities to begin with. If they don't believe in equities, they don't believe in you. Leave 'em ashore.

Doctor Noah's Fee, and What It Pays For

chapter eight

EIGHT

———————●———————

You'll have inferred from the two foregoing chapters that the huge preponderance of one's lifetime (and even of one's family's multigenerational) investment returns flow from one critical, binary decision — and from two corollary, behavioral decisions.

Realizing this, you may wish to pause here, take several deep breaths, and marvel at the liberating possibility that successful investing may be as simple as that: one threshold either/or decision, and two subsidiary do/don't decisions. Moreover, these three commitments, once made, need never be revisited: decide them once — correctly — and you not only don't have to decide them again, *you never have to think about them again.*

Virtually all other decisions that must be made in the context of a long-term/multigenerational financial plan are refinements. After a third of a century of studying the behavior of investments and — infinitely more important — the behavior of investors, I conclude that the three key decisions we've already made (however implicitly) govern around 85% of one's total long-term return.

A fourth decision, which we will consider shortly, accounts for upwards of another 10% of total return, and everything else — mutual funds vs. "wrap" accounts; indexing vs. active management; unit trusts vs. sector funds; the role of alternative investments such as hedge funds, managed futures and real estate; and all similar mechanical noise — everything else, soaking wet, *might* be the other five percent.

The threshold decision — binary in that it admits of only two choices — is, of course, **stocks/bonds.** If the last 200 years (and especially the last 75) aren't a fluke, there is good reason to think that an owner's real long-term return may exceed a loaner's by an order of magnitude...or more. Add to this (or turn it around into) the fact of equities' great incremental *safety* — in the only terms that matter: **purchasing power** — and it's clear that stocks/bonds is the governing, hugely preponderant variable in long-term return.

I place the next two behavioral decisions one full step below the threshold, but in positions of equal importance to each other. And even they are binary in their way, so that the decision-making process isn't at all complicated. They are to seek no timing advantage against the market, and never to abandon one's long-term equity investments because of *any* combination of temporarily negative economic/market circumstances. (And you may take the phrase "temporarily negative" to be the redundancy that it surely is.)

I'll identify these behavioral laws by their rightful, colloquial names: **don't try to time the market** and **don't panic.**

(Moreover, never let anyone tell you that he's not panicking, but rather protecting his capital until "this terrible crisis" passes. *He's panicking.* And if they get out, they either never get back in, or they get back in very late, and chase whatever's then currently hot, trying to make up for lost time — which just sets up the *next* panic cycle.)

The fourth decision, in turn, is one full step below the two golden "don'ts" that amplify and support the threshold issue. It is the decision to diversify your equity portfolio, by any or all of management style, capitalization and geography.

We know that growth and value tend to run on different cycles — if not downright countercyclically — and end up producing about the same long-term return. Big-cap and small-cap also like to run counter to each other, with small-cap outperforming big-cap by about 15% a year over the last 75 years. This is only as it should be, since small-cap is *both* more volatile *and* genuinely riskier, because more small-cap companies end up becoming genuinely worthless, as you'd expect. (That said, the small-cap premium seems to have compressed somewhat over the last few years; it used to be closer to 20%. I have no idea whether this phenomenon is cyclical or secular, but I felt it shouldn't pass without mention.)

Finally, although this too bears watching, foreign economies and their stock markets have in the past run on meaningfully different cycles from those of the U.S., effectively diversifying a preponderantly American portfolio.

Granted, in the industrialized world, the advance of globalization may work to homogenize the economies — and the cycles — of the major trading nations. We may never march in lock step, but the disparities between the U.S. and Euroland, for example, will probably continue to blur. And I'm not convinced that economic reality observes quite the same distinctions as do mutual fund classification systems. Is Atlanta-based Coca-Cola, which books most of its revenues and even more of its profits overseas, a U.S. equity or a global equity? How about DaimlerChrysler?

It's in the emerging markets, I believe, that really meaningful international diversification is still available — as are premium returns (with concomitant volatility *and* risk). And in multigenerational portfolios, the potential benefits of very high long-term development rates in those areas of the world should be of major interest — and not just (or even mostly) for reasons of diversification.

What diversification *cannot* do is produce higher returns than the weighted average returns of a portfolio's components. (This may seem obvious, but so does the fact that you can't turn lead into gold. Didn't stop a lot of really smart people from trying.) What diversification can (and will) do — because the portfolio components are running on so many different cycles — is to depress the overall volatility of the portfolio, producing a pattern of lower highs and higher lows *around the same trendline*. That is, you get the full, undiluted, long-term equity return of the portfolio's weighted average composition. But along the way, the disparate cycles of the different components exert some not inconsiderable smoothing effect on the peaks and valleys. This juxtaposition — the full return of the component equities without the full volatility — adds up, I'm reliably informed by people who care about such things, to a higher risk-adjusted rate of return...whatever the hell that is. (May God strike me dead — or at least force me to read the last six Tom Clancy novels while flying coach in a middle seat — if I ever say "higher risk-adjusted rate of return" to a poor, defenseless American family.)

In the real world, diversification is there to keep people from overconcentrating their portfolios in a mania, and getting wiped out in the subsequent crash. Simple as that. A well-diversified portfolio will not go up as much as will whatever sector of the market is the fad, craze or mania *du jour*. And it won't set a household/family's financial plan back 10 years when the bubble bursts, either.

The tech mania/dot.com bubble of 1999-2000, and the spectacular crash that followed, is merely one classic example. In 1999, the Nasdaq went up more than four times as much as the S&P 500. In 2000, the Nasdaq went down *more than four times as much as the S&P 500.* And neither of these statistics begins to capture the euphoria/terror cycle of dot.com — the tulipmania of the new millennium. (Indeed, when the stock market capitalization of an online travel agency exceeded those of the three largest U.S. airlines *combined*, the tulips started to make a lot of sense.)

An epic financial mania like dot.com doesn't come along every day — but it's no rarity, either. All revolutionary new technologies spawn investment bubbles; the Internet was actually the fifth in the twentieth century, after automobiles, airplanes, radio and television. There were also, in living memory, financial "engineering" bubbles like the conglomerates of the go-go 1960s, and the junk bond/leveraged buyout craze of the 1980s. One or another emerging market regularly serves as a sinkhole of speculative excess. And once in a while, mass hysteria even transmogrifies a commodity business into an illusory growth industry — look at oil in the late 1970s. There's almost always something on which to speculate — i.e. into which to underdiversify.

If you really understand the harmlessness of equity volatility — and especially if you're a long-term accumulator, consciously or unconsciously dollar-cost averaging by regularly funding your 401(k) or paying your variable universal life premiums — you may not need diversification that much. You may, quite rationally, take all the volatility you can get. Moreover, if you're immune to the speculative urge — if you never feel a compulsion to bet the ranch on some wonderful "new era" — diversification's antic charm may be lost on you. For the rest of us mortals, it's the fourth major arrow in our equity quiver, and the completion of as much as 95% of our total lifetime portfolio return.

As a quick reference guide to this chapter so far, I illustrate it as follows. (Remember that I said the four rules form a three-level hierarchy.)

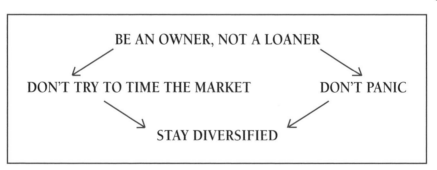

Everything else is commentary. Everything else is a refinement. Almost everything else is noise. And we will get to everything else in a few minutes. But right now, I'd like to suggest that you create, and carry with you everywhere you go, a sort of instant memory jogger, perspective restorer and anxiety buster.

There's an old story told about a humble cabin boy who rose, over a 50-year career at sea, to be the admiral of a great navy. When he retired, his successor opened his safe, and found that the old salt had left behind one small, yellowed scrap of parchment. On it was written, "Port, left. Starboard, right." We're about to formulate a similar document, which they'll find in your desk when you retire after 50 glorious years as Doctor Noah. And remember, now: this is for you, not for your clients, who wouldn't understand it (and whom your compliance cops will never let see it, even it they could).

(1) Get a 3x5 card.

(2) In the middle of one side, affix a beautiful new 1975 Apollo Soyuz 10-cent stamp.

(3) Over the stamp, print the question, "How are you defining 'risk'?" Below the stamp, print "How are you defining 'safety'?"

(4) On the other side of the card, print the three-line, four-rule hierarchy from page 221, complete with arrows.

(5) Get it laminated.

(6) Read both sides aloud to yourself at least twice a day, before you begin work and before you go home. A day may come when doing this saves your career.

We said that the first three issues in this hierarchy each required only one decision per lifetime (yes, I'll always own instead of loaning: no, I'll never panic, etc.) Diversification isn't so simple. There are infinite permutations of an intelligently diversified equity portfolio, none of which can be proven prospectively to be superior to another. Moreover, managers will move on, retire and even die, forcing you to reassess, and perhaps to change, portfolio components. What does a properly diversified portfolio look like? How often and/or why do you change it? These are bottomless questions, and are also a source of potential conflict between advisor and client through the years, unless everybody gets on — and stays on — the same page right from the outset. Herewith, an attempt to write that page:

(1) THE OVERALL PORTFOLIO WILL BE MADE UP OF MANAGED/ POOLED SUB-PORTFOLIOS, NOT OF INDIVIDUAL STOCKS.

This should go without saying, but rarely does. The New Financial Advisor must never be involved directly in stocks, but use managed and/or pooled portfolios — mutual funds, individually managed ("wrap") accounts, the sub-accounts of variable annuities and variable life, etc.

(If a prospective client tries to bring you a portfolio of stocks, politely decline to accept it, on the basis that you would not be able intelligently to manage stocks you know nothing about in a market you don't follow. Same with a hodgepodge of old mutual funds, which at least may have the benefit of having been taxed as they went along. In any event, offer to sell the portfolio out with no — or the minimum — charge, or invite the client to do so himself. *Only cash gets on The Ark.*)

Put all theological issues of portfolio construction (passive/active, fund/"wrap") aside for a moment, and see this defining issue for what it is. **Doctor Noah doesn't manage money. She manages people.** No one can do both supremely well. And since investor behavior is infinitely more important than investment performance, it just makes sense that the captain of The Ark would devote herself entirely to the higher function, and leave the lesser one to subordinates — portfolio managers — or to the markets themselves via indexing.

(2) DON'T OVERDIVERSIFY. DON'T UNDERDIVERSIFY.

Five accounts, each of which is pulling fairly hard against at least one other, should be plenty. Much beyond that, you're not an investor, you're a collector. (And what you really own is one big, expensive, inefficient index fund.) A nice, serviceable portfolio might start out with 20% of the assets in each of:

Big-cap growth	Big-cap value
Small-cap growth	Small-cap value
International/emerging markets	

I deliberately fudged the last category, for the reasons cited above. Have some tolerance for ambiguity, for heaven's sake; make a decision. It's your Ark.

(3) ALL INDEXES ARE NOT CREATED EQUAL.

In the first quarter of 1998, if you can believe it, 76% of *all* net equity fund inflows reported by the Investment Company Institute went into index funds. How much money must pour into an index until it becomes truly representative of nothing at all — until it's just 500 (or whatever) grotesquely overbought, hideously overvalued stocks that are virtually guaranteed to underperform as a group over the next block of time? (Never mind; ignore that question. I apologize. It's just that the whole issue of portfolio management, which accounts on its very best day for maybe five percent of anyone's real-life total return, bores me so utterly to distraction that I'm liable to go off on tangents.) In the first quarter of 1999 — as the performance maniacs, who had so recently sworn eternal fealty to indexing, flitted off to chase dot.com — *only six percent of net equity inflows indexed.*

This vignette would probably be awfully funny if it weren't so awfully true. I report it to you only (a) as a form of therapy and (b) to suggest, however anecdotally, that indexing — like The Shadow of old radio days — has the power to cloud men's minds. Investors and advisors alike, albeit for different reasons, have trouble seeing the indexing issue clearly. Let me therefore take a whack — one man's whack, which doesn't presume to be definitive — at framing the issue correctly, so that you can arrive at your own conclusion.

Indexing holds that stock prices are so efficient — the information so copious and complete, the analysis of that information by thousands of smart people so ferocious and relentless — that an active manager can't consistently find enough mispriced equity to overcome the costs of active management which his investors must bear. (Note that indexing is fundamentally an issue of *cost*, then, rather than some abstraction about right and wrong.)

An index, mathematically, will perform as well as the average dollar invested anywhere in it. But if that average dollar is laboring under a couple of percentage points of management costs, then the index must far outperform the average of the money invested in it. This doesn't suggest that no active manager can outperform. But, because *there is no statistical evidence for the persistence of performance* — and mark you, gentle reader, there surely isn't — indexers simply say that the prospective overperformers can't be systematically identified in advance. So, since the index return has historically been more than sufficient to build and maintain anyone's fortune, best to relax and just let the index happen to you.

I guess my problem with indexing is its spoken or unspoken assumption that it is equally valid, in some linear way, for any and all markets. This is not merely wrong, but counterintuitive.

The indexing argument is as right *as it gets* in the S&P 500, surely the most transparent companies in the most transparent market in the most transparent economy in the world. (The foregoing is not the same as saying it's right, period. I take no position in the matter, at least for the moment.) But can you suppose it equally — or even remotely as — true in, say, the Russell 2000: a huge pool of small, funky, spottily researched, haphazardly traded companies, the completeness of whose disclosure is not something to which a reasonable observer would stipulate? Might not an active manager select against *that* index with incrementally greater hope of success?

And what of the shooting-star technologies (not to mention the wildly uneven capitalization and management depths) of the Nasdaq 100? And above all, what of the emerging markets, where inexpert, distracted and sometimes corrupted government regulation, shallow and chaotic markets, idiosyncratic accounting conventions and managements with their own singular approaches to reporting the truth combine quite often to create the very antithesis of transparency?

My bottom line is that I think indexing has been academically over-sold, and that the further you get from the S&P 500, the more ragged the index argument gets. There are, finally, indexes and indexes. (Nor are all funds in the same index created equal: costs vary widely, and in indexing, costs are *the* issue.)

You want to use an S&P 500 index fund as the core holding in a diversified equity portfolio? I won't try to stop you. You want to index *all the way across the board?* I incline to the belief that you're potentially leaving a lot of money — even net of management costs — on the table.

Of course, the real reason advisors were frightened of index funds in the bad old commission-driven days was the belief that, if investors could consistently outperform most managers by indexing, they didn't need an advisor. The tragic flaw implicit in this reasoning is the assumption that investment performance governs real-life return. Of course, it doesn't: investor behavior does, and an advisor is first and foremost a behavior modifier. Is anyone less likely to panic out of an index fund in a major market crash than out of a managed fund? Of course not. So, since Doctor Noah's asset-based advisory fee is compensation for helping clients avoid The Big Mistake, it is charged — as we'll shortly see — on active and passive funds alike, with no distinction.

(4) CHOOSE ACTIVE MANAGERS ON THE BASIS OF CHARACTER.

Huh? *Character?* (What about "performance"? What about *stars*?) Yes, this is the kind of admonition which probably gives students of post-modern portfolio theory the vapors, but hear me out. If you're committed to the essential logic of equity diversification — the full long-term return with somewhat smoothed, multi-cycle volatility along the way — what you ask from any one manager isn't so much genius as it is *discipline.*

The enemy of diversification isn't "underperformance," whatever that means. (At any given time, in a diversified portfolio, a couple of things should *always* be underperforming, and a couple of others overperforming. *That's how you know diversification is working.*) No, the enemy of diversification is *style drift:* suddenly, *three* of your five accounts have huge positions in Microsoft, after Judge Jackson whacks them upside the head and the stock gets killed. And butter wouldn't melt in your value managers' mouths: they claim that Microsoft, with its $26 billion in cash, is a value stock at this point, when you and they know they're just trying to find a way to climb on the tech bandwagon without getting caught. *Style drift.*

So how else do you pick active managers for a diversified portfolio? (A) Well, even I would like to see that they've done better than the average of their peers for some meaningful period of time — say 10 years. And (B) as the former point implies, I'd rather they had been managing money for quite a while, and had some real combat experience. (C) Finally, as a long-term investor, I have an emotional bias toward managers who are also long-term investors. So I tend to set great store by low turnover. Buffett's dictum, "Our favorite holding period is forever," strikes a deep chord in me — and I don't mind the lower expense ratios, either. (Just don't make a religion out of this *or any* one variable, OK?)

Go to your screens. Crank up that Principia thing, whatever it is. If you believe in your firm, be guided to some significant extent by their select list. (If you don't believe in your firm, ask yourself why you're there.) Just don't make yourself nuts over this issue. There's no statistical evidence for the persistence of performance (which doesn't mean you and your firm can't identify long-term superior managers), and we're only talking about five percent of a real family's real-life return here, right? *Don't make yourself nuts.* Nobody ever ran out of money in retirement, or didn't run out of money in retirement, because of which small-cap value manager he picked. Manager selection can just never be the critical — or even *a* critical — issue, compared to the much larger questions of investor behavior.

(5) REBALANCE STATIC PORTFOLIOS — THOSE WITHOUT NEW MONEY COMING IN — ANNUALLY. PORTFOLIOS TO WHICH AC-

CUMULATORS REGULARLY CONTRIBUTE ARE, THROUGH THE GE-
NIUS OF DOLLAR-COST AVERAGING, REBALANCING THEMSELVES.

Blinding glimpse of the obvious: if you're truly committed to maintaining a diversification discipline, come back to your original formula
(five accounts at 20% each or whatever) once a year — at the same time
each year. (Otherwise, even if you don't admit it to yourself, you're market-timing.)

When money is still flowing regularly into the portfolio, rebalancing isn't necessary because dollar-cost averaging is already doing it, and to
a fare-thee-well. DCA is buying barrelsful of low-priced shares in your
"underperforming" sectors — before the sale ends — and thimblesful of
your "overperforming" ones. So the whole account is marching back toward its original formation without you having to do anything about it.

This is yet another reason — if one were still needed — why the
New Financial Advisor (fee-based, so there's zero incentive to make gratuitous portfolio adjustments) steadfastly but politely resists his clients'
suggestion that they sell out of their "underperforming" (read: underval-
ued) funds and chuck the money into their "overperforming" (read: overvalued) ones. Especially when DCA is doing its glorious work, *nothing is
almost always the right thing to do.* Which brings us to:

(6) CHANGE YOUR LONG-TERM DIVERSIFIED PORTFOLIOS AS
LITTLE AS IS HUMANLY POSSIBLE.

On Day One, tell your new clients that these five funds/accounts
are intended to go into their estates. *That* ought to get their attention.
(Yours, too.) Train them, in other words — right from the get-go — not
to expect (or demand) any but the rarest, most infrequent portfolio tweaking. This will go against all their instincts — which should tell you that it
must be the right thing to do (or, more accurately, *not* do).

No one will ever turn up in Doctor Noah's cabin demanding to
change his long-term care insurance. But someone will show up *nearly
every day* wanting to change his investment portfolio...and, not only that,

having a very specific idea *how* he wants it changed (sell value and buy tech, March 2000; sell everything and buy T-bills, September 2001). This is one of the classic American delusions: that, from reading magazines and watching CNBC, someone would be equipped to advise his own professional advisor about portfolio changes. It's right up there with the fact that, in survey after survey, 90% of all Americans rate themselves above-average drivers.

Hear me, ladies and gentlemen, as I offer you one of the great laws in investing — indeed, perhaps the $e=mc^2$ of portfolio management:

PORTFOLIO TURNOVER CORRELATES
NEGATIVELY WITH RETURN.

The more often you change your portfolio, trying to leap out of the way of something "bad," or into the path of something "good," the wronger you will be, and the more inexorably you will grind down your long-term return. Unless and until the client's goals change, nothing is virtually always the right thing — albeit the hardest thing — to do. *Tweaking is hazardous to your wealth.* Stand by your plan.

Yes, but what if a manager leaves, or retires, or dies? Then, make a decision. Consult the old manager, if she's still around. Consult the new manager. Consult your firm. Consult your heart. Then: make a decision. That's what you're good at. That's what you get paid for. That's what the folks are relying on you to do. You want me to tell you there's some statistical rule, here? You want me to tell you that you're predictably, reliably better off either moving or staying, whenever the issue is forced upon you? OK, here's the rule. (You may not immediately see how this rule solves your problem, but I promise that if you fast and meditate on it for three days and nights, the answer will come to you in a vision.) This rule was formulated by the greatest of all American Zen masters, the late, lamented Charles Dillon Stengel. The master said:

"Good pitching always beats good hitting.

And vice versa."

Are we just about done, here? Can we *please* stop talking about the thing that produces five percent of a household/family's total long-term real-life return, but into which people — clients and advisors alike — often put up to 95% of their time and energy?

Look: portfolio management is certainly a potentially interesting subject. And if it were at all scientific (i.e. if you could reliably predict *any* performance, absolute or relative), or if it were at all decisive (i.e. if the clients' success were actually driven by investment performance rather than by investor behavior), it might be a useful field of study for Doctor Noah. Since it is *neither* scientific *nor* decisive, portfolio management may not be a good use of too much of your time. (And to me, I confess, it's just narcoleptic, navel-gazing necromancy.)

I'm not sure how much the U.S. Marines need to study foreign policy. I think they would tell you that their job is, whenever the President tells 'em to saddle up and ride, to saddle up and ride. And so it is, after a fashion, with the New Financial Advisor. Since 100% of a family's financial planning success, and 95% of its investment success, are behavioral, I can't help but wonder if portfolio management isn't the tail, trying (and failing) to wag the dog.

That about covers what we can and can't know — and therefore can and can't control — about the behavior of a diversified equity investment portfolio in the context of a comprehensive financial plan. We can neither know nor control much about the behavior of investments, which is OK, because that turns out not to matter much. But we can control almost all of our total lifetime return through four decisions: stocks not bonds; don't try to time markets; don't panic; diversify and stay that way. Thus, this chapter so far has been an analysis of *what the fee-based New Financial Advisor **doesn't** get paid for.*

You are not paid by your clients to be "right" about the markets, nor to move your clients in and out. These are not only things you cannot do, but things which you believe it is terribly self-destructive even to attempt. You are not paid to anticipate the course of the economy, nor of interest rates, which you are quite sure no one can reliably do. You are not paid to move money from one sector of the market to another, as the former flames out and the latter gets ready to run — also quite impossible on a consistent basis. Finally, you are not paid to predict which mutual funds will "outperform" most other similar mutual funds, particularly over periods of the next year or two — again, something no one can do.

Once the greatest hurdle has been surmounted, then — once a plan is actually in place — what and how is the New Financial Advisor paid? And, most particularly — in view of the above litany of things clients pressingly want done and which the advisor refuses even to consider — what on earth is the advisor paid *for?*

(No, you didn't miss anything; we have *not* yet spoken about presenting the finished plan, answering questions/objections about it, and then keeping the plan in good repair while keeping the clients posted. We're coming to all those things. But *putting* the plan in place is the smallest part of what we do, and — absent insurance commissions and/or a fee for the plan itself — represents to the fee-based advisor little or no significant revenue. I'm just trying to complete the thought we've been unfolding for the last two-and-a-half chapters: *what is the nature of fee-based investment advice,* and what exactly does the client get for what he is asked to pay, year after year?)

Assume you took all the insurance commissions, any fee-for-service on the creation of the plan, and an ongoing investment advisory fee to your practice, put 'em all in a blender, and amortized them over the term of your relationship with the client household/family. Now assume that that number comes out to about one percent per year of the assets under management, over and above things like fees and expenses of the money managers and whatever third-party advice/service providers *aren't you.*

Now, for simplicity's and clarity's sake, forget about the components of the one percent — forget about where it's coming from — just assume that, at the end of the day, *your personal advice costs the clients one percent of their assets under your stewardship.* (I think that's about where everything's going to end up, at some point. Even life insurance commissions, I'd guess, will tend to levelize and become much more fee-like.) The questions then become:

(1) what does the client household/family actually get for that one percent a year, and

(2) would a reasonable person conclude that what he/she/they got in return for the one percent was worth at least that much, and more?

These may not seem like particularly *easy* questions to answer, but at least they're essentially *simple.* They frame the central issue in a potentially very useful way. I think the best of us advisors feel that our value is an absurdly — perhaps even unfairly — large multiple of our price. ("One percent?! They should be naming their *grandchildren* after me!") But we also know that we live in a no-load culture, deeply suspicious of our motives, let alone our cost. And in that media-driven culture, two stockbrokers who churn 40 greedy people into the ground trading margined dot.com stocks will merit a 4,000-word feature article in the Sunday New York *Times.* While some God-fearing, Cub Scout-leading, wife-loving, kid-nurturing planner out in Ames, Iowa — who's quietly turning a hundred families into multigenerational millionaires — will get his name in the local paper once: when he dies. That's not fair, but it is the way things are, and we're well-advised to deal with life on life's terms. (Besides, if life were fair, no prospect would ever say "no" to the likes of you and me.)

However, I would ask, in fairness, to be allowed to turn the above two questions around on my prospects, and effectively to answer those questions by asking one of my own:

"Does it seem probable to you that, with all the resources of my firm behind me, I will

(a) cause your long-term investment return to be at least one percent per year more than you might obtain on your own, *and/or*

(b) save you at least one percent per year in the cost of mistakes I might be able to help you not make, *and/or*

(c) save you at least the equivalent of one percent per year in time, energy, worry and/or record-keeping?"

Please note that no one of those three services has to be worth one percent to the prospects all by itself. The question carefully — and quite correctly — asks if the prospects think that *any combination* of those three great gifts to a family's financial and emotional well-being would, in all probability, be worth more than our one percent annual fee. We know we're worth multiples of a point — just as the New York *Times* intuitively if not specifically knows about that guy out in Ames, and a thousand more like him. But it isn't nearly enough that we know: *they* have to know, *and they have to say that they know.*

• *ADDING ONE PERCENT:* Some poor guy who was born in 1943 (as I was) into a Depression-scarred household (as mine was), who has a wife who'll probably live to be 100 (as mine will), kids in their 20s and early 30s (as mine are) and grandchildren just now coming into the world (as, God be thanked, mine are), might be planning to retire at 62 — *and think he has (at this writing) a four-year investing time horizon!* He might *already* be 50% in bonds! Suppose, with the stamp and the quarter, you could get him back to 80/20 stocks/bonds, much less all-equity. Suppose you could get him to put the bottom 10%-15% of his portfolio in emerging markets — because, when his grand-daughter is the age he and I are now, China and India might be as developed as Europe is in our time. Do you doubt that *either* of those portfolio enhancements, let alone *both*, could fail to raise his lifetime return going forward by at least one percent per year?

- *SAVING ONE PERCENT IN MISTAKES NOT MADE:* Suppose all you were ever able to do was to stop that client from getting out of the market *just once* in fear of "a correction" that doesn't come for 2,000 more Dow points on the upside, while he waits in agony? Or suppose you prevented him from being bitten on the neck by *just one* of these other hydra-headed manifestations of The Big Mistake:

(1) *Panic.* As we've seen, this is the mechanism for turning temporary decline into permanent loss, because the client didn't have your faith in the future standing by to overcome his fear of the future. And if history is any guide, you'll save him and his family from fear not just once, *but one year in five.*

(2) *Euphoria/Overconfidence.* How many people not only got taken in by the tech mania "new era," but went in with the proceeds of a home equity loan? Couldn't happen on your watch, could it? What's *that* worth, even once in an investing lifetime?

(3) *Underdiversification:* How many people junked a diversified portfolio and bet the whole ranch on technology's sacred cow, Cisco Systems, just before it went down 80%? Would you have countenanced that?

(4) *Overdiversification.* How many people have picked up bits and pieces of 10 or 12 mutual funds in their IRA and/or 410(k), buying whatever was hot when they made each year's contribution? You'd have had them dollar-cost averaging into the same five funds...right?

(5) *Speculating instead of investing, and not knowing the difference.* How many people — with how much of their core capital — genuinely believed they were "investing in the growth of the Internet" by buying start-up dot.com IPOs with no earnings, no revenues, and business plans that sounded as if they'd been written by Hans Christian Andersen or the Brothers Grimm? When this garbage hit even

20% of the portfolio, you'd have sounded the alarm. And on *margin? Fahgeddaboudit!*

(6) *Investing for current yield instead of for total return.* The silent killer, slowly and quietly — and even peacefully — destroying the family's real wealth...until Doctor Noah arrives with the equity serum.

Please see that, if this is all your one percent bought the household/family — that is, a Big Mistake insurance policy, in the person of you — it would already be worth multiples of what they're paying. If investment success is overwhelmingly behavioral, so is investment failure, brought on by the very terrible, very human impulses that lead to one or another form — or, serially, to several different forms — of The Big Mistake. Technology didn't kill people in 2000-01; overconfidence/underdiversification/speculation did — and that toxic trifecta became even *more* lethal when funded with borrowed money. *Couldn't have happened on The Ark.*

- *SAVING ONE PERCENT IN TIME, ENERGY, WORRY, AND/OR RECORD-KEEPING*: What's the millionaire next door's time worth? If he had three extra hours a week that he wasn't putting into keeping track of his mutual funds, because Doctor Noah does that — and he invested that time in his business, or in teaching his granddaughter to fish — what might those hours yield him, financially and emotionally? Heck, any *one* of the four benefits in this question might be worth a point to the right person. And, especially on top of Big Mistake insurance, we're practically throwing them in.

I hope you'll feel that this wonderful three-part question ("Does it seem probable to you...") is the perfect statement of your value, your cost, and the enormous extent to which the former exceeds the latter. *It is also, of course, the ultimate disqualifier.* If there is one supremely reliable test of whether a prospect deserves admission to The Ark, this question is surely it. Were a prospect able to say "no" in answer to it, or even to express very serious reservations, you'd have both reason and cause to excuse yourself without further discussion. I say again: the faster you disqualify marginal-to-unsuitable prospects, the more time and energy you'll have to speak to *real* candidates, and the sooner you'll sell out The Ark. Cajoling prospects slowly back to sanity isn't in your job description, and it isn't something you or any of us are ever going to be good at. Leave them ashore. They need the eggs. *Next.*

This "What I'm worth/what I cost" interrogative statement — there are such things — is just one way of appreciating how much healthier a fee-based investment relationship (based on behavior modification) is, compared to the sad, tired, shabby old commission-based interaction (based on "performance"). But there are a couple of other important aspects of the fee-based arrangement that are also well worth mentioning.

(1) FEES PUT US, FINALLY AND FOREVER MORE, ON THE SAME SIDE OF THE TABLE AS OUR CLIENTS.

Once upon a time, if I recommended a stock to you, and you bought it, I'd have gotten a certain commission. If the stock went up 10 times over the next several years, you'd have all the appreciation, and I'd still have the same commission. Even putting the fairness issue aside, I had no *direct* financial interest in your investment success. (Indirectly, of course, I tried to recommend things I thought would work out, if only because I didn't want to lose your account.)

The converse was, perhaps even more pointedly, also true. If you bought a stock I recommended, I got my commission — and, if the stock subsequently declined 50%, still had that same commission. That is, I might have felt, but did not share in, your pain.

I was *somewhere* in the room with you — not exactly on your side of the table, but somewhere. (And certainly not on the *opposite* side of the table: a potential conflict of interest is still not an actual conflict of interest, no matter what our dear Trotskyites at NAPFA think.)

A fee-based arrangement puts the advisor solidly and squarely on her client's side of the table, in that there is a direct, linear, inelastic relationship between her fee income and the value of the client's investments. And if, in the long-run, the value of the account is a proxy for the quality of the advice — which it most assuredly is — then we may well and truly say to our prospects and clients the 10 most liberating words I've ever gotten to speak in this profession: *I prosper as you prosper; I suffer if you suffer.*

(2) FEES FAIRLY COMPENSATE US TO ADVISE OUR CLIENTS TO DO NOTHING — WHEN, AS IT ALMOST ALWAYS IS, NOTHING IS THE RIGHT THING FOR THEM TO DO.

In the bad old commission-based days, when a $400,000 stock account asked me if we wouldn't be better off getting out of a falling market, and buying back in when "things settle down," my whole life flashed before my eyes, as you can well imagine.

Today, our entire strategy of diversified, managed/pooled equity investing should aim for the goal of zero turnover — or as close as we can humanly get. In a fee-based world, we can both believe *and* practice the great law that portfolio turnover correlates negatively with return. And we can also resist our clients' genetically encoded, CNBC-inflamed impulse to tinker, time and tweak.

Once a portfolio is in place that is truly calibrated to the lifetime/multigenerational goals of a client household/family, the best advice we can give them is almost always not to do anything — except, of course, to add more money to their accounts, even — and especially — when the world's in flames. ("I buy," said one of the early Rothschilds, "when blood is running in the streets of Paris.")

We deserve to be paid for life-changingly, life-savingly good advice. And our clients should *want* their financial arrangement with us maximally to incent us to offer them just such great advice. Fees incent *and* reward us for giving what is nearly always the best advice: stand fast;

change nothing. Therefore, *our clients should love a fee-based arrangement every bit as much as we do.*

All of the above is perfectly straightforward, and quite easily practiced in *prospecting* situations. The plot thickens considerably if you're now going back to existing, commission-based clients, and trying to convert them to a fee basis.

The Catch-22 here, of course, is that it's difficult to recommend fees as being fairer than commissions (though they surely are), nor as eliminating commissions' built-in potential for conflict of interest (though they do that, too). A client, presented with this reasoning, would be hard-pressed *not* to wonder aloud why you hadn't gotten around to mentioning these commission issues before.

Moreover, in some very low-turnover stock accounts (where the advisor is basically being used as a custodian, whether he admits it to himself or not), conversion to a fee basis will merely be a price increase, with no value added (nor sought, for that matter). I'm still a pretty fair country salesman when I have to be, but I don't think I could have sold that on my best day — which was probably a while back.

Finally, there's the not uncommon case of the advisor who's got, in the word of Forrest Gump, a gozillion dollars worth of "A" shares out. He's not even between a rock and a hard place; *he's pinned under the rock.* Having obviously (and not at all wrongly) sold his clients on the fact that they'd never have to pay a commission again, he can hardly break faith with them now. Though he can — and, in my view, must — tell them that all *new* money has to go into "C" shares, as he transitions to a fee-based practice. ("C" shares are sort of the entry-level fee, and thus OK in my book, *as long as they're very thoroughly disclosed.*)

You're not going to be able to just turn around, in any of these or many similar situations, and simply change the pricing of your relationship. (Nor should you, I mustn't fail to mention, try to sell a fee basis to somebody who trades actively, on the grounds that fees will end up being cheaper. In fact, you shouldn't *have* active traders. They're all crazy.) **Rather, first change the product, *then* change the pricing.**

That is, you have to go to clients with a different product/service platform before you can alter the compensation basis through which you relate to them. And in approaching existing clients with any combination of a new product/service platform and its delivery on a fee basis, the key point to make is that *you would always have done it this way if it had been available*. That is, the healthier, more goal-oriented, fee-based relationship isn't some new marketing gimmick, but a hitherto unavailable, highly desirable improvement for all concerned.

In *any* client situation, I think you're always best advised to go for the plan. There might be intermediate steps, but why bother with them? Sure, you can try to get someone who's only done individual stocks and bonds into a "wrap" mutual fund program, or all the way up — if he has the wherewithal — to individually managed fee-based accounts. But you're still acting only as an investment advisor, and if you're seriously committed to not watching the market or the economy anymore, do you think that's going to work?

Similarly, you might try to get a family with a hodgepodge of different accounts onto one of those new platforms where virtually all of a firm's retail products and services are available for, say, one percent of the assets. But that's still not a plan, and Doctor Noah is, at the end of the day, a planner.

I think these kinds of incrementalism are most appealing to experienced advisors who are afraid they're going to lose the account. Best to be brutally honest with yourself — not to mention the client. If they're not ultimately going to get on The Ark, there really isn't that much you can do for them, because you owe it to yourself and your family to expend your finite reserves of time and energy looking for people who *will* get on The Ark. So although my basic principle for experienced advisors is "change the product, *then* change the pricing," unless you're trying to change the product into the plan, my guess is you're spinning your wheels.

I've mentioned professionally managed "wrap" accounts of individual stocks a couple of times now, and though my eyes glaze over at the whole issue of product comparisons, I do seem to get an awful lot of e-mail traffic asking if I think these accounts are "better" than mutual funds, or vice versa. So perhaps you'll allow me to deliver my short homily on this subject, and then we can all take the nap we'll suddenly feel desperately in need of.

The benefits of "wrap" accounts, in order of *perceived* importance, are (1) tax efficiency and (2) greater focus. I have to confess, as Stalin said about hearing the word "intellectual," that every time I hear an equity investment praised *first* for its tax advantage, I reach for my gun.

"Tax efficiency" just means that, in a low-turnover "wrap" portfolio, you may not get capital-gains taxed for many, many moons. Fine: neither will you in a low-turnover mutual fund...of the kind for which I've previously confessed a bias. (Comparing low-turnover "wrap" accounts to *high*-turnover mutual funds isn't quite fair, is it?)

Next, the *timing* of long-term capital gains taxation, if you'll permit me to say so, rather egregiously misses the point — which I always thought, and still think, is the *amount*. And I haven't yet heard even its most enthusiastic supporters suggest that you *make more money* in "wrap." (Personally, I devoutly hope I pay $20 million in long-term capital gains taxes next year, no matter whence it comes.)

Finally, I'm all for intelligent focus, and I think it's a perfectly wonderful thing — right up to the point (and that point surely differs for different clients) where it slides over into underdiversification.

I can only hope that, just before this discussion puts you into deep REM sleep, you see that this is not a brief for or against either of these forms of equity investment. (Just remember that equities are your birthday present; the shape of the box your present comes in can never be the critical variable.) That you own equities and that you remain adequately diversified are what counts. I've suggested that five countervailing equity styles may be about the optimum. So if "wrap" account minimums are still $100,000 when you read this, I think you'd need to have at least $500,000 in order to implement an intelligent "wrap" equity strategy — and even then, if you were ending up with fewer than, say, 75-100 stocks, you'd want to think long and hard about whether you were sufficiently diversified. Short of that amount — and that spread of risk — I'd strongly vote for staying with low-turnover, concentrated-portfolio funds.

So, good night, then.

IN SUMMARY

- Four decisions — three of which are once-in-a-lifetime, and the fourth of which should be revisited as infrequently as is humanly possible — govern upwards of 95% of your total lifetime return. Illustrated as a hierarchy to demonstrate their relative importance:

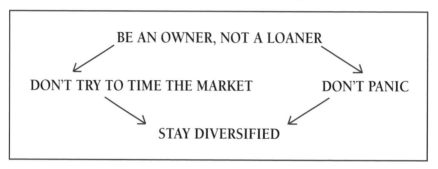

- Everything else — *everything else* — accounts for the other five per-cent. It is one of the enduring mysteries of human perversity that nearly everyone puts 95% of his time and effort into the other five percent.
- When all is said and done, diversification is there to keep people from blowing themselves up by betting the ranch on the "new era" *du jour.*
- Five countervailing styles ought to do it: big-cap growth and value, small-cap growth and value, and international/emerging markets.
- You don't seem to get as much bang for your buck in mature-market international diversification as you used to. Think of the grandchil-dren, and think about emerging markets.
- Indexing isn't a panacea. The less transparent a market or market sector, the better active management looks.
- With active management, the enemy of diversification isn't "underperformance," it's *style drift.* So what you ask of your manag-ers isn't so much genius as it is discipline — *style discipline.*
- You can make yourself really nuts about fund selection, and sooner

or later most advisors do. Just keep intoning your mantra: *five percent...*

- Rebalance static portfolios annually on the same day. Portfolios that receive regular inflows are rebalancing themselves, through the genius of dollar-cost averaging. (*Do not,* however, dollar-cost average with lump sums. Don't, in other words, hold money back from a market that goes up 80% of the time. It may at times seem prudent to do so, but it's really the worst species of closet market-timing — against *very* long odds.)

- Once diversified, aim for zero turnover. (You won't get to that ideal, but it's a noble goal.) Otherwise, you'll just end up outsmarting yourself. *Portfolio turnover correlates negatively with return.*

- Portfolio management (a) can't matter that much and (b) isn't how you earn your fee.

- Assume that you (over and above all the experts) cost the family one percent of their assets a year. Will you:
    - (a) add a point to their do-it-yourself return, *and/or*
    - (b) save them a point in The Big Mistake not made, *and/or*
    - (c) save them a point in time, energy, worry and/or record-keeping?

- If you will — and heaven knows you will — hiring you is a no-brainer...assuming, which you can't always do, that the people of whom you ask this question are sane.

- The Big Mistake can be any one, or a combination, or a consecutive series of: overconfidence/euphoria; panic; underdiversification; overdiversification; speculation that thinks it's investing; investing for current yield instead of for total return; and leverage. Your one percent fee would be cheap if all it bought were Big Mistake insurance.

- Fees put us, finally and forever more, on the same side of the table as the client. *"I prosper as you prosper; I suffer if you suffer."* Moreover, fees fairly compensate us to advise our clients to do nothing — when, as it virtually always is, nothing is the right thing for them to do.

- The plot thickens when you're trying to convert existing accounts from commissions to fees. The general principle is: first change the product, then change the pricing. Present fees, above all, as the way you would always have chosen to go, if they'd been available.
- Gradualism is probably just postponing the inevitable; change the product to the plan, or plan to punt.
- Individually managed accounts are a potentially useful alternative to mutual funds if — and only if — you have the wherewithal to achieve sufficient diversification. At $100,000 minimums, that probably means at least $500,000, in five different accounts containing no fewer than 75-100 stocks. Otherwise, low-turnover, concentrated-portfolio funds ought to do you fine.

Presenting The Finished Plan

chapter nine

NINE

———————•———————

In the reconnaissance phase of financial planning, once the household/family has evinced an active interest in taking the necessary steps to secure its future, we seek to establish three things:

(1) understanding and agreement as to which of The Seven Glorious Outcomes — and any other aims which may not fit neatly into The Seven — the prospects need/wish to pursue;

(2) at least a ballpark quantification of those needs/ wishes, particularly with respect to retirement income goals and other investment-driven outcomes;

(3) a general sense of mutual respect, and of at least incipient trust on the prospects' part.

When you've gotten all the subsequent information you and the experts need, and a plan has been formulated which you reasonably understand *and are proud of,* it's time for the moment of truth: the presentation of the finished plan.

In this chapter, we'll set some attitudinal and behavioral guidelines for presenting the plan in its most easily digestible form, and for responding to the most common types of questions/reservations/objections which can be expected to surface. I make no attempt, in this latter context, to anticipate nor answer technical questions/objections of any kind, for two simple reasons.

First, the technicalities are not the New Financial Advisor's job — unless and until she elects to make them her job — and are best hammered out between your experts and the prospects' technical advisors.

(Let the lawyers talk to the lawyers, if need be; let the accountants talk to the accountants.) Second, and perhaps even more important, where good will and a genuine desire to complete a plan are present, a way through (or around) any technical difficulty will always be found. But in the absence of either or both of those critical values, even the most trifling problem will get blown up into a dealbuster, or someone will keep pulling on one loose string until the whole fabric unravels. *No essential problem is technical, and no technical problem is essential.* Stay focused — and keep the prospects focused — on essentials, and leave the how-to issues to staff people.

Until you develop your own preferred style for conducting this all-important meeting, you may wish to consider the following suggestions for its setting, cast of characters, and basic agenda:

(1) IF AT ALL POSSIBLE, CONDUCT THE MEETING IN YOUR OFFICE. Generally, top quality professionals don't make house calls. You would expect to have a critical meeting with your physician or attorney in his office, where he could consult his files, support staff, library and other resources on your behalf. Presenting the completed plan in your office reinforces your own high-level professionalism and gives you maximum access to your own staff and resources, which may become very important once Q&A gets going.

(2) ALL KNOWN DECISION-MAKERS FROM THE PROSPECT'S SIDE MUST BE PRESENT. Not all meetings end in a decision, but it *is* the desired (and even deserved) outcome, and you shouldn't ever feel obligated to make your presentation where no decision can be made — because someone with a decisive say in the matter "can't" be there. Wait 'em out. If the meeting never gets scheduled, or keeps getting put off, that's your answer: they need the eggs. *Next.*

(3) ALL OBVIOUSLY NECESSARY EXPERTS FROM YOUR FIRM MUST BE PRESENT OR REACHABLE BY PHONE. Any attorney,

advanced underwriter or asset manager whose strategy is key to the plan, and whose expertise is probably going to be called on, obviously has to be present or in range — unless/until you feel you can advocate for his decisions as well as or better than he can. Just survey the field, as any good general would, and make sure no key position is undefended — because Murphy's Law says that that's exactly where you'll get hit. But don't overwhelm the household/family with a whole roomful of gratuitous experts, either.

(4) RUN THE MEETING. Do not cede the central role in presenting the plan to an expert, or any gauntlet thereof. The prospects have to know that you're Doctor Noah, not some kind of glorified master of ceremonies. (So, for that matter, do your own people. We don't need experts patronizing you in front of your prospects, and not even realizing they're doing so.) Remember: they don't buy the plan; they buy the planner.

(5) SAY AS LITTLE AS POSSIBLE, SO THAT EVERYTHING YOU *DO* SAY IS OF CRITICAL IMPORTANCE. During your fact-finding (and feeling-finding), two or three drop-dead critical issues — things the household/family regards as "musts" — will probably have come to light. Another couple of very desirable outcomes, not quite on the order of "musts," may also have surfaced. Organize your initial presentation purely around those deeply felt needs/ wants, ticking them off one by one and reporting that (*not how*) each one has been solved. This should just be a comforting litany of "You indicated that it was very important for you to.../We were able to..." If some explanation is critical to even a glancing understanding of the solution, explain just that much and no more. *Don't overexplain*; you'll sound defensive.

(6) STRESS THAT YOUR PROPOSED SOLUTIONS ARE NOTHING MORE OR LESS THAN THE MOST EFFICIENT, LEAST COMPLEX, LEAST EXPENSIVE WAYS TO ACCOMPLISH WHAT THE

PROSPECTS SAID WAS IMPORTANT. Even before they buy the plan, make them *own* it, if you see what I mean. Don't let them, even in their own minds, separate your proffered solutions from their stated problems. Hold the moral high ground of planning, which is that we're just doing what they said they wanted done — the best way we know (read: *the best way we believe there is)* to do it.

(7) IN GENERAL, DON'T ANSWER QUESTIONS NOBODY'S ASKED YOU YET. BUT IF YOU SEE AN OPPORTUNITY TO SHOOT ONE BIG OBJECTION IN THE HEAD WITHOUT WARNING, BE MY GUEST. In the obvious example of a portfolio that's probably much heavier in equities than the prospects may have expected, consider saying something like, "You indicated that you wanted to build a retirement income of $50,000 over Social Security. We were able to create a portfolio whose historic return would do that, and it may be just a bit more weighted to equities than you might have anticipated, but again, using historical rates of return, there's no other way to get where you want to go in the time you have left to retirement."

(8) MAKE IT CLEAR THAT YOU ARE SIMPLY STATING AN EXECU-TIVE SUMMARY, THAT YOU'RE VERY CONCERNED ABOUT NOT BURYING THEM IN A MOUND OF DETAIL BEFORE THEY'VE HAD A CHANCE TO ABSORB THE PLAN'S KEY AC-COMPLISHMENTS. In other words, give them permission to like the fact that you are keeping it simple enough for them to understand, without their having to worry that you're somehow over-simplifying.

(9) GIVE THEM A SYNOPSIS OF THE COSTS, BEING CAREFUL TO RELATE EACH MAJOR ITEM OF EXPENDITURE TO THE KEY PROBLEM IT SOLVES. Again, the issue here is that you be clearly seen standing up proudly for what everything — including, and

especially, you — costs. You can't ever put yourself in the position of appearing to be trimming on the costs, trying to downplay them, or in any way exhibiting fear of them.

(10) CONCLUDE BY REASSURING THE PROSPECTS THAT THE PLAN ISN'T CARVED IN STONE, THAT IT'S A WORK IN PROGRESS. STATE CLEARLY, HOWEVER, THAT THE CONSENSUS OF YOU AND THE EXPERTS IS THAT **THIS IS WHAT YOU WOULD IDEALLY DO IF YOU WERE THE PROSPECTS.** You don't want the household/family to feel that they're being put in the position of "take it or leave it." Any first draft of a plan may err on the side of funding the hopes and dreams so completely that the prospects just can't afford to do it all. Leave everybody some wiggle room, but remind the prospects that a lot of good people — some of them right here in the room — put a lot of quality time into the plan, and that you/they stand enthusiastically behind it. Conclude by saying, "I feel that we ought to just ease up at this point and give you folks the opportunity to ask some questions — or just tell us what you're feeling."

If this process takes a whole lot more than about 15 minutes, you may be doing it wrong. The ideal is probably about 12-15. But look at the immensity of what you can accomplish in that time. And see, above all, that you establish a very specific, non-technical, non-"selling" tone to the interview, which says, in effect:

> *You told us what you needed/wanted. We believe this plan does those things in the optimum way. We don't want to bore you with too much detail, except to the extent you'd like us to. Do you have any questions/ how do you feel about all this?*

This style of presentation presumes understanding. That is, its premise is that the plan is a more or less perfect vehicle for the hopes and dreams — and an effective antidote to the fears — of the household/family, *but it doesn't labor under any burden of "proof."* It never says this plan is better or cheaper than anyone else's. It makes no representations about how strong the insurance companies are, or how proficient the investment managers. It doesn't seem to feel challenged to demonstrate anything at all, beyond the serene conviction on the part of you and your firm that, in the prospects' position, it's what you'd do. Simply stated, *this presentation refuses to "sell."*

It does, however, give the prospects permission to *buy* the plan, pending receipt of any and all answers which they may now seek. Before examining what that Q&A process may sound like, however, I think it's time for you to get out another one of those big index cards, and transcribe the 10 presentation guidelines to be followed at the plan delivery meeting. Laminate this one, too. And plan to outline every presentation according to this system — until you develop a system all your own.

Take care, as you create this very spare, presumptive, almost minimalist presentation, not to oversell anything. What you're offering is a plan for the future, *not a guarantee of it,* which isn't within human power. Especially with respect to the plan's accumulation targets, premised as they must be on some trendline rate (or rates) of return, you need to make brief but clear reference to the cybernetic way any investment program travels toward a target.

You'll never get exactly the assumed rate of return; in real life you'll earn a long-term return either higher or lower. Therefore any number of mid-course corrections in the accumulation program may be warranted, and even necessary. If you get better-than-anticipated returns, especially in the early years, you have the luxury of either overshooting your goals or of trimming back your contributions — at least as long as the net effect leaves you about on plan. If, on the other hand, you earn below-trendline returns, especially in those early years, you'll have to raise your contributions or count on less of an accumulation (and therefore, in retirement, less income).

This is just another reason to build your financial plan's assumptions on historically defensible rates of return. *The key to a consistently successful financial planning practice is giving the clients reasonable expectations.* And the one thing your clients should never be is surprised.

A comprehensive financial, investment and estate plan, regardless of how economically it's presented, is just a huge amount of material to throw at people — possibly the greatest volume of information, and certainly the most *important* information, they've ever been given in one sitting in their entire lives. Moreover, you aren't asking them to master that information in any rigorous, intellectual sense, not least of all because they can't. You're inviting them, in essence, to make an act of faith that the plan is as complete and as beneficial as you say it is — which is an act of faith in you, and in your firm.

No matter how credible you are when making the opening presentation we outlined above — and no matter how good you may already be at reading people's reactions — I don't think you can really have any idea how this process is progressing until you start getting some feedback. Until, that is, the moment when — under your gentle guidance — Q&A breaks out.

Amateurs fear Q&A as an obstacle course, at the end of which lies a question they can't answer, and therefore a lost "sale." Professionals welcome Q&A as the only real way to discover what the prospects are thinking — how they're reacting to this blizzard of information. (A real professional, if she thinks about it at all, has absolutely no fear of questions she can't answer, reasoning that (a) if she doesn't know the answer, the question is probably technical and therefore non-essential, and (b) that's what the experts are for.)

Most "sales training" I've encountered says that a sales interview has three phases: the presentation, Q&A and "the close" — a mysterious endgame in which the prospect, at a given signal, decides to buy whatever we're selling. My own experience suggests that the decision to adopt your plan is made in one of two places: either before the prospects walk in the door for the plan presentation interview, or during Q&A.

If you've disqualified non-prospects hard enough — if you've made people qualify, in some very real sense, to even see a plan drawn by you and your firm — some of the best of them will already be "closed" when they arrive. Indeed, some closed themselves, in effect, when they made the difficult decision to turn over all their documents to you, and to disclose the most private details of their financial lives. Respect how far they've had to come just to get to the plan, and consider the possibility that the decision has essentially been made already. This is just another reason to offer a very economical, very presumptive executive summary, and then move straight into Q&A: to allow the prospects, after getting clarification on a few items, to tell you that they're ready to go.

If they're not already closed when they walk in, prospects make their decision, I'm convinced, during Q&A. For a few, it happens when they ask one or two questions about points in the plan that are the real essentials to them. When they get confirmation that the plan has indeed taken care of those critical elements, they're ready to stipulate to just about everything else.

For the rest, the decision comes somewhere in the Q&A process, but not in the way you might think. I don't believe that prospects in this group ask a specific question, hear an intellectually great answer, and the light goes on. Rather, even when the prospect's conscious mind thinks it's looking for objective answers, *his unconscious is watching to see how you react emotionally to being challenged.* If you don't get rattled — if your demeanor says, "This is what you said you needed, and this is the best if not the only way to get you what you need" — then sooner or later they blow the meeting up and leave, or they accept you and your plan. In neither event, I'm convinced, is the decision consciously made — you didn't "win" or "lose" an intellectual debate of some kind. Indeed, the concept "this is what you said you needed" is, in essence, a refusal to debate.

PROSPECTS: We want to retire comfortably, but we don't want this much exposure to the stock market.

NEW FINANCIAL ADVISOR: (Smiling, a little sadly) That's a bit like saying you want to go to Australia, but you don't fly in airplanes.

P: What do you mean?

NFA: If you need to go down to the corner for a loaf of bread, I recommend you walk. If you need to go visit your children in the next county, I recommend you drive. If you need to go to Australia, even if you don't like flying that much, I have to recommend an airplane. No other way to get there, that I know of.

Same with your retirement income goals. You say you need $50,000 a year, over Social Security and your pension plan payout, to live the retired life of dignity and independence you've worked for and dreamed of. And I agree with you: you deserve it.

And, given the time you have left until retirement, and the amounts you've said you can put away, it's do-able... at the long-term rate of return of high quality equities. And not any other way. Equities are the airplane. Your lifestyle in retirement is Australia. Simple as that.

P: But what about volatility?

NFA: It's the mother of return, as we've discussed. If the volatility went away, the premium long-term return we're relying on would go away as well, heaven forbid. And volatility has no power to hurt the truly long-term investor...like you.

You have five years to go until retirement, and we've

agreed that retirement for one or both of you could easily be a 30-year process. Even forgetting about what your appreciated capital could mean to your children and grandchildren — and we mustn't *ever* forget that — try to take a 35-year perspective.

One way to do that might be to look *back* 35 years. (Hands them the bear market chart; see page 170) It's 1967. We're just recovering from a 240-day bear market in 1966. The Vietnam war is turning into a quagmire. Next year — 1968 — will begin with the shock of the Tet offensive. By spring, Robert Kennedy and Dr. King will be dead, and the cities will be in flames. And a *new* bear market will be starting around Thanksgiving. Indeed, from 1967 until 2001, there'll be *eight* bear markets — which is pretty normal. OPEC, Watergate and stagflation are still to come. And where are we now?

The cost of living is up perhaps four times. The dividend of the S&P 500 is up about five times. And stock *prices* are up more than 10 times. Interest rates? Say they're about the same.

Can you doubt that everyone who invested primarily in bonds in 1967 is destitute? Can you doubt that everyone who invested primarily in equities gives thanks every day? (Catching himself, and laughing) Sorry; didn't mean to go off on you like that...

P: No, that's all right. You've put it in perspective. We see now why you're so passionate about this issue...

I hope you will also see implicit in the NFA's rant the core answer to all current-events-based cavils. It always looks like the wrong time to invest, because to the media, bad new is good copy. So whatever is even remotely wrong with the economy, the markets or the world will get reported as the precursor of Armageddon. And this reportage will *always* be hyped with the word "crisis." (When no crisis exists, the media will simply imagine one, like the massive coverage of shark attacks in summer 2001 — when there were statistically no more shark attacks than in any other recent summer.)

If there's no Cuban Missile Crisis, you'll get 24/7 coverage of the ethnic strife in Kosovo — which, not in any way to belittle the very real sufferings of its people, is roughly the size of Ohio. *It's always something.* There's always an apocalypse *du jour.* But name any "crisis" of the last 50 years, and anyone in his right mind now regrets not having invested right in the middle of it — indeed, on its very darkest day.

The critically important things to remember about the current events/apocalypse *du jour* objection are threefold:

(1) Never engage with it directly; don't analyze or debate it. Each "crisis" is just a different species of the same genus: people rationalizing their nameless fear by focusing it on something — *anything* — specific. The "crisis" is never the problem: *fear* is the problem.

(2) Twenty years from now, everyone will pray for one more chance to invest today — no matter how awful today looks *today* — but heaven will not answer. So thank heaven that Doctor Noah is here today, reminding you (a) that today is always the hardest day to invest, and the only day we have; and (b) that the only thing we have to fear is fear itself. Doctor Noah doesn't have to know *how* the apocalypse *du jour* will get resolved; he need only know, with perfect faith, *that* it will. For the antidote to fear isn't knowledge, but faith.

(3) This time, it's *not* different. It's just different enough in the details to frighten people into *thinking* it's fundamentally different. We saw earlier that since the end of WWII, the S&P 500, punctuated

by no fewer than a dozen absolutely devastating bear markets, went up 50 times in 55 years. I guarantee you that every single crisis in this period — and there were more than a few epic and very real ones — *looked different.* And, in the end, none was sufficiently different to derail the inevitability of democratic capitalism.

Over the years, I found one very effective way of inoculating people against the often dramatic but ultimately transitory effects on their portfolio of the apocalypse *du jour.* When I handed a recommended portfolio to prospects, I also listed the last three big declines in each of the funds (or at least in relevant indexes). I call this process "lifeboat drills." Volatility is an abstraction; it's a word that means different things to different people. You've seen that the bear market chart is standard issue to all Ark passengers, but I wanted people to know what real-life declines in their particular investments were going to look like — or at least what they had looked like.

If I wanted part of the portfolio to be in emerging markets, I'd show clients the effects of the two phases of the Asian contagion in 1997 and (with Russian's default) in 1998. And I'd round this out with a look at the emerging market meltdown surrounding the Mexican peso crisis of 1994. There's nothing particularly scientific about this: you can't step into the same river twice, as Heraclitus said, and the next three declines aren't going to look exactly like the last three (although they'll probably give us just as little warning). But I found — and believe you'll find — that passengers on The Ark are markedly less susceptible to panic once they've been through their lifeboat drills. (This is also, I think, something of a gut check for the advisor. If you'd be at all reluctant to show potential investors what a series of perfectly normal temporary declines might look like, you are, *ipso facto*, overselling.)

Another genus of questions/objections that breeds many different species is the issue of your compensation. As a general rule, though, you can assume that **your price is only an issue to the extent that your value is in question.** And that becomes the key to responding to this whole panoply of objections: reinforcing what Doctor Noah's fee buys The Ark's passengers.

PROSPECT: Why shouldn't we just buy index funds?

NEW FINANCIAL ADVISOR: You can buy index funds, if you want. I don't recommend buying *only* index funds, but I wouldn't oppose you if you did. It doesn't matter that much, and I wouldn't let the whole plan founder on a relatively minor issue like portfolio construction. (Silence)

P: So then we wouldn't have to pay you a fee for picking funds.

NFA: You're *never* going to pay me a fee to pick funds, actively managed or otherwise. *Picking* funds is the smallest part of my job. And I don't know how any advisor would go about demonstrating to you that his fund selections would out-perform anyone else's *in the future.*

P: Then why are we paying you an advisory fee, again?

NFA: For good behavioral advice, which you believe will help you make better behavioral decisions, which you further believe will produce a return for you and your family which is greater than you'd get on your own *by more than the cost of my fee.* Otherwise you shouldn't hire me. Or anybody, for that matter.

P: But you just said you couldn't prove that your funds are better than anyone else's.

NFA: (Serenely) And indeed, I can't. (Silence)

P: So where is your value?

NFA: Right here. (Taps the list of the seven manifestations of The Big Mistake) Do you remember that I said that, as ingredients of lifetime return, investor behavior is to investment performance as 19 is to one?

P: Clearly. It was the thing you said which struck us the most.

NFA: (Taps the list again) Well, I'm your behavioral coach. And that coaching is what the fee is for. But there's no sense paying it if you're not convinced that, *even after the fee,* you'll do better with the coaching than without.

P: We're convinced, we're convinced...

This issue may also come up when the clients realize that you never react to markets, and never tinker with the portfolio.

PROSPECT: If this portfolio's never going to change much, why are we paying you an advisory fee, year after year?

NEW FINANCIAL ADVISOR: (Kindly) Well, not for portfolio management, that's for sure!

P: My very point.

NFA: (Tapping the list of Big Mistakes) It trivializes what I do to some extent, but think of my fee as a Big Mistake insurance premium. You pay your premium every year, and hope you never need me. That's a little bit of an oversimplification, but it's not inaccurate. In fact, I think it's helpful.

P: How, exactly?

NFA: Do you have fire insurance on your house?

P: Of course.

NFA: Auto insurance?

P: Sure, you have to.

NFA: OK, and you also have Big Mistake insurance on your investment portfolio. You pay your fire insurance premium every year, and hope it's wasted — that your house doesn't burn down. You pay your auto insurance and hope your car doesn't get totaled. And you pay one percent of your portfolio's value every year to me and my firm, and hope you're never tempted to make The Big Mistake.

Where this analogy breaks down, of course, is that the other insurances pay off only *after* disaster strikes, while Big Mistake insurance pays off *beforehand.* I come to your house *before* it burns down, to help you not bail out of a crisis market. I steer your car out of harm's way *before* a wreck, when I help you not to put too much of your portfolio in a hot sector, like technology was a couple of years back. In that sense, Big Mistake insurance isn't there to fix the damage, but to prevent it.

P: So the reason I pay you to keep telling me not to do any-thing...

NFA: ...is twofold, really. (1) It's virtually always the best advice for long-term, goal-oriented investors like you. And (2), even more important, human nature being what it is, *you might not be able to keep doing nothing on your own.*

P: Sure, sure...I knew that. I was just...

NFA: ...testing me?

Ladies and gentlemen, sometimes they're just...*testing you.* They're sending out a sonar ping to verify the depth of your conviction. Why don't you calmly presume that Q&A is just that sort of gentle exercise — a good person, simply seeking reassurance — unless it develops other-wise? That may keep you from tensing up and/or overanswering what may be a relatively innocuous question...a sonar ping.

I hope you've come to see two things about Q&A in a planning context. First is that virtually all the serious questions you're ever going to be asked will reflect one or more of the same five basic concerns:

- How financial planning works in general, and the implications of your specific planning recommen-dations.

- Why it costs what it costs — especially your as-set-based advisory fee — and whether that cost is worth it.

- A morbid fear of the equity markets, rooted in deeply flawed notions of "risk" and "volatility."

- Little or no clear sense of the implications of long-term erosion of purchasing power.

- Whether, and to what extent, you can be trusted.

Second, with the exception of the last issue (where you can't *give* the answer; you have to *be* the answer), virtually this entire book serves as the response — or, more accurately, as an encyclopedia of the responses — to these concerns. So instead of me rolling a lot of iterations (or species) of the first four genus issues, I'd urge you to make index card summaries of *your own* versions of the most comfortable answers you found in the book — answers that line up both with your beliefs, and with the ways you like to express those convictions.

If you found, for instance, that you were often asked how the portfolio managers were chosen, you'd want to have a crisp, clear answer which showed that this was something to which you and your firm had given a lot of conscious thought. You might say, if you believed it:

> "To the greatest extent possible, I use money managers here in our own firm, on the basis of two issues: *accessibility* and *accountability*. I encourage my clients to rely a lot on me personally, so I want to be in a position to stay in very close contact with their investment managers. That's *accessibility*. And *accountability* is implicit in the fact that my colleague advisors and I can go to our senior management if we're not happy about the way a particular fund or portfolio is being managed, in the knowledge that we can get a fair hearing, and get action if it's warranted. That's how I feel I get to do the best possible job for my clients and their families."

On the other hand, if you're someone who thinks "proprietary products" are a carcinogen, you might say something like:

> "Well, as we've discussed, my criteria for the five managers in my portfolios are character and discipline, reasonable longevity with their funds, and some clear record of producing results better than those of most of their peers. I work closely with the fund analysts in my firm to search out managers who best fit those descriptions, whichever fund family they happen to be with. Manager selection — particularly on variables as subjective as character — is an art, not a science. But I'm proud of our objectivity, and I would stack my — and your — five managers up against anyone's."

Please see, once again, that at this point it doesn't matter what *my* answers are to any of these questions. All that counts is that *you* have cogent answers that (a) you believe in strongly and that (b) you can express clearly and warmly.

How long should it take to "close" a financial plan? If you've thoroughly prepared the ground, if you've kept the family and especially its advisors in the loop, how many meetings should it take before the prospects start signing documents and applications, and start writing checks? My answer, assuming you've followed the meeting guidelines at the beginning of this chapter with respect to the cast of characters: one meeting, two at the most.

We've all heard stories about how some persistent advisor worked his way into an account after years of trying relentlessly to be of service. In general, I think this is a bad use of your time and energy. Grinding away at a difficult prospect is, most often, just staying with the prospect we've got instead of seeking out the prospect we really want. In other words, it's merely another form of prospecting anxiety.

Years ago, the legendary life insurance salesman Frank Bettger (author of the classic book *How I Raised Myself from Failure to Success in Selling*) told Dale Carnegie that he closed 70% of his cases on the first interview, 23% on the second — and seven percent on the third, fourth, fifth, etc. I think that's just about right for a financial plan, as well. If all the key players are present at that major presentation of the plan, and if all the necessary documents and information were in the hands of the planners in plenty of time beforehand, there should be few issues which survive the first meeting, and none still standing after the second. One never says never in our business, but thereafter I think any case becomes a very, very long shot. Yes, long shots pay off sometimes — but unless you're desperate, which you oughtn't ever to be, that isn't the way to bet.

Looking ahead to a time when you have a rapidly growing number of completed plans running, questions of the frequency and content of your client contact become important.

As with most aspects of practice management, there's no one right way to do client contact. There are, however, any number of wrong ways to handle it, or to let it manhandle you. So a word or two about both the upside and downside of continuing client/advisor interaction seems in order here.

The general rule for client contact in a long-term, low-turnover planning/portfolio strategy may not be intuitively obvious. I would state it thus: *as little formal contact as possible,* outside of a highly structured annual "state of the plan" meeting, with a written report as its basis.

Quarterly reports are at best a waste of time, in this view, and at worst they send a potentially very misleading signal, i.e. that anything important or even noteworthy can happen in a 90-day period. There are (or ought to be), on the other hand, plenty of opportunities for *informal* client contact — interactions of various kinds which have no specific plan-oriented agenda.

I've previously indicated my personal enthusiasm for newsletters; let me repeat it here — provided that your newsletter is interesting, personal up to a point, and that it conveys some sense of who you really are. Extended economic and/or market commentary is a huge no-no (for reasons that should be obvious), and dry reviews of abstruse tax legislation/regulation are also out of order. On the other hand, if you felt that some specific tax law event had widespread implications for your class of Ark passengers, that would be well worth commenting on. (The 2001 tax act's repudiation of meaningful estate tax repeal, and its enhancement of the already-remarkable benefits of Section 529, are great examples.)

I've always found, too, that nice, informal Client Appreciation Nights — with perhaps one interesting speaker and some classy desserts and coffee — are something that clients...really appreciate. And finally, in the relatively close confines of Doctor Noah's metaphorical Ark — where the Doctor competes by caring — you should be learning enough about the enthusiasms of family members to keep personal notes, appropriate newspaper/magazine clippings, and even the odd sporting event or theater tickets in the mail from time to time.

The annual meeting, with all hands on deck, should be the formal event of your plan year. (Just be careful not to let it degenerate into an orgy of "performance" comparisons, for that way lies madness.) The essential agenda of the annual meeting ought to be threefold:

(1) An extended review of the plan's goals, and whatever updating of the goals seems necessary or even advisable.

(2) A review of the progress of the plan in the past year (especially as to accumulation targets), relative to budget.

(3) A review of any anticipated events in, and especially of budgeted contributions to, the plan for

the coming year, including any mid-course corrections dictated by (2), above.

Clearly, an unwritten agenda item of the annual review is to make
sure that everyone who needs to be is still emotionally as well as financially "on board." It's also an ideal time for you to make an impassioned
restatement of your faith in the plan and its portfolios. Beyond that, my
formal client contact program may be summed up in four words: same
time next year.

Would that all our clients were either disciplined or docile enough
to accept this approach. But in the retail financial advisory profession, as
John Lennon sang, life is what happens to us while we're busy making
other plans.

Circumstances change; people change. When these things occur,
there is often a genuine need for revision of a financial plan. But it's not
the real ebbs and flows of life which prompt most incoming calls to advisors. Far more often, it's the rise and fall of markets, or the vagaries of
relative "performance."

When those issues surface, the client usually calls looking for permission to do the wrong thing...and that's on a good day. On bad days,
somebody runs screaming onto the bridge of The Ark and tries to tear the
wheel completely out of Doctor Noah's steady, capable hands. At that
point, the good Doctor may have some decisions to make.

Even with the inoculations of the historical bear market chart and
specific "lifeboat drills," even with a long-term planning perspective and
the twin commandments of "don't time" and "don't panic," even with
Doctor Noah's transcendent faith in the future...sometimes raw, naked,
panic-prone human nature wins out. And people want to sell out of their
equities, "for now" if not forever.

When everything about temporary declines that we've learned thus
far fails to carry the day with a client, I recommend one last-ditch effort.
First, make the point that equities *appear* to be so volatile because *they're*

quoted all day, every day.

NEW FINANCIAL ADVISOR: Do you think quality common stocks are more volatile in price than, say, single-family homes?

CLIENT: Of course they are!

NFA: How do you know?

C: Just look at the paper! The market's down 30% in a year!

NFA: You don't think that's ever happened to your house?

C: Of course not!

NFA: How do you know? Remember how quiet everything got after the Crash of '87? Remember the recession of 1990-91? Remember when long-term interest rates went up 50% in late '93, early '94? You don't think the price of homes cratered then, because they were unfinanceable?

C: Well...you know, I *do* remember houses going begging in those times...

NFA: Less than today's stock market? More? The same?

C: I don't know!

NFA: (Gently) Do you know why you don't know?

C: (Really getting fried) No, I don't know why I don't know!

NFA: Because the price of your house isn't listed in the paper every day. Much less on TV every second. If it were, I'll bet you'd have sold it three times in the last 20 years.

C: But my house didn't change in value!

NFA: They why do you think your investments are?

C: Because...oh, wait a minute, now. I was going to say, "because I see them quoted every day in the paper."

NFA: (Very gently) My point, exactly.

C: OK, OK. Say the price of my house *did* decline as much as the stock market, a couple of times.

NFA: Yes, *do* say it. Because it's surely true. But you liked your house, and you liked your neighborhood, and you needed

	a place to live...
C:	...and I knew it'd come back.
NFA:	Yes, especially that: *you knew it'd come back.*
C:	Have I ever asked you to forget about a conversation we were having?
NFA:	(Serenely) Not that I remember.
C:	Thank you. Mind forgetting about this one, too?
NFA:	This one what?

If, on the other hand, the client still wishes to sell, ask permission to let someone else in your office handle the orders, and refuse to accept any compensation for placing them. It is marginally possible that your insistence in good conscience not to be involved in a terrible decision, and your refusal to be paid for executing it, may snap the client out of it.

In the not entirely dissimilar happenstance of a client wishing to switch his investments in a way you consider inappropriate, (a) do the sell side with no commission and (b) ask the client to do the buy side online, or with another advisor. Because you can't in sound conscience (or even sound business practice) take an advisory fee for an investment you know nothing about and/or disapprove of.

When pressured to go along with a portfolio decision I couldn't countenance, I always made my "funeral speech." You may wish to consider adapting it to your own style.

"I've always operated on the assumption that my client relationships are for life — that one of us is going to the other one's funeral. You may very well go to mine. But if it turns out the other way around, some days later I'm going to be sitting down with your family, telling them where they are.

"If what you want to do today turns out not to have been a good decision, your family's going to

ask me how I could have let you make it. And I'm
not going to have an acceptable answer.

"I'm sorry, but I'm never going to have that conversation with your family, because I'm not ever
going to put myself in that position. It's your money,
and you can ultimately do with it what you want.
But I won't help you do this, and I sincerely hope
you'll reconsider."

Like declining to write a passel of suicidal sell orders, the funeral
speech doesn't work all the time, and it may not even work most of the
time. But you'll always feel great for having made it. And if it just saves
one family's financial life one time, it'll be well worth all the occasions on
which you made it in vain.

I hope I don't need to add that — on those relatively rare occasions
where you draw a line in the sand with your sword, and the client crosses
it — you must immediately begin arranging to resign the account. Someone who's sold or switched after you've put all your credibility into dis-
suading him is like a dog that's bitten you. He's going to bite you again.
They never bite just once. Head The Ark up into the wind. Prepare to
lower a boat. It's over. He needed the eggs. *Next.*

I suggested earlier that if you're to sell out The Ark in three to four
years, the last 100 or so households/families may very well have to come
in through referral. I also said that I know of no reliable "technique" for
getting referrals, and don't believe anything of the kind exists. The only
reliable way I ever found to get a steady stream of quality referrals was
to do absolutely superlative work — relentlessly, single-mindedly
underpromising and overdelivering — for people who actively and vocally appreciate it. This is yet another reason (even though, at this point,
none should be needed) not to accept difficult, strained client relationships. Even if you can keep some passive/aggressive ingrate on The Ark,

(a) why would you need or even want to, and (b) he's not going to refer you. (He has no friends, and wouldn't give you the satisfaction.) Do great work for great clients, and great referrals will surely abound. *Res ipsa loquitur.*

But not, of course, *only* great referrals. From time to time, you will surely run into situations where a terrific client refers you to someone who doesn't meet your minimum account size. The general principle here is, of course, don't compromise, because that's always a slippery slope. Find a "good" reason to compromise today, and you'll surely find another tomorrow...and then another, until you've no standards left at all — just "guidelines" waiting to be compromised.

The procedure to be followed in this case is:

- Complete the fact-finding interview in which you discover that the referral doesn't meet your minimum. Don't raise the issue with the referral.

- Immediately call the referring client, and make it clear that you can't take the referral because you are trying to maintain standards *which enable you most efficiently to serve great clients like him.* Let the referring client know, too, that you haven't said *anything* to the referral before you two had a chance to get on the same page.

- Tell the referring client that you have a colleague with capabilities and attitudes similar to yours who isn't quite as far along in her career as you are, and who would be very well qualified to handle the referral. Offer to serve as a backstop to your colleague as necessary, to reassure the referring client. Above all, make clear that *you would never take this step without first securing the referring client's blessing.*

In every case where I personally followed these steps, the referring client was perfectly content. But I can't tell you that no one will ever say, "It's both of us or neither." In the very improbable event that this happens, bite the bullet. *Never* knuckle under to *any* ultimatum. *Never* compromise your standards, or one day The Ark will surely be lost.

And so it's time for me to leave you to your glorious work. I wish I had some ringing valedictory message of my own, but I find that David Bayles and Ted Orland said it best, in the last paragraph of their wonderful book for artists called *Art & Fear:*

> "In the end, it all comes down to this: you have a choice (or more accurately a rolling tangle of choices) between giving your work your best shot and risking that it will not make you happy, or not giving it your best shot — and thereby *guaranteeing* that it will not make you happy. It becomes a choice between certainty and uncertainty. And curiously, uncertainty is the comforting choice."

IN SUMMARY

- It's time to present the plan. Don't sweat the small stuff. Where good will and a genuine desire to complete a plan are present, no essential problem is technical, and no technical problem is essential.
- Ten golden guidelines for the plan presentation meeting:
  (1)   Your turf.
  (2)   All client decision-makers present, or wait 'til they are.
  (3)   All your experts present or reachable.
  (4)   Your meeting. Not your side's meeting: *your* meeting.
  (5)   Speak little; tell them that (*not how*) the plan accomplishes all their most cherished goals.
  (6)   Hold the moral high ground: your plan is simply the optimum way to do what they said they wanted.
  (7)   Don't answer questions no one's asked you yet, but if you can bushwhack one big, obvious objection, fire away.
  (8)   Let them know you're just summarizing; let 'em like it, too.
  (9)   Be very upfront about costs; relate them clearly to specific benefits.
  (10)   Leave room for downsizing the plan in case it's just too ambitious, but stress that this is what you'd do if you were they.
- Don't try to prove anything, and don't "sell."
- Don't get backed into appearing to guarantee returns. Accumulation targets, in the real world, are reached cybernetically — lots of mid-course corrections.
- If they haven't made a decision already, Q&A is where it happens — and not necessarily intellectually or even consciously.
- For most everyone, equities are the plane to Australia: you may not like flying, but it's too far to row. Or swim.
- Help people to see into the future of equities by looking back equally

far into their past.

- There's always an apocalypse *du jour.* There's always a "good" current-events-driven reason not to invest today. And 20 years from now, everyone will wish he'd invested in the depths of the current "crisis." When there's no "crisis," journalism will hallucinate one. *Shark!*

- "Lifeboat drills" — showing investors the last three big declines in their actual investments (not just in the market as a whole) — may inoculate them against the next panic.

- Your fee isn't for portfolio management. It's for behavior management.

- At the end of the day, all legitimate (and most illegitimate) questions and objections center on five issues:

  (1) how planning works/why your specific recommendations

  (2) cost, especially your one percent

  (3) fear/ignorance of equities

  (4) missing the erosion of purchasing power

  (5) trust, or the absence thereof

- Record the questions you get asked a lot; perfect your own personal, deeply felt answers.

- If you haven't closed a plan in two major meetings, you're almost certainly not going to.

- One formal, written annual "state of the plan" event. No formal quarterly noise. Lots of nice, real, human, informal contact.

- Sometimes people crack up in a storm at sea in the stock market. Try analogizing equity volatility to home prices: they'd probably be just as volatile if you could quote 'em every day. And/or make the funeral speech. If people are *still* trying to bite you, set 'em adrift.

- Everything I ever learned about getting referrals, in 10 words: do great work for great clients who actively appreciate it. Carefully, gently but firmly farm out substandard referrals.

- Choose uncertainty; choose excellence. "Uncertainty is the comforting choice."

THE
THOMAS
CROWN
AFFAIR

epilogue

●

EPILOGUE

———————●———————

This book advises and even urges you to seek out relationships with ever more affluent Americans. And it insists that these people are every bit as financially doomed as anyone — perhaps more so, because they are so much more susceptible to the illusion that they have "enough" money.

You, too, are in danger of being overly impressed with apparent wealth, and daunted by prospecting those who possess it. This is very natural, very human — and very bad for you. (It's also particularly bad for the affluent, because their need for sound advice is so great but so subtle.) As an antidote to these feelings, I recommend that you own, and watch as often as you need to, the original 1968 film *The Thomas Crown Affair.*

The film stars Steve McQueen as the plundering plutocrat Thomas Crown, and Faye Dunaway as his nemesis and love, the insurance investigator Vicky Anderson. (The crackerjack direction was by Norman Jewison, and the soundtrack features Noel Harrison singing a medley of his hit, "The Windmills of Your Mind.")

The film begins with a beautifully organized $2.66 million bank robbery, executed by five men who have never met each other; the heist is masterminded and literally overseen by the title character. What differentiates this from all other caper movies, and really gives it its bite, is that Thomas Crown is already fabulously — and quite legitimately — wealthy. *He doesn't need the money*; he seems, rather, to need the intellectual challenge.

When Ms. Vicky begins almost immediately to suspect Thomas Crown, the policeman heading the investigation rejects her theory out of hand, on the grounds that Crown is already worth...**four million dollars**! (How the audiences in 1968 must have gasped at this; it probably seemed like all the money in the world.)

Thomas Crown, age 36, is living in a 150-year-old gated mansion on Boston's Beacon Hill, filled with art and antiques. He drives a new Rolls Royce, and is building a beach house — on what must be quite a lot of beach, because there are no other houses around, and he can take Vicky for a long spin in his dune buggy without seeing another living soul. This guy is *rich*.

Or was...and here is my point. Let's imagine that the story ends right there. Thomas and Vicky retire to a life of love and luxury. (Couldn't happen: neither of these two narcissists could stand the other — or anyone else — for six months.) Let's say that, on top of four million dollars of liquid net worth, the robbery netted Thomas $2.5 million. (It didn't: there were the five thieves to pay off, plus expenses, not to mention the tender mercies of the Swiss bankers to whom Crown entrusted the cash.) Finally, let's suppose the happy couple invested the whole $6.5 million in high quality, tax-free municipal bonds at six percent. (They couldn't: rates weren't that high then and aren't now, though they were for a while in between.)

At this writing, Thomas Crown would be a hale and hearty 69 years old. And his income would still be a tax-exempt...$390,000 a year.

The mansion is gone; its fine art is gone. The beach property is *long* gone. A whole year's worth of bond interest couldn't replace the Rolls. And I see Thomas Crown living in a two-bedroom condo in a nice, upscale development somewhere — with every other upper-middle-class retiree in town, all trying to figure out what hit them.

Reality hit them. The postage stamp hit them. The toxic fiction of currency hit them. The realization that the only sane long-term definition of money is purchasing power hit them...but far too late to do them any good.

This, then, is your mission. This is the great long-term/multi-generational financial planning need that's so pressing because it's so insidious. This is the pure essence of your potential to do well by doing good.

Now, go do it.

BIBLIOGRAPHY / RESOURCES

ACKNOWLEDGMENTS

BIBLIOGRAPHY
———————●———————
RESOURCES

- Emerson's essay "Compensation" appears in virtually any and every collection of his essays, as does his other greatest hit, "Self-Reliance."

- Tom Stanley's and Bill Danko's *The Millionaire Next Door* belongs in every advisor's library. Pocket Books puts out a very inexpensive paperback edition.

- Roger Lowenstein's *Buffett: The Making of an American Capitalist* (Main Street/Doubleday) is the best biography available of the man. His methods can and should be studied from *The Essays of Warren Buffett*, edited by Lawrence A. Cunningham. Professor Cunningham has brilliantly selected and arranged sections of Buffett's letters to Berkshire Hathaway shareholders into a rigorous but accessible format. Buffett himself has said that this is the best presentation of his beliefs and practices. (ISBN 0-9664461-0-0; cunning@ymail.yu.edu)

- *Attract and Retain the Affluent Investor* by Stephen Gresham and Evan Cooper (Dearborn) has little to recommend it other than the story of "George K." But those 13 pages are not to be missed.

- Frank Maselli's *Seminars: The Emotional Dynamic* is the best single resource I've seen on how to organize and give a great seminar. (ISBN 1-57502-412-8; www.powerspeak.com)

- Aaron Hemsley's basic behavioral approach to prospecting is in the audiotape program "The Psychology of Maximum Sales Performance." (801-356-0830, www.aaronhemsley.com)

- On stories and analogies, I like Scott West's and Mitch Anthony's *Storyselling for Financial Advisors* (Dearborn). Just ignore the psychological "profiling."

- The Apollo Soyuz 1975 10-cent stamp is catalog number 1569 in both the Scott's stamp catalog and *The Postal Service Guide to U.S. Stamps*, published jointly by the Postal Service (www.usps.com) and HarperResource (www.harpercollins.com). Any good stamp dealer can obtain the stamp for you inexpensively in quantity, or you can contact the dealer who supplies me, Joseph Kardwell (800-233-0828). I always try to use a stamp that clearly shows both the price and the year; the *Guide* lets you look at a whole year's output and pick the stamp you think works best.

- Jeremy J. Siegel's classic *Stocks for the Long Run*, with a foreword by Peter Bernstein, is published in hardcover by McGraw Hill. My *Simple Wealth, Inevitable Wealth: How you and your financial advisor can grow your fortune in stock mutual funds* (www.nickmurray.com) is a way of helping you explain to your clients/prospects not only the role of equities, but the absolute indispensability of an advisor in a lifetime program of equity investing.

- The Alzheimer's Association's website www.alz.org is a constant source of good information on the disease. Dr. David Snowdon, who conducted the landmark "Nun Study," chronicles it in *Aging With Grace* (Bantam Books). Another highly regarded book is David Shenk's *The Forgetting: Alzheimer's: Portrait of an Epidemic* (Doubleday).

- Mental accounting and many other manifestations of The Big Mistake are analyzed in a popular book on behavioral economics called *Why Smart People Make Big Money Mistakes* by Gary Belsky and Thomas Gilovich (Simon & Schuster).

ACKNOWLEDGMENTS

————————•————————

No book about succeeding in a profession to which one has devoted a third of a century can fail to be somewhat autobiographical. This book in particular — premised on the belief that money is love, and describing the quest for multigenerational wealth for our clients and ourselves — is very much so.

So my deepest gratitude is, as always, to the love of my life and the mother of my children, Joan Carrick Murray. Wife, mother, grandmother and now brilliant businesswoman in her own right, Joan took a passionate interest in this book. The book is much the better for it.

There can be few greater blessings on an entrepreneurial soul than to have a child join him in business. My daughter Karen is simply the best editor I've ever had, and the best business partner anyone *could* have; the job she did in getting this book out in record time was her finest hour. And all this while carrying her second child.

Keynes said, "I am a speculator so my children can be dancers," and I suppose I am what I am so that my other two children, Joan Eileen and Mark, can pursue their respective arts…and dreams. I learn daily from their courage.

Karen's husband David Dickerson, portfolio manager at Phoenix-Zweig, tracked down virtually all of the statistical information in this book, and offered sound advice on its judicious use.

At The Nick Murray Company, Heather Harris and Rhona Vandernoth continually make me look rather better organized than I really am.

Bob Leo, Vice Chairman of MFS Fund Distributors, Inc., offered his warm encouragement and the statistical material on systematic withdrawal. Karen Edmonds, a member of Bob's team, provided the detailed chart on page 211.

Rita Hagerman and her team at North Fork Press contributed a beautiful design to present my message in clear, readable form.

I owe the vibrant illustration of Doctor Noah on the book's cover to Stephen Hayes, a perceptive and intelligent, as well as extremely gifted, artist.

Without the efforts of Ruth Jordan and her staff at Overnight Type, this book would not have gone from handwritten manuscript to typed draft in anything like the time it did.

These terrific people contributed to whatever is good about this book. Any and all of its errors of fact and/or judgment are mine.